AFRICA
AND THE
GREAT
POWERS
IN THE
1980s

Edited by
Olajide Aluko

UNIVERSITY
PRESS OF
AMERICA

LANHAM • NEW YORK • LONDON

Copyright © 1987 by

University Press of America,® Inc.

4720 Boston Way
Lanham, MD 20706

3 Henrietta Street
London WC2E 8LU England

British Cataloging in Publication Information Available

Library of Congress Cataloging in Publication Data

Africa and the great powers in the 1980s.

   Bibliography: p.
   1. Africa—Foreign relations—1960-
I. Aluko, Olajide.
DT30.5.A352   1987   327.6   86-15924
ISBN 0-8191-5592-6 (alk. paper)
ISBN 0-8191-5593-4 (pbk. : alk. paper)

All University Press of America books are produced on acid-free
paper which exceeds the minimum standards set by the National
Historical Publication and Records Commission.

TABLE OF CONTENTS

List of Contributors

Akanmu Adebayo is Lecturer in History at the University of Ife
in Nigeria.

Olajide Aluko is Professor of International Relations at the
University of Ife where he has also served as Head of
Department and Dean of the Faculty of Administration.

Douglas G. Anglin is Professor of Political Science at
Carleton University in Ottawa, Canada. Dr. Anglin was
the first Vice-Chancellor of the University of Zambia
in Lusaka.

Babafemi A. Badejo is Lecturer in Political Science at the
University of Lagos in Nigeria.

Naomi Chazan is Senior Lecturer in Political Science at the
Hebrew University in Jerusalem where she directs the
Africa Research Program at the Truman Research
Institute. Dr. Chazan has twice been a Visiting Fellow
at Radcliffe College and the Centre for International
Affairs at Harvard University.

Jean Herskovits is Professor of History at the State
University College of New York at Purchase. Dr.
Herskovits has been a frequent visitor to and
commentator on Nigerian affairs.

Michael Leifer is Reader in International Relations at the
London School of Economics, England.

James Mayall is Reader in International Relations at the
London School of Economics.

Olatunde J.B. Ojo is Senior Lecturer in Political and
Administrative Studies at the University of Port
Harcourt in Nigeria.

Amadu Sesay is Senior Lecturer in International Relations at
the University of Ife.

Timothy M. Shaw is Professor of Political Science and Director
of the Centre for African Studies at Dalhousie
University in Nova Scotia, Canada.

Rainer Telzlaff is Professor of Political Science at the
University of Hamburg in West Germany.

iv

Africa, 1985

Foreword

Africa and the Great Powers at the End
of the Twentieth-Century

Timothy M. Shaw

"Looked at from the African standpoint, the states on the continent
are developing greater military
power, thereby raising their conflicts to higher levels of unilateral effectiveness but also to
higher levels of bilateral stalemate."
                    - I. William Zartman
                    Ripe for Resolution[1]

"...the issue of 'new influentials'
is too important to be brushed
aside, for it touches on some basic
questions of contemporary international affairs."
                    - Bahgat Korany
            "Hierarchy within the South"[2]

"The internationalization of
Africa's crisis areas is a function
of the disposition and capacity of
the United States and the Soviet
Union to penetrate them...
penetration is relatively uncon-
strained because the mechanisms for
controlling the escalation potential of superpower competition are
weak and ineffective...the penetra-
bility of Africa's crises is also a
function of the vulnerability and
reciprocity of the African adversaries involved."

                    - James S. Coleman &
                    Richard L Sklar
                    "Introduction"[3]

    Analysis of Africa and the powers is in flux
because of interrelated changes in i) the identity of
the powers, ii) the factors being treated, iii) the locus
of decision-making, iv) the character of the world

system, and v) the appearance of new inequalities in Africa itself. This volume of original essays on aspects of this range of issues reflects the mood of revisionism which goes well beyond assumptions of colonial legacies and neo-colonial linkages.

First, the present century has marked a cycle in Africa-great power relations: from "discovery" to "decolonisation" and on to disillusionment or disengagement. Whilst the political map of the continent seems to have remained intact the identity of the "great" powers has been transformed away from European metropoles and towards non-European super- and major-powers. Not that France and Britain can be dismissed altogether as influential actors on the continent, but their roles have been joined and even superceded by a set of non-EEC states, notably the US and USSR but also China and Japan, and even fellow "Southern" states such as Brazil and Cuba. And other EEC members like West Germany as well as major African actors such as Nigeria, let alone the distinctive case of South Africa, have come to play significant roles, often in association with other extra-African countries. In short, the pattern of alliances and counter-alliances is more complex and changeable than before.

Moreover, second, the range of issues has expanded the scope and shifted in balance. In the initial post-independence period, the emphasis was on continental economic development in a period of global strategic detente. This also coincided with a mood of or emphasis on transnational economic "interdependence" in both analysis and policy. However, the mid-1970s' conjuncture was one of the return (regression?) towards superpower stand-off as well as one of economic shocks--from a high price for energy to inflated debt burdens and fluctuating exchange rates. Thus the 1980s has seen a return to cold war-type rhetoric and alliance as well as to economic decline and dismissal. In short, Africa in the last two decades of the twentieth century is more marginal and vulnerable than ever: marginal in global economic and strategic calculations and vulnerable to pressures in both issue areas. Although the international hierarchy may have changed in some aspects, Africa remains dependent and external forces dominant. The effective metropoles may now lie outside of Europe but they do not yet exist within the continent itself. Discovery may have given way to decolonisation but development remains elusive, seemingly forever. Until Africa's economic self-reliance increases its strategic status will remain problematic.

Meanwhile, third, the ultimate determinant and definition of Africa foreign policy is neither collective PanAfrican or national development but rather presidential or regime longevity. Although disguised in rhetoric of continental or national good, the bottom line, particularly in hard times, is personal survival, in economic, political and historical terms. The continent's continuing economic crisis has encouraged this tendency: classes and fractions out of favour can endanger their physical as well as political survival in periods of drought and desertification. Whilst most analyses of foreign policy decision-making in Africa have gone well beyond inappropriate assumptions of democratic process and collective goods, only a few have situated choices over a set of issues in the context of constrained and contracting national political economies.[4]

Fourth, the global context of the African condition has been transformed during this century not only by the industrial and other revolutions and two world wars but also by post-war changes in technology, energy and money. Africa may have been incorporated into the global economy to produce primary commodities and to consume industrial products--the dependencia nexus--as well as to staff imperial armies, but by independence, the needs and patterns of industrialisation had changed. The mixture of post-industrial internationalisation and production, mainly through the global reach of a few multinational corporations, served to erode Europe's demand and price for African commodities. This initial post-independence economic shock was exacerbated by subsequent oil and debt shocks, often combined with unhelpful environmental conditions, so that neo-colonial assumptions were superceded by fears of marginalisation and isolation. But if Africa's economic status was problematic in the 1970s its strategic position was being reaffirmed as bipolar dialectics resumed following a brief decade of detente. Alliance shifts in the Horn compounded by struggles elsewhere in the Sahel (notably Chad and Sahara) and the mixture of South African destabilisation and superpower involvements throughout Southern Africa, let alone the Reagan Administration's preoccupation with Libya, all served to revive cold war tensions throughout the continent. In turn, extracontinental pressures combined with economic difficulties to induce a growing tendency towards militarisation of both internal and regional relations:

the diversion of personnel and financial resources toward regime security and stability rather than national development.

And finally, fifth, the above four factors have together produced a new pattern of inequalities on the continent both within and between states. Class formation internally and uneven growth externally have exacerbated latent differences to generate a new minority of major African powers. The bases of these states' influence may vary from size of territory, population and economy to strategic location or production but their relative affluence sets them apart from the majority in decline. Furthermore, the domestic correlates of their external effect reinforce their distinctiveness. The rise of national bourgeois factions in such states facilitates their regional hegemony and suggests a perpetuation of their new-found roles. African political economies like Algeria, Egypt, Ivory Coast, Kenya, Nigeria and Zimbabwe have always been _primus inter pares_. But this status has firmer roots than ever as economic, strategic and communications roles come to reinforce each other in the new international division of labour. Africa may be the only Third World region to lack one or more Newly Industrialising Countries yet its industrial and military capacities are concentrated in a handful of territories which tend to attract extra-continental attention. And the Berlin-defined continental map may yet be in flux as de facto informal economic exchanges undermine de jure political jurisdictions.

Thus this volume appears at an interesting time or conjuncture in the evolution of Africa's relations with the powers. It results from one in a series of annual international conferences arranged by the Department of International Relations at the University of Ife in Nigeria and was partially funded through a Ford Foundation grant to that Department. It brings together a leading group of African and international scholars which is testimony to the eminence of that Department and University in this growing field of study. It could not have been published without the invaluable editorial skills of Kirk Williams and Lee Parpart along with the word-processing of Rosamond Luke and Elfrieda Schneider. Although the conference at which these papers were presented occured in mid-1983 the salience of the subject matter is, if anything, ever greater now. Despite declarations of African national and collective self-reliance, the continent remains strategically important even if economically tenuous; such is the changing yet continuing dialectic between Africa and the global system.

Notes

1. I. William Zartman Ripe for Resolution: conflict and intervention in Africa (New York: OUP for Council on Foreign Relations, 1985) 5.

2. Bahgat Korany "Hierarchy within the South: in search of theory" Third World Affairs 1986 (London: Third World Foundation, 1986) 86-87.

3. James S. Coleman & Richard L. Sklar "Introduction" in Gerald J. Bender, James S. Coleman & Richard L. Sklar (eds) African Crisis Areas and US Foreign Policy (Berkeley: University of California Press, 1985) 11-12.

4. On this new wave of African foreign policy studies see Bahgat Korany et al How Foreign Policy Decision are Made in the Third World: a comparative analysis (Boulder: Westview, 1986), Bahgat Korany & Ali E. Hillal Dessouki et al The Foreign Policies of Arab States (Boulder: Westview, 1984), and Timothy M. Shaw & Olajide Aluko (eds) The Political Economy of African Foreign Policy: comparative analysis (New York: St. Martins, 1984).

INTRODUCTION

African Security Problems and the Great Powers

Olajide Aluko

On the face of it, one must wonder whether African countries have security problems when, unlike their counterparts in Latin America, Eastern Europe, and Asia, they do not lie in the shadow of any of the great powers. Moreover, in African countries--where the security of the state is often equated or confused with the continuation in office of the respective Presidents, Prime Ministers or Heads of State, and where the one party system or even the one-man state is the rule rather than the exception--can one really talk of the security problems facing the continent? Who knows what this really means, apart from what many African leaders believe it to mean?

Despite all this, however, there is no doubt that African states have legitimate security problems. In this chapter these are confined to direct or indirect military threats or challenge to the states, although it is realised that the current concept of security also involves economic, political, cultural and even psychological spheres. Not only does Africa have legitimate security problems; but such problems have intensified since the mid-seventies and have been so severe as to warrant heavy security expenditure within the continent. Indeed, Africa, which is the poorest and the most backward of the continents, has spent a higher percentage of its earnings on defence than any of the other continents as indicated below.

In 1968 Africa was a lightly armed region representing 4 percent of all developing countries' arms imports. Ten years later, this figure had risen to 32 percent. Spending on security had virtually doubled in real terms every two years. Even more startling, Africa's military expenditure per soldier ($8,383) exceeded that of Latin America ($5,621), South Asia ($2,380), and the Far East ($5,134) by 1977.[1] Since then there has been greater militarisation of the continent with even higher security budgets.[2]

From this a preliminary question arises. What has brought about the deterioration of security in the continent? In addition, I pose further questions to help our understanding of the subject. First, what is the nature of African security problems? Second, why and how have the great powers responded to such problems? Third, what have been the consequences of such response? And fourth, what are the future prospects for African security? These are the main questions I shall try to grapple with in the rest of this study.

i) **Deterioration of Security Problems**

A variety of complex factors has been responsible for the deterioration of the security situation in Africa since the mid-seventies. Among them four are most significant: a) the intensification of intrastate conflicts; b) the worsening socio-economic life at home; c) intrusion of the cold war into the continent; and d) the lack of respect for African opinion and the OAU by the great powers. I will examine each of these briefly.

In the early sixties, the level of intra-state conflicts, with the exception of the Congo (now Zaire), was not appalling, and in most cases these conflicts were resolved as much as possible by African states themselves. Thus, in 1964, it was the Nigerian troops that had assisted to suppress the East African mutinies. Even the Nigerian Civil War (1967-70) was largely resolved by the OAU. Likewise, the conflicts between the triumvirate of Maga, Apithy and Ahomadegbe in the then Republic of Dahomey (now Benin) in the early seventies were resolved chiefly by the leaders themselves and in 1972 by their soldiers under Colonel Mathieu Kerekou, the present Head of State. The civil war between the Ayanya fighters of Southern Sudan and the northern part of the country was resolved by an agreement in 1972 that owed much to late Emperor Haile Selassie of Ethiopia.

However, since the mid-seventies, the situation has changed dramatically. It took French troops, military aid from the US, and financial aid for security forces in the late-seventies and early-eighties to help in ending the civil war in Chad, however temporarily. Likewise, it required the French and Belgian troops and American arms and equipment to assist Mobutu Sese Seko in suppressing the Shaba invasions in 1977 and again in 1978.

The exacerbation of socio-economic life for the majority of Africans, especially since the early seven-

2

ties, has contributed to the sharp decline of security arrangements in many African countries. Since the early seventies, the economies of most African countries have deteriorated as a result of different forces: the quadrupling of crude oil prices in 1973/4 and another bout of price increases in 1979/80; the consequent increase in the prices of goods and services from the industrial countries; the world-wide recession which among other things brought down the prices of primary products to their lowest levels since the end of the Second World War; and the mismanagement, inefficiency and lack of financial discipline, and corruption in public life on the continent. As a result, the economic growth of Africa that recorded an average of 3.5 percent in the sixties dropped to a corresponding percentage of 0.5 in the early eighties. The balance of payments positions of most countries plunged in to heavy deficits by the late-seventies. Foreign exchange reserves almost vanished and became a major constraint on most African states in the seventies. External debts at $28 billion in 1970 had quadrupled in 1975 to $112 billion and to over $325 billion by 1979.

The social implications of all these were serious, especially for the vast majority of African peoples, the educated elite, and the opposition groups who were virtually excluded from "the good life." Standards of living fell sharply. Large-scale unemployment and runaway inflation became rife in the seventies in contrast to the earlier period. The quality of life deteriorated.

This situation ultimately led to large groups of people becoming alienated from the existing political system and from its ruling class. Where opposition parties, groups and leaders had relative freedom of the press and speech, as in Nigeria, they jumped to criticise the policies of government. In some cases such criticisms have been well taken; in others not. But in most other African states with a one-party system, or with one-man rule as in Banda's Malawi, the opposition groups usually went underground to plan ways to change the existing order and government by force. Some of these dissident elements sought military aid from abroad, while the governing elite might request foreign military support usually from the great powers. The stage was set for increased insecurity and threats. In many African states the result has been "coups" and "counter-coups" that has often heightened the sense of insecurity in such countries.

3

Inter-state conflicts have worsened since the seventies also. Whereas most of such conflicts in the sixties and even up to the early seventies were low-level and largely resolved by the African leaders themselves, more recent conflicts have had to be tackled with military aid from any of the great powers. For example, in 1963-64, the Moroccan-Algerian border conflict was resolved by African leaders. This was also true of Ethiopian-Somalia conflict up to 1973-4 when Somalia arranged a peace treaty in October 1972 to end the shooting war between Idi Amin's Uganda and Nyerere's Tanzania.[3] Although this conflict reemerged later in 1978-79, this has not set at nought the role of the Somali Republic in 1972.

By contrast, in the conflict between Algeria and Morocco over the Western Sahara since the mid-seventies, the US has been providing massive military aid to Morocco while the Soviet Union has been doing the same for Algeria. Similarly, in Libya's conflicts with Egypt, Sudan and Chad, the US has been providing unprecedented military aid to Egypt which under Foreign Military Sales (FMS) financing was to receive in 1984 the sum of $1.3 billion from Washington, making it the second largest recipient of US military aid after Israel.[4] And US military support and assistance to Sudan and Chad have been to some extent matched by Soviet military aid to Libya. Likewise, while the Somali Republic switched from dependence on Soviet arms in the late seventies, Ethiopia has switched to Moscow during the same period.

The open intrusion of the cold war conflict into the continent has been a major factor. Until the early seventies, except for the Congo (now Zaire) crisis, the cold war was largely kept out of Africa. This was not so much because the great powers were hamstrung by Africa's slogans of "Keep off Africa" and "Africa for Africans." Rather it was because the great powers believed that large-scale intrusion of cold war tactics would scare Africa away from them, and that the superpower's interests in the continent would best be served by not extending their mutual intense competition to the region. But two major factors changed this. First, a series of nonaggression and friendship pacts were signed between West Germany, the USSR and the other Eastern European countries including East Germany, between 1970 and 1972. East Germany was subsequently admitted to the United Nations (UN) in 1972 which not only effectively marked the end of the cold war in Europe but also shifted its theatre to

4

somewhere between the Red Sea and the East African coast. The Middle East War of October 1973 further underlined this trend. Second, the collapse of the Portuguese empire in Mozambique and Angola in 1975, and the subsequent arrival of the Cuban combat brigade and Soviet military aid, equipment and advisers were major factors which altered superpower involvement in the continent.

The lack of respect for African opinion and for the OAU that became more pronounced after the mid-seventies contributed to this trend. Before the 1970s, the great powers restrained themselves from getting deeply involved in the Nigerian Civil War (1967-70) largely because the OAU was solidly in support of the Federal Nigerian government's position on the principle of inviolability of a country's territorial integrity. Likewise, the great powers showed considerable regard for the OAU position on Somalia and Ethiopia up till the early seventies as shown above, as well as the border clashes between many other African countries.

Since then, however, the great powers have tended to pay scant attention to either African opinion or the OAU. For example, France and Belgium despatched paratroops to Kolwezi in Zaire in 1977 to save the Mobutu government in a venture that the London Guardian described as showing nothing but contempt for Africa.[5] It was sensitivity to African opinion that refrained the great powers from acquiring army, navy, and air bases in Africa in the sixties until the late-seventies. Part of the reason for this could be found in the continued weakness of the continent and the OAU. And in part it could be traced to the terrible decline of the OAU among its member states and as a continental body that can be counted upon to ensure the security of its member states.

ii) **Nature of Security Problems**

The security problems of Africa arise from two main areas: internal and external. The nature of such problems has varied. For those arising from internal sources, their nature could be ideological as with the Katangese gendarmes, Frolinat in Chad, and the Mozambique National Resistance (MNR). Problems could also be religious, as illustrated by the Frolinat Islamic forces that fought to unseat the predominantly Christian-dominated regime of ex-President Francois Tombalbaye and later that of General Felix Malloum from 1964 until 1979. The riots in Kano in December 1980

5

led by Maitasine and later in 1982 by his surviving
followers in the Maiduguri, Kano, Bauchi, Kaduna
states, that led to over 800 deaths and over 2,000
wounded, were also religious in nature. Sometimes,
problems may be ethnic as in the cases of "Biafrans"
against the Northern-dominated federal Nigerian
government or the predominantly Ndebele-dominated ZAPU
of Joshua Nkomo against the Shona-dominated regime of
Robert Mugabe in Zimbabwe.

Threats arising from the outside have been complex
in nature. Only the most notable ones will be mentioned here. Security problems arising externally may
involve territorial or boundary disputes, as between
Algeria and Morocco; Nigeria and Cameroun; or Nigeria
and Chad. These have arisen from the lack of properly
delimited boundaries by the former colonial map-makers
of the 19th century, which has led to armed clashes
involving at least 84 deaths and over 200 wounded by
May 21 1983.[6] A few, such as the conflicts between
Somalia and Ethiopia and Kenya, have involved not only
territorial disputes but also irredentist claims on
neighbours. A few have been largely ideological in
nature, such as the Tanzania-Uganda conflict from 1971
until 1979 when the Amin government was finally overthrown by the Ugandan Liberation Army with the help of
over 12,000 Tanzanian regular forces and militiamen.

On the other hand, the Libyan-Egyptian-Sudanese-
Chadian conflict has been ideological and political.
The nature of some security problems could be neo-
colonial expansionist adventures such as Morocco's
claim to Western Sahara and Mauritania's to the southern part of the same territory between late-1975 and
1979.

Furthermore, the continuing existence of the apartheid system in South Africa as well as the latter's
continuing illegal occupation of Namibia has constituted a major security problem not only for neighbouring
African states, but also for most of Africa south of
the Sahara.[7] Finally, the readiness of the great
powers since the mid-seventies to establish military
bases on the continent has not only complicated
Africa's problems, but has also roped some African
states into the respective cold war alliances of their
patrons. Apart from this there have been joint military exercises between Egypt and US combat forces, as
well as between US and Moroccan forces. In the sixties, such ventures would have been rejected by these
African states.

Before going on to the next section, it is pertinent to remember that some of the internal dissident elements have support from either neighbouring states, great powers, or both. For example, the Katangese gendarmes of Zaire had the support of the Angolan government in 1977 and again in 1978. The UNITA dissident forces in Angola had the active military backing of South Africa and the US, especially since Ronald Reagan was elected to the White House in January 1981. The Lesotho Liberation Army (LLA) stated recently that it had the military and financial backing of the Botha government, and it claimed responsibility for the act of sabotage in Maseru, Lesotho, in February 1983.[8] The guerrilla movement in Mozambique--the MNR--is not only fully-backed militarily by South Africa but it is also financed by Pretoria which has created a serious security problem for the Frelimo government. Finally, Ethiopia gave active support to the Western Somali Liberation Front, a group violently opposed to the government of Siad Barre.

The upshot of all this has been to compound Africa's security problems. We may now examine why and how the great powers have responded to these problems. Perhaps I should deal with why the giant industrial powers have chosen to get involved in African security matters. Although a number of reasons couldbe given, I will give a brief analysis of only the most important ones.

iii)   **Why Great Power Involvement?**

The first important reason for great power intervention is that almost all African countries produce very few arms for internal security not to mention external security. While in 1972 the South African Defence Ministry announced that Pretoria was self-sufficient[9] in arms production for internal defence, in 1983 no single member of the OAU could seriously make such a claim.[10] Largely as a result of this, almost all African states have had to turn to the great powers for arms and ammunition. For a number of reasons, the great powers have been eager to provide necessary military requirements, and in some cases more.

The sale and supply of arms by the great powers are seen by them as an instrument of their foreign policy. These include the promotion of their strategic, political and diplomatic positions on the continent <u>vis-a-vis</u>

7

other great powers or their adversaries, such as US
military support for the triple alliance of Egypt,
Sudan and Chad with cold war overtones against Libya
backed by Soviet arms. Likewise, US military bases and
installations in Kenya, Somalia, Oman, and Egypt are to
serve the requirements of the Rapid Development Force
(RDF), now called the US Central Command, which stands
against possible threats to the Middle East oil fields
from a Soviet-backed assault operating from their facilities in Ethiopia or South Yemen.[11] The vast American
naval and military communications installation in Diego
Garcia is intended to serve cold war ends and perhaps
preserve the safety of the sea lanes from the Middle
East through the Indian Ocean to the Atlantic. Heavy
US military support for Morocco and Tunisia has been
given for strategic reasons in the Mediterranean as
well as to neutralise possible military assaults from
Soviet-armed Algeria or Libya.

Soviet arms for Mozambique and Angola are designed
to serve ideological ends rather than any serious
security consideration. The existence of French bases
in 11 of its former colonies such as Senegal, Ivory
Coast, Central African Republic, Gabon, Djibouti,
Reunion, Mayotte etc., are meant to serve the historical, political, economic, diplomatic and cultural
interests of France. French military aid to other
African countries such as Morocco, Zaire, Chad etc., is
also intended to promote French interests. The same is
true of British military aid to Kenya, Zimbabwe,
Nigeria, Uganda, etc.

Some of the heavy military sales and supplies, such
as the US Foreign Military Sales (FMS), are undertaken
largely to improve balance of payments positions and to
create jobs in arms industry at home. Similarly, the
despatch of military training teams and advisers to
some African countries exists largely to provide
employment opportunities for the nationals of military
aid-giving countries. There is nothing wrong with
using the supply and the sale of arms to serve the
interests of such selling countries. What is wrong is
when such interests are allowed to negate the overall
interests of the recipients as is the case in many
developing countries.[12]

iv) **Response of the Great Powers**

The great powers have responded in a number of
ways to what they perceive to be the security problems

facing different African countries. The first is to
have a pact under which arms, ammunition and other
equipment could be made available. There is hardly a
single African country whose security is not heavily
dependent on arms from the industrial giants. Recently
this has involved the provision of sophisticated equipment to some African countries that can hardly be supported by their economic capability. These include the
supply of four Airborne Warning and Control Systems
(AWACS) to Egypt and F-4 fighter bombers to both Egypt
and Morocco while the Soviet Union has been supplying
Libya with the sophisticated MIG 23s and different
types of missiles.

There has also been the provision of military
training programmes in the recipient countries and the
training of African military personnel in the military
institutions of the great powers. The great powers'
intelligence services have been used to serve many
African leaders. Recently almost all the francophone
African countries were provided with defence advisers
from France.[13]

Furthermore, new developments in great power military involvement have recently taken place. First,
joint security pacts had been signed between two or
more great powers to defend the independence and sovereignty of certain African countries. The most notable
was the US-Franco-Belgian pact in 1977 and in 1978 to
save the Mobutu government. Likewise, the Soviet-East
German security arrangement for the defence of Angola
has been in effect since late-1975. Another recent
innovation is the holding of joint military exercises
between some great powers and certain African states.
Thus we had the joint US-Egyptian military exercise
late in 1982 and in early-1983 there was the joint
US-Moroccan military exercise. All these would have
been regarded as anathema by Africa in the sixties and
early seventies; if such joint military ventures had
taken place they would have been greeted with strident
strictures throughout the continent. Another recent
development has been the provision of military bases
for the great powers in some African countries.
Indeed, the joint military ventures between some
African countries and great powers as well as the
existence of great power bases in many African countries have made nonsense out of the principle and the
claim of many of these countries to the doctrine and
the practice of nonalignment.

9

But now both the times and the circumstances have changed, and only Gaddafi of Libya was able to condemn such joint ventures. Libya's denunciation was regarded by the Western powers as that of a lone disaffected voice in the whole of Africa.

v) **Consequences of Great Power Involvement**

Writing about the consequences of great power military involvement in the continent is not easy, for such assessment will depend on the perspective of the individual. To the African leaders whose survival has hung on such military support, the consequences will be beneficial. But such a view will not be uncontested. For the survival of some leaders has not necessarily meant peace and prosperity for their various nationals; indeed, it could mean the opposite. Therefore, we have to take a more critical analytical approach.

Thus, as in every other case, there are likely to be two sides to the question of arms supply and support for Africa: the positive and negative. One positive aspect of this is that in some respects, great power military involvement has contributed to the survival of some regimes such as those of Mobutu in Zaire, and the MPLA in Angola, and of a number of governments in Francophone Africa.[14] Another positive aspect is that a number of African states such as Ethiopia, Nigeria and Kenya, to mention a few, have retained their territorial integrity largely as a result of military support from some of the great powers.

The negative consequences of the involvement are varied and only the significant ones will be examined here. While it is true that great power military support has been used to prolong the life of some regimes on the continent, it is also true that in some cases such power has been exercised in a negative way to remove some leaders from office. This was the case of Jean Bokassa of the Central African Empire in 1979 and of Macias Nguema of Equatorial Guinea the same year.[15] Another more recent example is that of Goukhouni Weddeye of Chad in June 1982.

Another negative consequence of such involvement is the needless internationalisation of African conflicts. This was the case of the Shaba invasion in 1977 and again in 1978. In these two cases, the five major NATO powers--the U.S., the U.K., West Germany, France, and Belgium--had to meet on an emergency basis to coordi-

10

nate their response.[16] It was also true of the Ethiopian-Somalia conflict in 1977-8. The most spectacular of such instances was the reported Libyan-inspired revolt in Southern Sudan early in February 1983 that swiftly led the US to send four AWACs to Egypt, and to move the US nuclear aircraft carrier Nimitz into the waters off the Libyan coast.[17] To counter this, it was also reported that the USSR was prepared to despatch military aid and equipment to Libya.[18]

Another negative result has been the occurence of actual military clashes between some great powers and certain African countries. The most celebrated case was the shooting down of two Libyan bombers by US military planes off the Gulf of Sirte in 1981.[19] Such cases may arise again in the near future.

The demotion of the OAU to the back seat in such matters of security and international order in Africa since the late seventies has been one of the major negative consequences of heavy great power military involvement in Africa. As indicated earlier, prior to the early seventies the great powers deferred to a considerable extent to the Organisation on such issues. This has since changed. And the virtual paralysis of the OAU since February 1982 has further reduced its utility in matters of security on the continent not only before the great powers but also before many African countries.

Still another negative consequence has been the introduction of the cold war into the continent in a more crude and blatant way than in the pre-1970 period. Indeed, some African countries such as Kenya, Somalia, Sudan, Chad, Egypt, Morocco, and even Tunisia (all of which have recently been described by Harry Shaw as "key allies of the US") have virtually become part of the NATO alliance in the cold war struggle against the Warsaw Pact Organisation. On the other hand, a few countries such as Angola, Mozambique, Ethiopia and to some extent Libya, with Soviet SS-12 "Scaleboard" missiles on her territory, have become more or less appendages to the Soviet-led military alliance.[20]

Another negative aspect of great power military involvement has been growing dependencies by many African countries for the satisfaction of their military needs. While the actual value of the heavy and sophisticated equipment supplied by the USSR is not known, there is no doubt that this must have been

11

rising given the types of equipment provided by her to
some African countries. Since the late seventies, the
US administration has stepped up military sales and
support for some African countries. These have been
pushed up further under the Reagan Administration.
Under the Reagan proposals for 1984, Foreign Military
Sales (FMS) to Egypt alone would rise to $1.3 billion,
an increase of 136 percent over the $550 million pro-
vided in 1981. U.S. military assistance to Morocco
would rise by 200 percent to over $150 million,[21] and
to Sudan by 220 percent. Even Liberia was to receive
$5 million in military assistance from the US in 1983
whereas in 1981 Monrovia received little or no such
military aid. In return for this new agreement, the
Liberian government would grant landing and other
rights for US Air Force planes at Robertsfield airport.[22] As pointed out earlier, of late France has
provided more arms, military aircraft and helicopters,
as well as defence advisers to almost all the Francophone African states including the "socialist state" of
Benin.[23]

    Still another negative consequence of the enormous
great power arms sales to Africa will be to compound
their debt-burden and worsen their socio-economic life.
A great deal of military assistance and support has to
be paid for with interest. Although detailed figures
are not available on this on many African countries,
there is no doubt that the figure is growing at an
alarming rate. For instance, it has been estimated
that debt repayments to the US under FMS in 1983 would
amount to 46 percent of total Egyptian exports in 1983.
It has also been calculated that given current high
interest rates, interest charges alone might exceed the
original face value of the loan before the grace period
expires. In the case of Egypt it was reported that the
equipment purchased under such agreements will have
worn out or become obsolete by the time the loan is
finally paid off.[24] The case of Morocco is similarly
terrible. Rabat, since the late-seventies, has devoted
about 47 percent of its annual budget to security
matters. Ethiopia has since the late-seventies devoted
about 40 percent of her total budget to defence.[25] The
case of other African states may not be as serious.
But given the increase of their dependence on the great
powers for arms and ammunition their debt burden will
worsen. For instance Africa's total external debt
amounted to $28 billion in 1970, to $112 billion in
1975, and to over $420 billion in 1981. Given the
world-wide economic recession, the depression of the
commodity market, the glut in the oil market coupled

with mismanagement, inefficiency, lack of financial discipline, and large-scale corruption in public life in most African states, the debt burden will become worse. The upshot of all this will be Africa's greater dependence on the industrial giants.

vi) **Prospects and Conclusion**

The prospects for African security in the near future are not bright; indeed, they are bleak. Security problems are likely to worsen rather than improve, partly because of the exacerbation of the socio-economic condition of the continent. The economies of almost all African countries are in perilous conditions. There is no indication that this will be relieved soon. Worsening economic circumstances will in turn necessitate African requests for massive economic aid from the industrial giants which will further increase Africa's dependence on them.

Against a desperately sinking economy, barely any advance can be made in Africa on the level of military technology. In view of this, most African states will become heavily dependent on arms and equipment from the great powers throughout the rest of this decade, even more than in the past. The disarray of the OAU and its almost total impotence since early 1982 has weakened the Organisation's role in matters of security and order in the continent. Even though the 19th summit of the Organisation was eventually held successfully in early June 1983 in Addis Ababa, it will take years before the OAU can regain the ground it has lost in African and world affairs. The apartheid system in Pretoria will find relief during this decade. And as long as it exists, it will continue to pose serious security problems for its black neighbours and the rest of black-ruled Africa.

Finally, there is nothing to show that the great powers will not become more ready to get involved militarily in the continent in the foreseeable future. Nothing exists to deter them. And they have strategic, political, ideological, economic, and cultural interests to protect and enhance in Africa.

From the above, the conclusion is clear. Unless Africa can put its own house in order, restore the OAU to a position of strength, and reduce intra-state and inter-state conflicts that often create serious security problems, and unless there is significant improvement in the level of economic performance and an appreciable improvement in level of military technology, then the continent will for the forseeable future remain a veritable terrain for great power forays. Africa's dependence on these great powers may in such circumstances become worse than at independence. If this were to happen, Africa will not only become a pawn in the chess game of the great powers, it will also become ripe for re-colonisation by the industrial giants, albeit in a more subtle but surer way.

Notes

1. *World Military Expenditure and Arms Transfers 1969-78*, (Washington: US Arms Control and Disarmament Agency, 1983).

2. More will be said of this below under the section dealing with the consequences.

3. For further details see *Strategic Survey, 1972* (London: IISS, 1972), 59.

4. Harry J. Shaw, "U.S. Security Assistance: Debts and Dependency" *Foreign Policy* (New York) No. 50, Spring 1983.

5. *The Guardian* (London) 22 May 1978.

6. See *The National Concord* (Lagos) 26 May 1983.

7. This is well analysed by Robert S. Jaster, *A Regional Security Role for Africa's Frontline States: experience and prospects* (London: IISS, 1983, Adelphi Paper No. 180).

8. *Africa Research Bulletin* (London) February 1983.

9. *Strategic Survey, 1972.*

10. In 1964, a Defence Industries Corporation was set up by the Nigerian government to produce light arms for the country's armed forces; but nearly 20 years later, nothing tangible has been produced there.

11. *The New York Times*, 18 May 1983 and 20 May 1983.

12. I will say more on this below.

13. Interview, April 1983.

14. At times heavy great power military support for unpopular leaders could be counter-productive as in the case of Sadat assassinated in 1981 and the abortive "coup" in Kenya in August 1982.

15. It is possible, however, to argue that the removal of Bokassa and Nguema in 1979 was a positive move in view of their wickedness, cruelty and callousness to their own peoples. But it would have been preferable if they had been replaced by their own peoples without any external military aid.

16. For further details see Olajide Aluko, "African Response to Great Power Military Intervention in Africa since Angola", African Affairs (London) 80 (319); 159-179.

17. Africa Research Bulletin (London) February 1983.

18. It is pertinent to note here that the alleged Libyan-inspired rebellion in Southern Sudan was a ruse; and the truth of the case was that the Gaddafi forces were then supporting the Weddeye forces in the northern part of Chad against the Habre government in N'djamena. See The Times (London) 23 February 1983.

19. For details see Claudia Wright, "Libya and the West: headlong into confrontation" International Affairs (London) 58 (1), Winter 1981/82, 13-41.

20. Shaw, "U.S. Security Assistance".

21. Africa Research Bulletin (London) February 1983.

22. Ibid

23. Interview, April 1983.

24. See Shaw, "U.S. Security Assistance".

25. West Africa (London) 2 May 1983.

Chapter One

Nigeria and the United States: an historical view[1]

Jean Herskovits

In the larger context of "Africa and the Great Powers," to examine relations between Nigeria and the United States is to choose one term out of each side of an equation larger and more complex on both sides. Further, each of the two countries has foreign policy priorities, and for neither does the other come at the top.

Nonetheless, Nigeria and the United States have increasingly had to take each other's existence, interests, and goals into account, even if not in equal measure. And each carries special weight within the sphere of its greatest impact: the United States as leader among the Western powers, with their long colonial and post-colonial histories in Africa; and Nigeria, as a leader in Africa, sharing the colonial experience and legacy of competition and at times conflict among former colonizers.

There is no doubt that historical relations between Europe, African countries and the United States have altered and complicated relations that might otherwise exist. A major contradiction in those relations is the inherent tension between the universal democratic and anti-colonial (and neo-colonial) ideals inherent in American ideology on the one hand and, on the other, America's commitment to a military, economic, and ideological bond with its NATO allies in the larger context of bi-polar superpower rivalry. For historical reasons and geopolitical self-interest (but not usually to its own economic advantage), the United States has long deferred to its NATO allies on African matters. Though the degree of deference has declined, it continues to surface, encouraged by European nations acting in their own self-interest.

That theme joins global super-power rivalry to intrude and ebb with a kind of tidal regularity into relations between the United States and Africa generally. But if there is one nation in Africa where a potential to break through to a nearly independent bilateral relationship, one where impact can take place in either direction, it is, I would argue, Nigeria.

17

Instances of it have already occurred. This is not, of
course, to overlook constraints raised in the lively
debate over Nigeria's foreign policy, constraints inherent in such matters as what it may mean to be a
"middle power," or to be caught in the ever-clearer
interdependence of the world's economy.²

It is in this context that an historical examination of the relation between the United States and
Nigeria should raise major points touching broader
relations between the great powers and African nations
in general. I hope to illuminate in that examination a
pattern of actions, reactions, and options on both
sides.

i) **From Ignorance to Interaction**

At the end of 1960, a few months after Nigeria's
independence from Britain, the description of Nigerian-
American relations was simple: there were virtually
none. The U.S. had warmly welcomed Nigeria's admission
to the United Nations in October, though Secretary of
State Christian Herter was overdoing diplomatic court-
esy when he said, "...the world has watched Nigeria's
progress toward independence with unparalleled attention. Certainly few recent events have so captured the
imagination of the American people."³

During the early 1960s bilateral relations continued to be embryonic. Nigeria had placed one of its five
overseas missions in Washington, clearly wishing to
expand those relations. On its side, the United States
government had just begun to discover Africa; only in
1958 had the Senate created an Africa subcommittee of
its Foreign Relations Committee. That Senator John F.
Kennedy, its first chairman, would become President in
1961 was as unpredictable as it was fortunate for newly
independent African countries. Their early years could
have seen the United States with a President neither
knowledgeable nor interested, whose appointments would
have kept attitudes and policies unquestioningly Eurocentric. Instead, Kennedy's first appointment was of
Governor G. Mennan Williams as Assistant Secretary of
State for African Affairs. With him and his deputy, J.
Wayne Fredericks, in the Africa Bureau (itself only four
years old), understanding of African issues would be
subtle, sophisticated and complex. The assertion that
Africa's problems would be dealt with accordingly, and
not just fed into a computer programmed for Europe and

18

would be heard, if not always heeded, throughout the State Department and official Washington.

Although what preoccupied Americans most about Africa was the Congo crisis, President Kennedy made time for numerous African heads of state and government, seeing and talking substance with more than any President has since. Nigeria's Prime Minister was one, making an official visit to the United States at his invitation in July 1961.

The communique at the end of the talks in Washington had two themes: bilateral economic relations and shared concerns about African issues. Then, as now, these were the bases of the relationship. But in 1961 the economic thrust was from the US to Nigeria, and it centered on aid. The other interest was the United Nations. It suited the economic and international realities of the early 1960s and the policies of both countries that it should be so. Nigeria, like most newly-independent African countries, laid great stress on the United Nations, and in the Congo the U.N. was a central actor, with full American support designed explicitly to head off East-West confrontation there, and to preserve the territorial integrity of that country. President Kennedy "praised the strenuous and effective efforts made by Nigerian statesmen toward a peaceful solution of the problems of that country, and the exemplary performance of Nigerian troops and police serving with the United Nations in the Congo."[4] The communique continued that the President and the Prime Minister "agreed that the Congo's political and economic problems must not be used for cold war purposes," a fundamental position later enlarged to include all of Africa.

Trade and investment received only passing mention in an exchange of economic missions in 1961.[5] By 1965, Nigeria was to have the largest USAID programme--and also the largest Peace Corps programme--in Africa, a measure of confidence in Nigeria's future. Americans, at least those few who thought of Nigeria at all, saw in Nigeria economic promise, commitment to democracy, and a conservative inclination; this they found an attractive counterpoise to the leadership of Ghana's Kwame Nkrumah, whose non-alignment many saw as rhetorically-overlaid Marxism. Even in the 1980's, few Americans understand the inappropriateness of imposing bipolar ideological labels on new nationalism; still fewer understood twenty years earlier.

19

In the 1960s Nigeria's political and economic
orientation was directed towards Britain, which suited
most American policy-makers. In all African cases, not
just Nigeria's, the U.S. looked for advice from former
colonial powers, who were, after all, NATO allies.
Only the State Department's Africa Bureau, working
ceaselessly, made small inroads into that dominant
government view during the Democratic administrations
of the 1960s. Never were the difficulties more starkly
apparent than when Secretary of State Dean Rusk said at
the start of the Nigerian Civil War that Nigeria was
"the primary responsibility of Great Britain,"[6] and
thus the U.S. would sell arms to neither side.

U.S. policy-makers, faced with a continuing conflict, had to focus on the issues. They heard echoes
from the American Civil War, and also from Katanga's
attempt to secede from the Congo. They saw a fragmenting Africa, unstable, and offering the Soviets opportunities for "adventurism." They picked up an emerging
African commitment to inherited colonial boundaries,
sharing the African fears of "Balkanization." Thus
Joseph Palmer, who had succeeded Williams as Assistant
Secretary for African Affairs after serving as the
first U.S. Ambassador to independent Nigeria, and his
successor in Lagos, Elbert G. Matthews, argued vigo-
rously in support of the "One Nigeria" of general
Yakubu Gowon's government. This was consistent with
the position American diplomats in Lagos and Kaduna had
taken against the idea of Northern secession in July
1966 (Dissent came from the consulate in Enugu, which
not surprisingly put forward the Biafran case).

In August 1967, the Nigerian government, having
tried to buy arms from the United States and been
refused, announced an agreement to purchase them from
the Soviet Union. The New York Times editorialised the
American reaction:

> ...unusually clumsy tactics have
> spotlighted the schizophrenia in
> Washington's behavior toward a
> civil war that is wracking the
> biggest and most important country
> of black Africa.
>
> In that conflict, the United States
> recognizes only the Federal Govern-
> ment in Lagos and hopes that a way
> may be found to keep Nigeria intact

as a country. That means
Washington hopes the attempt of Ibo
leaders of the East to set up a
separate state of "Biafra" will not
succeed. Yet Washington goes out
of its way to publicize its refusal
"to provide arms and ammunition to
either side." And when the Soviet
Union moves into the vacuum to
supply arms to the Federal Government to help it put down the
secession, the State Department
promptly calls this "a matter of
regret."[7]

ii) **The Strains of War**

The "schizophrenia" was to persist throughout the
war, but the strains within it would intensify. The
U.S. maintained its position, which it sometimes described as "neutrality," at least in respect of arms
sales. That stance, however, infuriated both sides and
became increasingly difficult to maintain as civilian
starvation, widely-publicized in the Western press,
drew a mounting public outcry for support of Biafra.
Without British as well as Russian arms sales to the
Federal Government, an argument to give military aid to
Biafra would have compounded the difficulties of the
African Bureau.

But in the 1968 Presidential campaign, Republican
candidate Richard M. Nixon and Democratic near-
candidate, Eugene McCarthy, insisted that genocide was
taking place in Biafra, a refrain heard repeatedly in
the Congress as 1969 wore on.[8] Pressure to shift support to Biafra on humanitarian grounds became ever-more
intense. But the American government did not yield;
President Nixon, faced with Nigeria's realities, did
not talk further of genocide, though he did recognize
humanitarian concerns, by appointing in February 1969 a
"Special Coordinator on Relief to Civilian Victims of
the Nigerian Civil War." This followed a study of
policy options by the National Security Council Interdepartmental Group for Africa, whose paper examining
the political consequences of possible U.S. actions led
with this assessment: "The U.S. has no vital interests
in Nigeria or Biafra." As illuminating, however, is
the concise elaboration that followed:

21

Broadly, there are two opposing
views of our interests, with many
variations. Designed deliberately
to heighten the contrast, these
are:

1. We have a major interest in the
   future stability of the region
   all Africa: We favor the unity
   of Nigeria to avoid:

   a) A blow to the Federation likely
      to fragment it;

   b) An environment of continuing
      hostility that would result in
      an arms race between the frag-
      ments;

   c) The prospect of great-power
      rivalries;

   d) A precedent for sucession
      elsewhere;

   e) Opposing the majority of Afri-
      can states on a crucial African
      issue...

2. The overriding U.S. concern is
   to save as many lives as
   possible...To the extent that
   we can, of course, we should
   keep in mind the important
   political considerations
   involved...These problems must
   not, however, be permitted to
   stand in the way of saving
   human life...

     Details of relief policy aside, it is clear that
the first view of U.S. national interest prevailed. It
shows a continuing concern to prevent great-power
rivalries (presumably East-West; not, for example,
French-U.S.), and it shows the successful injection of
African thinking on an African issue as an
element--even if the last--to be considered.

     After the Civil War ended with Biafra's surrender
in January 1970, a new dimension to Nigeria's import-

ance began to emerge: it was becoming one of the
world's principal oil producers. Nigeria's potential
had been known for some time; major oil companies had
been actively exploring since the 1950s, and, but for
the war, its weight as a producer would have been felt
earlier. From 415,000 barrels a day in 1966 (which
dropped to 142,000 in 1968), Nigeria was producing
560,000 in January 1970 and by August 1972 had reached
2 million.[10] Further, by 1972, Nigeria was already the
United States's third largest supplier of crude oil,
moving by 1974 into second place, a position it occupied until 1982.[11]

This fundamental change in the economic relationship between the United States and Nigeria went almost
unnoticed in the early 1970s. Relations between the
two countries were not particularly cordial. Nigeria's
view was that in its time of trial, Nigeria had been
betrayed by the United States, a country that, having
itself had a civil war against secession, should more
than any other have understood its needs and come to
its aid.

Americans outside the State Department lost
interest as soon as the war ended. Indeed, they could
not maintain an interest, for the press did not follow
the war's aftermath, neglecting--even refusing--to
report the phenomenal reconcilation and lack of repri-
sals.[12] In Lagos, relations were correct but cool.
The Peace Corps, widely seen in Nigeria as having
rallied American opinion to Biafra's side, had been
phased out during the war. The AID programme was
shrinking (and finally disappeared in 1974). Nigerians
were preoccupied with rebuilding their country, while
turning their attention to a more prominent role in
Africa, though the style of the Gowon government was to
do that very quietly.

The Organisation of African Unity, recognizing
Nigeria's importance and as a tribute to its new
stature, elected General Gowon its Chair in 1973, and
in that capacity he came to New York in early October
to address the UN General Assembly. Nigeria was
already a major oil supplier to the United States. If
for no other reason than that, the visit of its Head of
State to the UN provided an opportunity for him to discuss, as they say, matters of mutual interest, with
America's president.

Americans knew that having their country's stature
recognized was important to Nigeria's leaders. Assist-

23

ant Secretary of State for African Affairs, David
Newsom, had seen this in January 1970 when he had gone
to discuss post-war relief with the Lagos Government.
He had come back:

> ...with a feeling that the rela-
> tionships of the United States and
> other governments with Nigeria will
> have broader significance. The
> Nigerians stressed to me their
> feeling that the ability of an
> important black African nation to
> manage its affairs is at stake.
> There is an acute sensitivity about
> advice and actions which do not
> acknowledge Nigeria's sove-
> reignty.[13]

The State Department clearly understood that a meeting
should take place. But appointments for Gowon and
Nixon to meet were scheduled, cancelled, rescheduled,
and again cancelled--all from Washington or Key
Biscayne. Finally, the Nigerians said they had had
enough and their Head of State left without seeing
America's president.[14] Ironically, an oil boycott and
an OPEC decision quadrupling oil prices came only days
later. At that point the U.S. suddenly did have "a
vital interest" in Nigeria. Just moving into second
place among oil suppliers and providing nearly 14
percent of imports, Nigeria, though a member of OPEC
since 1971, did not join the Arab oil boycott that came
in the aftermath of the Six Day War. Thus it was
Nigeria that saved Americans from the traumatic disrup-
tion of oil supplies. Economic self-interest for a new
oil power was central to Nigeria's decision, not the
interest of the United States, whose government did not
even publicly acknowledge Nigeria's role in lessening
the crisis. Instead, Nigerians would see only continuing American neglect of their and Africa's international concerns, especially in southern Africa.

iii) **Recognition of Africa's Major Power: the
       Kissinger doctrine**

By the time Gowon was ousted in the bloodless coup
of 29 July 1975, the basis of the relationship between
Nigeria and the United States had, however, begun to
change--because Nigeria's position in the world had
begun to change. The reasons were twofold: most
importantly, oil, giving Nigeria a new prominence in

24

the world's economic equations; and second, Nigeria's emergence from the civil war as one nation, but now a confident nation, whose claim to leadership in Africa was the greater because of the way it had emerged from its ordeal.

Economically, the United States was dealing with a new relationship. The idea of aid had vanished from Nigerian thinking even before it did from American policy. Donald B. Easum, Assistant Secretary of State for Africa, recalls that in 1974 when, after OPEC quadrupled its oil prices, U.S. policy makers decided to bring what had been Africa'a largest aid program to an end on the grounds that Nigeria no longer needed it. Washington had nervously prepared for an angry reaction from Lagos but Nigerians greeted the news with amiable unconcern, proud to be paying their own way. Nigeria was also moving towards a more active African role, even if a far less visible and forceful one than would come after 1975. General Gowon would have no part of South Africa's wish for "dialogue" with states of black Africa, reaffirming instead Nigeria's commitment to the liberation movements. And by 1975 it was possible to note that "U.S. economic stakes in Nigeria are now as great as in South Africa and growing faster";[15] suggesting that one day Nigeria's policy makers might ask Americans (and West Europeans) doing business with South Africa and Nigeria to make a hard choice between the two.[16]

Nigeria's initiative with Togo to create the Economic Community of West African States (ECOWAS) added to its weight and leadership. The potential implications for the economies of the West could be considerable, and though the U.S. would be slow to recognise the fact, Nigeria as ECOWAS's centre of gravity grew harder to overlook.

Ignoring it would become harder still with the government led by General Murtala Muhammed. Internally and internationally both substance and style changed dramatically. The Murtala government did recognise, however, the importance of Nigerian-American relations; the other side of the oil coin, after all, was the ever-growing U.S. market for Nigeria's petroleum exports. The new leaders stated their wish to diversify American investment in Nigeria and to acquire American technology in line with plans for economic development. And so when the foreign minister, then-Colonel J.N. Garba, had his first discussions with the American Secretary of State in September 1975, he

25

suggested that Kissinger ought to consider visiting
Africa and that he would be welcome in Nigeria.

But a confidential transcript containing
Kissinger's comments about the invitation reveals an
attitude which would compound later difficulties in
communication. Said Kissinger, "I have never been to
Africa. I know nothing about it. I must go sometime.
I have told the Nigerians I will come, but they are
suggesting a day and a half. What can I do for a day
and a half in Nigeria?"[17]

Instead, without the insight Kissinger might have
gained from such a trip, American policy-makers made
decisions that managed both to bring U.S.-Nigerian
relations to their lowest point thus far and, ironically, to give the Muhammed Government the issue that
would thrust Nigeria into new prominence in Africa and
the world.

Nigeria, along with most OAU members, had hoped
that Angola would come to independence with a government of national unity, incorporating the three
liberation movements: MPLA, FNLA, and UNITA. What
abruptly changed Nigeria's position, indeed transformed
it into one of leading the OAU to sole recognition of
the MPLA, was the movement of South African troops deep
into Angola to insure, on the contrary, a government of
FNLA and UNITA.

The American Ambassador in Lagos, Donald B. Easum,
was not surprised at Nigeria's reaction. He had been
trying unsucessfully for some time to persuade
Kissinger and others in Washington that African views
needed hearing and understanding, not out of charity
but in the self-interest of the U.S. For his efforts
he'd been fired as Assistant Secretary of State for
Africa in December 1974 and then sent to Nigeria in May
1975. There his previous record brought him credibility and later important access to Nigeria's leaders,
who, however, had no illusions about his influence with
the Secretary.

But Washington was surprised and angry. In the
aftermath of December passage in Congress of the Clark
amendment prohibiting further covert aid to FNLA-UNITA,
a circular letter went from President Ford to African
heads of state, to "persuade' them not to push for recognition of MPLA at the forthcoming OAU special summit
meeting scheduled for January 1976. Nigeria saw the
persuasion as pressure, was deeply offended and took

the unprecedented step of publishing the letter in the
newspapers, thus escalating the campaign for MPLA's
recognition.

This issue was clear then, as it has been since:
Nigeria will see the South African government as the
foremost enemy of Africa; and it will not support any
government or movement in Africa who supports South
Africa. It will not understand the American argument,
that comes and goes like the tide, that the main threat
to Africa is a communist southern Africa, and the most
important enemies are the Soviet Union and Cuba. Whenever that argument gains primacy over majority rule and
human rights issues then relations between the U.S. and
Nigeria (and other African states) will worsen.

Thus, by the time Kissinger did want to visit
Lagos, in connection with his Lusaka speech in April
1976 following his "discovery" of Africa and the
importance of some of its problems, it was "not conven-
ient" for him to come. In fact, the matter was more
serious than diplomatic inconvenience, for after the
assassination of General Murtala Muhammed in an
unsuccessful coup on February 13, xenophobia directed
towards both Britain and the United States had scarcely
abated. A visit by the American Secretary of State,
with Nigerians newly aware of recent CIA involvement in
Angola and American encouragement of South Africa's
invasion, would produce more violent student demonstra-
tions.

Kissinger apparently understood neither the tense
situation facing the Nigerian government, now led by
Lieutenant-General Olusegun Obasanjo, nor its continuing refusal to accept his East-West view of Africa's
problems. As Nigeria refused further requests from
Kissinger in June and September 1976 that he visit
Lagos to explain his Rhodesian initiatives, the Secretary's anger and the distance between the two governments grew. That communications were kept open at all
between the U.S. Ambassador and the men at the top
level of Nigeria's government is best explained by the
qualities and efforts of the men involved.

iv) **Demonstrative Administration, Advocacy and Advent**

An important relationship, with its residue of substantial goodwill that had survived the late 1960s, was
severely damaged. But its resillience emerged after
Jimmy Carter was elected President in November 1976.
In early December Senator Dick Clark, then Chairman of

the African Subcommittee of the Senate Foreign Relations Committee, visited Lagos. He had raised the
first objections to covert American assistance to the
anti-MPLA forces in Angola and, of course, the Clark
Amendment was his. His warm welcome, and the open and
cordial discussions he had with top Nigerian officials,
foreshadowed vast changes evident when U.N. Ambassador
Andrew Young visited Lagos two months later.

What had changed? Perceptions and attitudes.
Nigerians saw Americans inside and close to the new
administration who approached Africa in a different
way: people who saw value for the U.S. in finding
points of common interest with Nigeria. Ambassador
Young said he would treat Nigerians as equals, and he
did. The view was born again that Americans want
Africa's problems seen first as African, whatever other
perspectives might also come into play (and Nigerians
did not deny other perspectives). And Nigerians also
saw that the Carter position on human rights was bound
to effect the new administration's view of Southern
Africa, bringing it closer to their own.

In February 1977 came the meeting between Andrew
Young and Olusegun Obasanjo which Easum describes as
"the most momentous of my foreign service career. It
was thrilling to see a strong, powerful leader with
control of his country changing the whole relationship
between it and the United States." Out of their discussion came agreement that the two countries could
find points of mutual self-interest, permitting cooperation rather than confrontation.

The emphasis was on seeking solutions to pressing
Southern African problems; the important long-term
bilateral economic questions would recede for the
moment. What had changed was a perception that, in
regard to Southern Africa, goals thought previously to
be in conflict were--or could be seen to be--the same.
That is, if the aim was to keep communism out of
Africa, which it was as much for Carter and Vance as it
was for Ford and Kissinger, there was a way to do it
that meshed with the goals of Nigeria and other African
states. This was to find truly democratic solutions in
Rhodesia and Namibia; the governments that would emerge
would, rhetoric aside, be profoundly nationalist, and
not Soviet allies or wedges into the continent. It was
delaying democratic solutions that would draw the
Soviets in further.

28

In short, Nigerians did not want a Soviet sphere of influence in Africa any more than the U.S. did, and American leaders could, while educating their public in complexities never before understood, make that shared interest clear.

The Carter Administration did not seek Nigerian cooperation for symbolic or sentimental value, as some detractors would later try to suggest. Nigeria had shown its weight in January 1976 over Angola, and its foreign minister, Jo Garba, had already gained the respect of Kissinger, who was increasingly conscious of Nigeria and its potential.[18] By August 1977, when Garba presided over a U.N. Conference Against Apartheid in Lagos, the Carter Administration well understood Nigeria's new role. The U.S. delegation included Ambassadors Andrew Young and Donald F. McHenry, and Assistant Secretary of State for African Affairs Richard Moose; it was the first time the U.S. had been present in Africa at an international meeting on such a scale and on such an issue.

The climate of mutual respect meant that when Nigeria's Head of State came to address the U.N. General Assembly in October 1977 the contrast with the 1973 fiasco was stunning. His concurrent visit to Washington was a full dress state visit, and the discussions between Carter and Obasanjo brought movement on both bilateral economic issues and those of southern Africa, both men being more comfortable with substance than diplomatic pleasantries.

Further, when Carter went to Lagos at the end of March 1978, it marked the first state visit an American President had ever made in Africa. Again the results were substantive, though the symbolism drew an irate reaction from South Africa's then Prime Minister, John Vorster. He denounced Carter's criticising his country's exclusionary politics from the platform of what he called a military dictatorship" with "no press freedom."[19] The attempt to demonstrate American hypocrisy only revealed South African ignorance.

The Carter visit accelerated cooperation, making possible other unprecedented initiatives. With Secretary of State Cyrus Vance in the party, the Nigerians decided to call together in Lagos the foreign ministers of the Front Line States. The subject would be Rhodesia, and Vance would join the talks. There followed only days later another meeting in Dar-es-Salaam, again at the Foreign Minister level,

with David Owen of Britain, Nkomo, and Mugabe also
participating in an Anglo-American plan for Rhodesia
quite different from the one Kissinger had proposed and
the Nigerians (and others) had rejected in 1976. Such
a gathering provided an opportunity to tackle approaches to Namibia, with, on this as on other occasions,
Nigeria's physically locating and bringing SWAPO's
leader, Sam Nujoma, into the negotiations.

The intricacies of the search for peaceful, democratic routes to Zimbabwe's and Namibia's independence
are not my concern here. But it is important that from
1977 those efforts, spearheaded on the Western side by
the United States, had actively involved on the African
side the Front Line States and Nigeria; that involvement was radically new, and was the pivot on which
improved Nigerian-American relations turned. For the
U.S. working with Nigeria would not have been possible,
or even been imagined, in 1976. It was, indeed,
unthinkable during the Nixon-Ford years to have foreign
ministers and other high officials from the two countries on a first-name, protocol-free basis, accepting
divergences of views as well as agreeing on issues.

The sense of mutual confidence extended beyond
Southern Africa. To give only one example, in the 1977
Shaba crisis, Nigeria played an important mediating
role between Angola and Zaire (having first, however,
ascertained that the U.S. would not intervene to give
lethal military assistance to Zaire), insisting that
this, like all African problems, must have an African
solution. From the American side, Nigeria's initia-
tive--which the U.S. could not have engineer-
ed--provided a way to resist pressure to intervene.

Improved communication and coincidence of some
interest did not mean, however, that either country
could take the other for granted--an American more than
Nigerian tendency. Jealously guarding the independence
of its policy as of its identity, Nigeria differed profoundly at times with the U.S., as with Britain, France
or the Soviet Union. For instance, in July 1978 at the
OAU summit meeting at Khartoum, General Obasanjo spoke
against all foreign intervention in Africa in forceful
terms that remain basic to Nigeria's policy:

> To the Soviets and their friends, I
> should like to say that having been
> invited to Africa in order to
> assist in the liberation struggle
> and the consolidation of national

independence, they should not over-
stay their welcome. Africa is not
about to throw off one colonial
yoke for another...

To the Western powers, I say that
they should act in such a way that
we are not led to believe they have
different concepts of independence
and sovereignty of Africa and for
Europe...Paratroop drops in the
twentieth century are no more
acceptable to us than the gunboats
of the last century were to our
ancestors. Convening conferences
in Europe and America to decide the
fate of Africa raises too many ugly
spectres which should be best for-
gotten both in ours and the
Europeans' interest...[20]

He was speaking with what was called "Shaba II"
fresh in his mind, as was referring to the sudden
American shift to the rhetoric of big power chess,
complete with support for French orchestrated
intervention on behalf of Zaire. Nigeria's leaders
were no longer confident of their understanding of
American policy, and by August members of the Supreme
Military Council were characterising government-to-
government relations as merely "correct."[21]

Stalled efforts in Southern Africa, especially over
Rhodesia, moderated the earlier cautious optimism, and
soon Obasanjo would be pronouncing the Anglo-American
plan "dead." Though communication would not end, the
pace of agreed-upon efforts would slow and their number
diminish. But the U.S. and Nigeria would one more time
play critical, if not coordinated, roles having profound effects on the future of Zimbabwe: Carter
resisted mounting Congressional pressure in May and
June of 1979 to lift sanctions against Rhodesia and
recognise the so-called Internal Settlement, which
Nigerians publicly applauded. For its part Nigeria
sent on the 1st of August the strongest possible message to Britain's new Conservative government of the
economic cost of such measures by nationalising British
Petroleum (BP) (with compensation to be paid) and taking other unpublicised but equally persuasive steps.[22]
When the subsequent Lancaster House Conference cleared
the way to Zimbabwe's April 1981 independence, both

31

countries could see results from their individual and joint roles. With a continuing stalemate over Namibia, Zimbabwe provided the most visible example of success in working towards shared goals.

The other interest which Nigeria and the United States shared was, of course bilateral economic relations. Throughout the period when Africa's crises commanded headlines, this aspect of the relationship simply moved ahead quietly. Where the two sets of issues intersected, was, predictably, over a potential Nigerian-South African economic counterpoise.

For the most part, the Nigerian government was as eager for expanded economic ties as the American administration which was concerned about the growing balance of payments deficit over oil imports. Both governments were rather more eager than the American private sector. The reasons for private sector indifference to Nigeria's booming economy were several. Some lay in the lack of adventurousness and African experience of potential U.S. investors; Americans tended to want to export equipment and consumer goods to Nigeria, while Nigerians wanted investment in the various sectors outlined in their Fourth Development Plan. Americans complained of the difficulties of doing business in Nigeria; mainly, but not only, bureaucratic tangles and delays. They had not much liked Nigeria's indigenisation programme, started in 1972 and revised in Nigeria's favour in 1977. From it Nigeria would take control of "the commanding heights of the economy" and individual Nigerians would acquire a larger stake in their economic growth. Although it was not a programme of nationalisation, it made American investors reluctant and nervous, whereas their European and Japanese counterparts were not.

But Nigeria wished to increase the American business presence, partly to diversify external economic activity further, and partly because of genuine admiration for American technology, whose transfer was a primary goal. The exchange of visits between Obasanjo and Carter initiated a continuing series of bilateral economic talks (those of July 1980 and September 1981 held at the Vice-Presidential level), and the meetings of joint working groups.

After 1978, the American government concentrated particularly on the economic side of the relationship, for Nigeria was entering the critical final stages of the transition to civilian rule, so that its government, while not abandoning its wider role, was focused on intricate and vital internal matters. Further, the American Embassy had recognised Nigerian sensitivities about even the appearance of external interference in the process, and chose to distance its people from political events. Instead, as Ambassador Easum put it, the U.S. made use of the good communications established in the political sphere to improve and advance economic relations.

Further, the Nigerian government's wish to scrutinise the possible South African activities of American companies[23] wanting to become active, or more active, in Nigeria was thwarted by U.S. boycott legislation. This had been designed for Middle East purposes, but was drawn up in general terms. Paradoxically, this legislation—which in brief made it illegal for a U.S. company to disclose, or even discuss, its business activities in a "boycotted" country with a "boycotting" country[24]—sometimes worked not for but against the interest of American companies, who legally could not argue their own case. As Obasanjo once commented, "We have our own ways of finding out, after all." But the Nigerian government, perhaps because of the legal tangle, did not often press the issue. In any case, in the two-and-a-half years between President Carter's visit to Lagos and President Shehu Shagari's visit to Washington in October 1980, the expansion of the economic relationship between the two countries continued.

v) **Towards Two Democracies**

Indeed, after 1 October 1979 there were more reasons than ever before why relations between the U.S. and Nigeria should have been excellent. On that date, Nigeria became a democracy of some 90 million people, the world's fourth largest and one with a new American-style constitution.

Nigerians did not chose that constitution because it was American, but rather because they decided that it suited their own complexities, which had parallels in the United States. But the fact that they chose it, and more, that they had to operate it, predisposed especially their leadership in both executive and legislative branches to have a new interest in how the American government works. As many travelled to the

U.S. to see for themselves, communications opened on a broader basis than ever before. More and more Nigerian students were coming to the U.S., some 25,000 by 1983, up from 10,000 only four years before.

Understanding would not, however, mean automatic agreement, as Jimmy Carter found out, when he dispatched Mohammed Ali to "persuade" African countries to boycott the Moscow Olympic Games of 1980 over Afghanistan. Despite Nigeria's expressed disapproval of the Soviet invasion, Ali's reception was cold and the results negative, though not seriously damaging to the relationship which through 1980 grew with the increasing economic importance of each country to the other.

President Shagari's visit to the United States in October 1980 was primarily to address the UN General Assembly; in the context of U.S.-Nigerian relations, however, the timing was unfortunate. The Presidential election campaign, reaching its climax, commanded public attention, and surely preoccupied President Carter and others in Washington. That an official visit took place at all showed the importance the U.S. had come to place since 1973 on Nigeria. But it was not a time to chart new bilateral directions, though circumstances might otherwise have been propitious. For Nigeria's economic weight with the U.S. was apparent even to those in Washington who scarcely thought of Africa: it seemed that in 1980 Nigeria might be America's largest balance of payment creditor. (In the event Nigeria was a close second to Japan).

By the 1983 elections, however, the relationship had changed. Divergence on Southern African issues was again pronounced, and even more important in a year critical to Nigeria's democratic future, the economic relationship had shifted dramatically. The reasons were external to Nigeria: in the first case, Reagan's assumption of the American presidency in 1981; in the second, the impact of the world-wide recession, combining with other political and economic factors, drove down the demand for oil.

The Reagan Administration is resolutely ideological in its view of international relations. Its approach to Third World countries was confrontational from the start, as bold downgrading of the UN demonstrated, along with a dismissive policy towards the Law of the Sea negotiations and towards dialogue on North-South economic issues. Its major figures are more insistent than were even Nixon and Kissinger on an

East-West or "globalist" approach to African (and other world) problems.

In Africa, this produced a radical change in approach to Southern Africa in particular from that taken by the Carter Administration. The prime "enemy" is again communism, which translates into Soviet aid for liberation movements and the Cuban presence in Angola. This has combined with an attitude towards the South African Government called "constructive engagement," in which the U.S. substitutes friendly discourse for confrontation in dealing with the Namibian question and with relations between South Africa and its other neighbours. Chester Crocker, author of this policy and Reagan's Assistant Secretary of State for African Affairs, initially saw it producing a quick and internationally acceptable settlement in Namibia; it has instead prolonged the stalemate of over two decades. The role of the Front Line States has been diminished in the search for a solution, and Nigeria has been, if not excluded, only sporadically included in that role.

Further, the Reagan Administration has produced out of its ideological assumptions the single issue that can delay resolution of the issue indefinitely and escalate the level of intervention and violence: "linkage" between the withdrawal of Cuban forces from independent Angola and Namibia independence, a connection which the South African Government quickly took over as its sine qua non.

Thus in assumptions about what is of vital importance, and in predictions of the consequences flowing from implementing policies resting on them, the United States and Nigeria are in profound disagreement. Nor does Nigeria approve of other U.S. actions that the policy has spawned: loosening the arms embargo against South Africa, refusal to condemn South African invasion of Angola in September 1981, forcing Angola to call for Cuban and Soviet reinforcements are two examples. Apparent U.S. condoning of South African efforts to destabilise its neighbours are profoundly disturbing to Nigeria, as to other African countries.

Though South Africa and Namibia have all but eclipsed the rest of Sub-Saharan Africa for the Reagan Administration, it has, through its ideological approach, injected itself into a matter much closer to Nigeria: Chad. Insisting that Libya is an agent of Soviet influence in Africa and the Middle East, the U.S. suddenly increased its concern over Chad's 20-year-long

civil war. Sharing a border with Chad, Nigeria had
since 1978 been very active in looking for a resolution
to the conflict to bring political stability to its
neighbour.

What could have been a chance to cooperate in
achieving compatible (if different) aims became instead
an attempt to solve America's problem at Nigeria's
expense. The cost to Nigeria was considerable, both in
money and in credibility, as principal participant in
an OAU force that could not, and did not, succeed in
fulfilling its mandate. Even with the Habre government
installed, the U.S. continued its pressure, persuading
Chad to bring Libya's incursions before the U.N. Security Council in March 1983, contrary to OAU policy of
keeping African issues within Africa, an approach
Nigeria would not support, whatever its own concern
about Chad's stability.

This ideological, globalist view of countries and
conflicts makes seeking nuanced U.S. policy to suit
particular circumstances all but impossible; for countries like Nigeria that must deal with this stance,
there is little room for manoeuvre. There is even less
room in such critical economic times as those facing
Nigeria in 1983. A combination of recession, fuel
conservation and stock-piling of oil in the industrialised countries had brought, in 1981, the beginning of
downward pressure on oil prices through declining
demand, and oil still provided 90 percent of Nigeria's
foreign exchange.

President Shagari has summarised the broader context:

> The objective of the industrialised
> countries...was to break OPEC.
> That was their aim, and nobody can
> convince me that it was not. I am
> not, however, blaming them for
> wishing to protect their own
> interest, but in the process they
> were fully aware that they were
> indeed harming us...But while try-
> ing to protect their own national
> interests, some of them failed to
> consider how their actions affected
> their foreign policies. These
> powers deliberately try to des-
> tablise the economies of the deve-
> loping countries in order to

36

strengthen their own. Inevitably
it boomerangs because the destabi-
lised countries always become
hostile to them...It has happened
in Latin America, for example.[25]

What, concretely, were the effects on Nigeria? The
precipitious decline in oil exports, and consequently
in revenue, and the two sets of austerity measures
taken by Shagari in April 1982 and January 1983 were
the salient ones. When Britain cut its North Sea oil
price in February, Nigeria was forced to drop its own
and was able to rally the support of OPEC to the new
lower price. OPEC was not broken yet.

But in 1982 Nigeria suffered particularly from U.S.
policies. For the first time in nearly a decade,
Nigeria was no longer America's second-largest supplier
of crude oil. In January 1983 it dropped to fourth
place, overtaken by Mexico and Great Britain, neither
one a member of OPEC. Americans, talking in the media
of secure supplies (and ignoring Nigeria's consistent
reliability, even in 1973-4), welcomed Britain into its
new position. The case of Mexico, far more complicated
politically and financially, demonstrated the unsur-
prising fact that its stability was of far greater
importance to the U.S. than was Nigeria's.

Though Nigeria soon moved into third place ahead of
Britain, this new situation under-scored what some
Nigerian leaders had quietly pointed out long before:
the obverse of Nigeria's being a major supplier of oil
to the U.S. is that the U.S. is Nigeria's principal
customer. That relationship can create leverage either
way.

Thus in a year in which Nigeria's fragile democratic institutions face a test in economic conditions
that would be disastrous in a Western democracy (inter-
war Europe comes quickly to mind), those very democracies are engaged in divisive and fragmenting modes of
dealing with most issues, foreign and domestic alike.
In the U.S. tension has escalated in the racial climate, and understanding of any sympathy for the problems facing "Third World" countries has diminished
markedly from its never-high point. Economic self-
interest is gauged ever-more narrowly, while acclama-
tion for the advance of democratic institutions is
loudly rhetorical and always in the context of East-
West confrontation.[26] This approach glosses over
essential complexities about what democracy means and

does not plumb the logical consequences of wanting its institutions maintained. It sidesteps the question of what a democratically-chosen government anywhere might choose to do that conflicts with what the U.S. would like to to do, implying that such a question should not arise.

Economic recession rarely stimulates generous impulses on the part of individuals, interest groups, or politicians, especially those who must respond to their constituents. In the United States, it has contributed to neo-protectionism, a gleeful and simplistic reaction to OPEC's difficulties, and, critically, lack of public understanding of the complexities of international finance, with growing hostility towards the measures--through the IMF, or the World Bank, or commercial banks--to assist developing countries through their short-term debt problems.

Nigeria is in fact "under-borrowed" as bankers look at it; its problem has not been in servicing its long term debt (which, in the terms of late-1970s possibilities for borrowing, is modest), but revenues have dropped preciptiously. Nor has the popular hostility towards extending further credit derived from Nigeria's case, but rather from the high publicity surrounding the need to reschedule Poland's and Mexico's and Brazil's debt. Nonetheless, Nigeria is caught in that negative climate, only heightened by press and television portrayal of the explusion of its illegal aliens early in 1983, reporting reminiscent in its judgemental over-simplification of how the Western media covered the Nigerian civil war.

The climate of opinion matters to relations between the countries because, contrary to the assumptions of many Africans, American policy is not made solely in the executive branch of the U.S. government. As the Clark Amendment demonstrated in 1976, Congress can have a decisive impact on a specific policy. Indeed, Congress in the spring of 1983 was again demonstrating this potential in seeking a similar prohibition on covert U.S. activities in Nicaragua.

But to focus Congressional attention requires an active constituency within the United States and the presence of legislators receptive to arguments (on African issues pressure can rarely be great enough) from such a constituency. In the first case, that constituency with black and whites in it has certainly grown for Africa in the last twenty years. It has also

38

become more focused, with at least one full-time organisation, Trans-Africa, lobbying for Africa, and a growth in other organisations that seek understanding of African issues and points of view.

But when one looks at the changing effectiveness of the Congressional Black Caucus and at the changing roster of Senators and Congressmen, it becomes clear that the effects of broader political and economic considerations weigh heavily. The Black Caucus is more effective with some administrations than others, and Africa's place on their agenda drops when an administration is unreceptive over domestic policies affecting Black Americans. Also important has been the 1980 defeat of a number of liberal Democrats in both Senate and House. They, like Senator Dick Clark two years before, fell before political forces minimally related to African matters, but their interest in Africa had been long-nurtured and they could be rallied at critical times.

vi) **Conclusions and Projections**

Taking all these conditions into account, 1983 is not a propitious time for good relations between Nigeria and the United States, though there are indications that the State Department understands in a non-ideological way the connection between alleviating short-term economic instability and minimising any potential threat to political stability. Nothing would please the government of South Africa and its ultra-conservative friends and advocates in the United States more than the failure of Nigeria's democratic institutions; it would give that ever-active lobby in the U.S. and Western Europe its best possible ammunition. The generality of American leaders do not want that, just as Nigeria's do not.[27]

Nigeria has never wanted too close a relationship with the United States; no Nigerian government has done the bidding of U.S. policy makers, and none is likely to do so. There are those in Nigeria who think the ties--economic and political--have become too close, that the U.S. takes Nigeria for granted; yet, as we have seen, the U.S. is repeatedly surprised when it tries to do so. Arguably, Nigeria benefits from America's lack of interest; many countries look nervously at what happens when Americans do get interested, especially in the developing countries. And yet in its own national interest and for broader African

reasons, Nigeria cannot ignore the U.S., especially at a time when America's economic policies have failed to ameliorate significantly a world-wide recession whose consequences for Nigeria, especially in an election year, are momentous.

But 1983, though important, is after all just another year in relations that span decades past and to come. Economic cycles will turn up as they have turned down, and administrations will come and go in both Nigeria and the U.S. There has been one period of a few years (1976-80) in which circumstances did allow a bilateral relationship in which Nigeria's impact on U.S. policy was clear and, perhaps, greater than the reverse. During some of that time Europe did not lead U.S. policy on most African issues; the U.S. and its allies, working together, even at times followed Nigeria's lead.

Important variables seem to be of two kinds: leadership in both countries and the degree of realism on both sides, and the economic position of each in relation to the other. It is clear that some American policy-makers are more receptive to the views of Nigeria than others. It is clear also that when Nigeria has economic leverage, its leaders receive a more careful hearing.

Those conditions may occur again, and in the aftermath of their recurrence historians may become more comfortable in analysis. But whatever the conditions, no American administration will again hold a view that Nigeria is "in Britain's sphere of influence," or that the U.S. "has no vital interest" there. That change in itself is progress when an African country deals with this particular great power.

Notes

1. Much of the material on which I base this account comes from extensive and frank discussions with those in the centre of events and policies. They have given their time, knowledge, and insight, many of them repeatedly over more than a decade, so that I might better understand the complexities, challenges, and possibilities of relations between Nigeria and the United States. They include successive Nigerian Heads of State, Foreign Ministers, and Ambassadors; American Assistant Secretaries of State for African Affairs, Ambassadors, Senators, and Congressmen; and many others in both governments. I am deeply grateful to them all.

2. The following works contain many of the salient arguments put forth in the last few years: A. Bolaji Akinyemi (ed), Nigeria and the World: readings in Nigerian foreign policy (Ibadan: Oxford University Press, 1978); Olajide Aluko, Essays in Nigerian Foreign Policy (London: George Allen & Unwin, 1981); Billy Dudley, An Introduction to Nigerian Government and Politics (Bloomington: Indiana University Press, 1982); Ray Ofoegbu, The Nigerian Foreign Policy (Enugu: Star 1978); Alaba Ogunsanwo, The Nigerian Military and Foreign Policy, 1975-1979: processes, principles, performance and contradictions (Princeton: Center of International Studies, Woodrow Wilson School of Public and International Affairs, Research Monograph No. 45, June 1980); Oyeleye Oyediran (ed), Survey of Nigerian Affairs, 1975 (Ibadan: Oxford University Press, 1978), and Survey of Nigerian Affairs, 1976-77 (Lagos: Macmillan Nigeria, 1981); and Timothy M. Shaw and Olajide Aluko (eds), Nigerian Foreign Policy: alternative perceptions and projections (London: Macmillan, 1983).

3. Department of State Bulletin, 24 October 1960, in Jean Herskovits (ed), Subsaharan Africa, Vol. 5 in Arthur M. Schlesinger, Jr. (ed), The Dynamics of World Power: a documentary history of United States foreign policy, 1945-1973 (New York: Chelsea House-McGraw Hill, 1973), 764.

4. Joint Communique, 27 July 1961, Department of State Bulletin, 21 August 1961, XVI (1156), 324.

5. *Department of State Bulletin*, 24 July 1961, XVI (1152), 156.

6. Quoted in *West Africa* (2616), 22 July 1967, 970.

7. Herskovits, *Documentary History*, 766.

8. *Ibid*, 773-809.

9. NSC Interdepartmental Group for Africa, Paper II, 1-2. NSCIG/AF 69-1, 4 February 1969.

10. Asiodu, P.C., "Nigeria and the Oil Question", Presidential Address to the Nigerian Economic Society, Lagos, February 1979, 6.

11. The PIMS (Petroleum Industry Monitoring System) *U.S.--OPEC Petroleum Report, 1973* (Washington: Federal Energy Administration Office of Policy and Analysis, 1 July 1974, and subsequent FEA/IEA monthly analyses of imports of crude oil for the year 1975-1978).

12. Commented the editor of a widely-read monthly in rejecting an article on post-war Nigeria in early 1971: "We know all we need to know about what's going on in Biafra. And anyway, if it's not genocide, our readers aren't interested." Not until January 1973, when *Foreign Affairs* published the author's "One Nigeria", 51(2), did any piece appear in a major American publication.

13. Statement by David D. Newsom, Assistant Secretary of State for African Affairs, testimony on "Relief problems in Nigeria", 21-22 January 1970, in Herskovits, *Documentary History*, 809.

14. A generous man, General Gowon commented at the time to a chagrined and apologetic American: "Running a big country is a complex thing; you can't tell what may have come up." What came up was not, as some surmised, the Middle East; it was, as Americans could subsequently piece together, Nixon's mounting anxiety that Archibald Cox was closing in on the Watergate tapes.

15. Jean Herskovits, "Nigeria: Africa's New Power", *Foreign Affairs*, 53(2), January 1975, 314.

16. Jean Herskovits, testimony before Subcommittee on African Affairs, Committee on Foreign Relations, U.S. Senate, July 29, 1975. U.S. Policy Toward Southern Africa (Washington: U.S. Government Printing Office, 1976), 432-3, 440, 449.

17. I am grateful to Bruce Oudes for this transcript of a conversation between Henry Kissinger and Shirley Temple Black, then U.S. Ambassador to Ghana, on 25 October 1975.

18. In August 1976, Garba needed to speak urgently to Kissinger on East African matters; despite strains in their country's relations, the Secretary interrupted his schedule on the West Coast to fly to Washington to meet Nigeria's Foreign Minister.

19. John F. Burns, "Vorster Criticises Carter", New York Times, 2 April 1978, 8.

20. General O. Obasanjo, "Address to the 15th Ordinary Session of the OAU Assembly of Heads of State and Government, Khartoum, July 1978, "A March of Progress": collected speeches of General Olusegun Obasanjo (Lagos: Federal Ministry of Information, 1970), 320-1.

21. Jean Herskovits, "The Dangers of Falling in Love: U.S.--Nigeria Relations", Nigeria Survey, Financial Times (London) 29 August 1978.

22. Nationalising BP was not, however, to be seen as a general precedent. It was aimed at a particular target, and its immediate cost was negligible, though the Government was aware that it could chill the investment climate for the future, which it has done. As important was the quiet end to accepting British companies' bids for Nigerian Government contracts and talk of finding alternative sources to British imports.

23. The Nigerian Government has "set up an economic intelligence unit" to deal with companies operating in South Africa. General O. Obasanjo, "Speech before the World Conference for Action Against Apartheid, August 1977", in Obasanjo, A March of Progress, 179-180. Brigadier Garba, speaking in February 1978, said, "We have introduced a clause in our contracts whereby companies that are operating in this country as well as in

South Africa have to give us an undertaking that
they will symstematically reduce their involvement in South Africa. There is also a stipula-
tion requiring a heavy fine of up to five times
the amount of a given contract if Government
finds out about its involvement in Apartheid
South Africa: "Address at Ahmadu Bello University: Nigeria's Foreign Policy and the National
Interest", February 1978.

24. Office of the Secretary of the Treasury, "New
     Boycott Guidelines". Federal Register
     (Washington, D.C.), 42(159), 17 August 1977,
     41504-17.

25. "Shagari: the man behind the image"; an inter-
     view with Peter Enahoro, Africa Now, 19 November
     1982, 58.

26   President Ronald Reagan's address before the
     British Parliament on 8 June 1982 took up this
     theme; he refers in it to Nigeria as follows: "In
     Africa, Nigeria is moving into (sic) remarkable
     and unmistakable ways to build and strengthen its
     democratic institutions" New York Times, 9 June
     1982.

27. This chapter, like the rest in this collection,
     was written before the end-1983 coup in Nigeria
     which brought the Nigerian military back to
     power.

Chapter Two

The Soviet Union and Nigeria

Olatunde J. B. Ojo

As African states gained independence in the 1960s
and were beset with coups and civil wars, the United
States could no longer rely on the sub-imperial role of
the colonial masters: the United Kingdom, France,
Belgium and Portugal. Direct American involvement
became imperative as the colonial powers could no longer vouch for the conduct of their erstwhile colonies.
The acceleration of the struggle for emancipation of
territories still under colonial rule and for black
majority rule and the collapse of the Portuguese colonial empire heightened the need for direct American
involvement. With increasing American direct interest
and involvement came the Soviet Union's increased activities, thus interjecting traditional Soviet-American
rivalry into sub-Saharan African affairs.

The interjection of Soviet-American rivalry into
African affairs has had a tremendous impact on Soviet
policies towards Africa as a whole and towards certain
African countries (Nigeria, Angola, Uganda and Zaire,
for example) and regions (Southern Africa, the Horn and
West Africa) creating, as it were, a hierarchy of
Soviet interests based on military-strategic, politico-
economic and socio-ideological calculations. One critical change in Soviet policy, for instance, was that,
whereas before the mid-1960s ideological affinity formed the basis of close political ties, in the next ten
years or so (1965 to 1975 approximately) pragmatism
formed the basis of policy. At this time close relations were established and fostered with any leader
willing to play ball irrespective of his ideological
persuasion. Since about 1975, however, there appears
to be a reversion to the earlier ideological phase.
These changes are largely the product of operational
experiences in Africa and of the escalated importance
of Third World affairs in general in Soviet international perspective.

In this chapter, I analyse one such operational
experience in Nigeria. What objectives were sought in
Nigeria and what instruments of policy were employed?
How successful have been the Soviets in achieving their

objectives, and what factors have been responsible for
success or failure? What are the prospects for the
future and what implications for Nigerian (and African)
foreign policy may be drawn?

i) Soviet Objectives

Soviet objectives in Nigeria derive from the opportunity the country offers as the ascendant "first major
black power in modern international politics"[1] to
strengthen Moscow's superpower role in East and Southern Africa and, through it, to increase the strength of
the world socialist system. An alliance with Nigeria
on the issue of national liberation, for example, would
indirectly foster the "anti-imperialist" goals of
Moscow, and strengthen its diplomatic hands and political ties in Angola, Ethiopia and Somali where gains in
the expansion of the world socialist system appear permanent. Such gains would reduce American- West
European influence in the region and constitute a
threat to their oil supply lines and their access to
the rich minerals of the area. In Soviet perspective,
"the identity of anti-imperialist aspirations within
the national liberation struggle is the corner-stone of
the Soviet Union's cooperation with developing countries. These countries have an ever-growing influence
in world politics and economics that Moscow could no
longer ignore".[2] The Third World has thus "become a
major setting of Soviet policy initiatives."[3] A country like Nigeria, therefore, acquires significance as
an instrument in the realisation of Soviet objectives
in the Third World in general and Africa, especially
Southern Africa, in particular.

The specific Soviet objectives in Nigeria as
garnered from Soviet pronouncements and behaviour are
inter-related but can be analytically separated and
described as follows:

a) Enlist Nigeria as an ally in strengthening and
supporting national liberation movements in
Southern Africa and opposing and eliminating the
remaining vestiges of colonialism, neocolonialism
and racism there. This entails, at the minimum the
encouragement and support of positive Nigerian diplomatic efforts that at once maximise the impact of
the Front Line States, reduce the influence of the
United States (and its ally Britain), and condone
Soviet presence and influence without the charges
of "Soviet expansionism," "Soviet domination" or

neocolonialism. Given African nationalism and
sensitivity to foreign activities that smack of
neocolonial domination, this requires delicate
Soviet diplomacy.

b) Enlist the Nigerians as partners in curtailing
American (and Western) presence and influence in
sub-Saharan Africa and stopping Peking from gaining
a foothold there. Since Sekou Toure sent the
Russians packing from Guinea and Nkrumah's overthrow in Ghana, the Soviets had lacked a foothold
in West Africa. In East Africa where there had
been gains in Tanzania and Zambia, Sino-Soviet
competition had been keen and China appeared to be
gaining ground there, and to be favoured in Zaire
and by the FNLA and UNITA in Angola until the victory of the MPLA. Apart from this "China factor,"
the Soviets see the American/Western influence in
Africa as detrimental to their interests in the Red
Sea/Indian Ocean area and in the South Atlantic
region. Curtailment of Chinese and Western influence would make room for easier expansion of Soviet
influence. For this purpose Nigeria is as good as
any other place to have a foothold. In any case,
the "growing Soviet naval role around the periphery
of Africa requires access to ports for the purpose
of repairs and refueling and the Soviets have
managed to secure the right to use facilities in
Algeria, Guinea, Nigeria, Congo, and other
states."[4] The Soviets would like to continue to
have this practical assistance that Nigeria's port
facilities offered and at the same time encourage
Lagos to take economic, commerical and diplomatic
decisions that help to weaken the influence of the
West and China.

c) Encourage the Nigerian government, as a leader in
Africa and the Third World, to take international
positions as close as possible to those of the
Soviet Union. As Robert Donaldson observes with
respect to Soviet-Indian relations, at stake here
is not only the target state's "posture in the
rhetorical arena (public statements, communiques,
etc) but also its behaviour in various international bodies, where the Soviets would like to have
support."[5] Accordingly the Soviets seek to promote
the image of a Soviet-Nigerian identity of views
for its impact not only in the Western capitals but
also in the Third World. Thus Nigeria should support Soviet initiatives in such forums as the
United Nations and the non-aligned movement and its

reward should itself serve as a showcase of what
friendly ties with the Soviet Union can produce for
Third World countries. As we shall see, the iron
and steel industry, so critical in the industrial-
ization of any country, became the symbol of
Soviet-Nigeria cooperation and achievement.

d) Encourage a non-capitalist path of socio-economic
development (socialist economy) and the "national-
democratic state" (progressive polity). Although
the Kremlin had always had low ideological esti-
mates and expectations of Nigeria, the overthrow of
the civilian regime in January 1966 raised hopes of
politico-ideological gains. Vladimir Yordanski
commented that "revolutionary and demoratic elements in the army officers' ranks [would hopefully
avoid] the mistakes of the ousted governments and,
together with domestic progressive forces closer to
the working class, would initiate radical internal
reforms and carry out much of the programme advocated by Moscow." These hopes were encouraged by a
number of Soviet theoreticians such as G.L. Mirsky
and A. Iskenderov who opined that the general emergence of the military and the intelligentsia in
much of Africa had very high revolutionary and
"progressive" potential, the overthrow of Soviet
favourites[6] such as Nkrumah and Ben Bella notwithstanding. The Nigeria civil war offered the
Soviets a great opportunity not simply to "take
advantage of mistakes the British make"[7] but also
to press the Nigerians directly and indirectly in
the direction of a socialist economy.

e) Build strong and lasting economic, commercial and
cultural ties with Nigeria. This is a concomitant
of the foregoing four basic objectives. Kosygin
had written to Gowon in October 1967 that the
Soviet Union would take measures to develop relations of friendship and cooperation in the economic
and cultural sphere "for the benefit of our
peoples" and in the interest of the complete
liberation of Africa from the bond of colonialism.
And certainly Soviet-Nigeria economic, commercial
and cultural ties would weaken by that much the
fabric of colonial and neo-colonial exploitative
relations, and serve to reinforce Nigeria's political and diplomatic orientation and exert an
influence on the direction of her internal development.

This is an objective consonant with research findings and recommendations. Research reports way
back in 1965-66 had urged the USSR to stabilise and
expand trade with the developing countries by
offering them long-term credits, preferably in connection with joint extraction or processing of
natural resources, and by forming mixed companies
with them in which she would take lower profits for
her shares than would a Western partner. Even the
23rd CPSU Congress of 1966 called for structural
changes in trade with the developing countries
through expanded exports of machinery and equipment. Nigeria obviously offered a very large
potential market not only for long-term credit in
connection with extractive or manufacturing indus-[8]
tries but also for Soviet machinery and equipment.

f) Create attitudes among Nigerians that are favourable to the USSR and the attainment of its objectives. Moscow has sought to build a reserve of
influence in Nigeria--create a predisposition to
support Soviet positions--via its material and
diplomatic support of Nigeria's territorial integrity, its financial and technical support of
progressive economic development plan and its propaganda[9] and cultural exchange programmes. As in
India, the USSR tries to create such an attitude
by attempting to foster a sense of need among
Nigerians, a feeling that continued Soviet support
and asistance is vital to the realisation of
Nigeria's own objectives. Again, the iron and
steel industry is a unique, instrumental project in
creating such a reserve of influence if used dis-
creetly.

Three observations on the foregoing Soviet objectives in Nigeria are in order. First, they are
post-civil war phenomenon. Before the civil war
Soviet objectives were inchoate, in part because of
the unflattering images and perceptions Soviet and
Nigerian leaders had of one another, and in part
because of an ideological gulf: Nigeria was not
seen to be a "progressive" country but one whose
leadership comprised "bourgeois reactionaries" and
"local feudals" incapable of a widespread national
liberation movement and one whose citizenry was
apathetic, without a single communist in its ranks,
the main socialist group--Socialist Workers and
Farmers Party founded only in 1963--having a
membership of only 22,000 by Moscow's own estimate
around 1966.[10] With the civil war and with the UK

agreeing to sell only limited arms and ammunitions while the US prohibited supplies, the Soviets saw a revolutionary potential to be exploited. The emergence of Nigeria as an African power--thanks to Soviet help in winning the war and thanks to petroleum and OPEC--made her a cinderella to be courted by small and medium powers in Africa and elsewhere and by the great and super powers. A pattern of objectives that have been pursued for the past several years now becomes discernible and articulated; factors for and against their realisation can be analysed and assessed.

Second, Soviet objectives in Nigeria fall into eight basic parameters of the overall evolution of Soviet policy toward Africa viz: preservation of the territorial integrity of African states; acquisition of logistic rights; direct involvement via military technicians in civil conflicts; informal alliances through treaties of friendship and cooperation; the use of Cubans or other proxies in vital conflicts in vital areas; competition and rivalry with the Chinese; active support of liberation movements; and a neo-ideological approach to relations, a return to the view that long-lasting political bonds must be based on a common ideological perspective.[11] As we shall see the lack of such a common ideological perspective and disagreement over the closeness of relation with the Chinese have been a problem in Nigeria--USSR relations.

Third, and finally, some Soviet objectives parallel those of succeeding Nigerian governments, thus presenting the Soviet Union with opportunities in its Nigerian policies. So, Nigeria's policy objective of defending the country's sovereignty, independence and territorial integrity is evidently compatible with putative Soviet objectives; indeed it offered Moscow the opportunity not only to assist Nigeria to win its civil war,[12] but also to establish a growing special link with the air force going back to that war. Similarly the Nigerian policy objective of creating the necesary political and economic conditions in Africa and the rest of the world which would foster Nigerian national self-reliance and rapid economic development, and facilitate the defence of the independence of all African countries, parallels Soviet socio-economic and politico-strategic objectives.[13] And it offers the Soviets great opportunity to assist in

50

Nigeria's economic development, to liaise in the non-aligned movement and in the Southern Africa liberation struggles and, obviously, to exercise tremendous influence on Nigerian attitudes towards the Soviet Union and on the scope and direction of Nigeria's socio-economic transformation.

But there have also been certain evident incompatibilities in the implications of the Nigerian and Soviet objectives to suggest a relationship that is unlikely to be permanent or free from tensions. Thus, in the area of security, Nigeria, to the chagrin of Moscow, will want more balanced dependence on the great powers and without ideological commitments as a quid pro quo. Similarly, in the socio-economic and politico-strategic areas, Nigeria will want "to promote relations and strengthen economic ties with friendly countries all over the world" including China,[14] it will want to strengthen its influence and leadership in Southern African affairs and it will resent Soviet independent initiatives in the area.[15] It will want to stake out its own positions in international relations especially in the various Third World forums and in the North-South dialogue; and it will resist Moscow's pressure to move the polity and economy in a socialist direction. It will decline to adopt a socialist ideology; on the contrary, it will take offence at Soviet propaganda and efforts to create lobbies in Nigeria for ideological reorientation.[16] Skilful diplomacy and forebearance and ideological differences are called for to prevent an open break. Luckily the need for a tactical alliance between the two countries for the realisation of their disparate if convergent strategic objectives in Southern African looms large and may sustain the uneasy bilateral relations.

ii) Instruments of Soviet Policy

The Soviet Union has employed several policy instruments orchestrated in pursuit of its objectives. Among these are military support and assistance, trade and aid, diplomacy and propaganda.

a) Military Support and Assistance

Before Nigeria's civil war, the Soviet "presence" in Nigeria had been limited to trade, economic aid,

technical assistance and diplomatic and cultural relations. As late as 1966 the USSR exported no arms or
ammunitions to Nigeria although it was the major supplier of arms to Africa. With the outbreak of the civil
war, and with the United Kingdom agreeing to sell only
limited arms and ammunitions while the US totally prohibited supplies, the Soviet Union had a great opportunity to realise one of its policy objectives. A communique from Tass of 21 July 1967, following a series
of Nigerian visits to Moscow begining in January that
year, declared:

> The USSR proceeds from the premise
> that attempts to dismember the
> Federal Republic of Nigeria run
> counter to the interests and aspi-
> rations of the Nigerian people and
> the interests of peace. The Soviet
> Union, guided by the peaceloving
> principles of its foreign policy,
> considers foreign interference in
> Nigeria's internal affairs inad-
> missible. The Soviet Union in its
> relations with Nigeria will con-
> tinue to render it support in its
> independent national development on
> the basis of equality and mutual
> respect.[17]

The extent of Soviet assistance to the war effort
remains a guarded secret. The United Kingdom no doubt
supplied nearly all the arms and ammunitions despite
the opposition of about two-thirds of the British public. The Soviet bloc, for its part, supplied almost
all the military aircraft, the extent of which remains
a matter for speculation. There is little doubt, however, that for Nigerian leaders such as Brigadier
Kurubo, head of the air force and ambassador to Moscow
during the war, the provision of Soviet military aircraft "was the most important factor in the defeat" of
the secessionists.[18] The extent of Soviet military
support and assistance since the war is indicative not
only of the extent of Soviet aid to the war effort but
also of how far the Soviet military presence has come.
Data for the immediate post-war years are not readily
available; but between 1974 and 1978 the USSR supplied
$80 million of the total N200 million arms transfer to
Nigeria or 40%.[19]

The Soviet presence has been predominant in the
Nigerian Air Force. Before the civil war and under the
Air Force Act of 1964 Nigeria signed contracts with
West Germany to train its air force personnel in
Germany and locally at Kaduna and to supply equipment.
Some training was done in Ethiopia as well. Transport
planes were acquired and Nigeria was going for jet aircraft when Germany cancelled its contract on account of
the war. Czechosolovakia temporarily filled the gap
until Moscow saw the opportunity not only to sell its
Mig 17s and, when their fire-power proved inadequate
for the war, its Ilyusin 128, but also to make Nigeria
align its foreign policy to boot.

The war over, Nigeria's emphasis on African liberation in its foreign policy, led to a decision to moder-
nise the Air Force and re-equip it to enable it to ward
off any aggression that might occur on account of any
new foreign policy posture. Accordingly, a large arms
deal with the USSR was concluded in 1974 and in October
the following year deliveries of a first batch of
Soviet MiG 21 fighters were made. Several Soviet military advisers came along to train Nigerians to fly and
maintain the war planes.[20] At the end of the military
regime in Nigeria these advisers were still in Nigeria,
albeit drastically reduced in number. And, as we have
noted, the Soviets managed to secure the right to use
port facilities in Nigeria.

Despite these gains in the military aspect of
Soviet objectives there have been problems. Lagos has
been uneasy about Soviet attitudes and the performance
of their obligations. In the civil war years the
Nigerians had been alarmed at the apparent administrative laxity of the USSR as for example the "cases of
rifles flown in by air while their magazines came much
later by sea [and] vehicles sent into Nigeria without
spare parts."[21] In the late 1970s the Nigerians were
constrained to order a reduction in the number of
Soviet military advisers on the MiG deal (from 40 to 5
in August 1979) due to the Russians' "inefficient
performance" and their "condescending attitudes."[22]
But it may very well be the case that inefficiency and
condescension were the product of Soviet frustration
over their remaining a sub-ordinate foreign power in
the polity, diplomacy and economy of Nigeria and over
the latter's lack of movement towards socialist ideology as well as their coquetting with China. Whatever
the case the Nigerians have seen a danger in relying
solely on the USSR for the training and supplies of
their Air Force, especially at a time when the Entebbe

Raid pointedly led to considerations of radar and sophisticated communication system including command and control. Accordingly, diversification of sources of equipment is being undertaken, as for instance, the order for twelve Alfa jets in place of Czechoslovakian L-29 jets that are being phased out. Training is also being localised; that is, foreign experts bring their men and equipment to train Nigerians in Nigeria, thus making training relevant to local needs and circumstances.

b) Trade and Aid

Nigeria's trade with the USSR and the Soviet bloc has remained very modest. While the volume has generally continued to increase into the 1980s, the relative weight of USSR and Soviet bloc imports and exports in the total Nigerian trade picture has fallen off since the peak of the civil war years. Between 1960 and 1966 Nigeria's trade with the Soviet bloc rose from 1.2 per cent to 2.2 per cent of its total imports and from a negligible amount to 1.2 percent of its total exports. During 1967 - 1971, Nigeria's trade with the Soviet bloc reached its peak, averaging 4.2 percent of its total imports and 3.9 percent of its total exports. But the share of the Soviet Union itself remained meagre, attaining the peak of 1-1.08 percent of total imports in 1970/71 and 2.7 percent of total exports in 1971 (Tables 2.1 and 2.2). After 1971 Nigeria's trade with the USSR and Communist East Europe rapidly declined to the insignificant level of the pre-war years.

The insignificant USSR and Soviet bloc trade with Nigeria is surprising in view of the efforts to increase trade and in view of the Soviet belief that trade, along with aid, is an instrument for "strengthening national and economic independence"[23]and is therefore a useful weapon against imperialism. Between 1968 and 1971 new bilateral trade agreements were signed between Nigeria and a number of Soviet bloc countries to replace those signed before the war. Typically these agreements (Rumania 1968, Bulgaria 1969, USSR 1971, and Poland 1976) provided for most favoured nation treatment for exchanges at the prevailing international prices, which were to be paid for in a mutually agreed convertible currency.[24] Other efforts to increase Nigeria-Soviet trade have centred upon trade and industrial exhibitions, principally by the Soviet

Table 2.1

Communist Bloc Shares of Nigeria's Imports
1960-1979

Year	Total Imports (Nm)	Soviet block Shares (Nm)	% of total	USSR Shares (Nm)	% of total	China's Share (Nm)	% of total
1960	431.8	8.6	2.0	—	0.0	3.5	0.8
1961	445.0	10.9	2.4	—	0.0	N/A	N/A
1962	406.0	11.0	2.7	0.08	0.02	N/A	N/A
1963	415.2	11.4	2.3	0.18	0.04	N/A	N/A
1964	506.0	12.8	2.5	0.10	0.02	N/A	N/A
1965	550.4	11.4	2.0	0.60	0.10	9.7	1.8
1966	512.8	11.4	2.2	1.00	0.20	N/A	N/A
1967	447.2	15.6	3.5	2.20	0.50	12.6	2.8
1968	386.4	19.0	5.0	1.80	0.50	7.4	1.9
1969	497.4	19.2	3.9	3.20	0.60	11.0	2.2
1970	756.4	31.6	4.6	7.60	1.00	14.0	1.9

Table 2.1 (cont'd)

1971	1079.0	40.6	3.8	11.60	1.08	20.2	1.9
1972	990.0	23.0	2.3	3.60	0.36	17.4	1.7
1973	1224.8	33.6	2.7	5.70	0.46	23.6	1.9
1974	1829.6	50.4	2.8	14.94	0.82	30.5	1.7
1975	3975.1	69.2	1.7	15.04	0.38	42.9	1.1
1976	5392.1	78.3	1.5	10.15	0.19	88.3	1.6
1977	7093.7	184.7	2.6	16.25	0.23	94.6	1.3
1978	8139.9	181.5	2.2	20.23	0.25	130.5	1.6
1979	6165.2	130.6	2.1	N/A			

Source: Nigeria Trade Summary, December of relevant years to 1973 UN Yearbook of International Trade Statistics 1979, Vol. 1 for 1974-78.

UN African Statistical Yearbook 1976 Part 2: West Africa Central Bank of Nigeria Economic and Financial Review Vol. 18 No. 1 (June 1980) p. 86.

Central Bank of Nigeria Annual Report and Statement of Accounts 1979 p. 76.

ECA Foreign Trade Statistics for Africa Series C No. 2 1980.

56

Table 2.2
Communist Bloc Shares of Nigeria's Exports 1960-1979

Year	Total Imports (Nm)	Soviet block Shares (Nm)	% of total	USSR Shares (Nm)	% of total	China's Share (Nm)	% of total
1960	339.4	1.3	0.4	–	0.0	–	0.0
1961	347.4	1.3	0.3	–	0.0	N/A	N/A
1962	337.2	3.4	1.0	–	0.0	N/A	N/A
1963	378.6	2.9	0.8	–	0.0	N/A	N/A
1964	421.0	7.8	1.8	3.0	0.7	N/A	N/A
1965	526.6	6.6	1.3	4.2	0.8	1.6	0.3
1966	555.0	6.8	1.2	0.6	0.1	N/A	N/A
1967	476.2	15.0	3.1	8.0	1.7	1.8	0.4
1968	413.0	24.0	3.8	11.0	2.6	0.4	0.1
1969	639.4	24.6	3.8	16.4	2.6	–	0.0
1970	877.0	20.8	3.5	17.6	2.0	0.8	0.1

Table 2.2 (cont'd)

Year							
1971	1280.8	44.6	3.4	35.0	2.7	0.4	0.0
1972	1421.8	25.4	1.8	19.5	1.3	3.2	0.2
1973	2268.4	31.6	1.4	23.0	1.0	5.1	0.2
1974	6038.9	80.8	1.3	59.5	1.0	3.6	0.2
1975	5253.1	82.3	1.6	74.8	1.4	4.8	0.0
1976	6392.3	32.0	0.5	22.5	0.4	6.4	0.1
1977	7630.8	18.4	0.2	—	0.0	7.6	0.1
1978	6324.8	21.0	0.3	—	0.0	6.3	0.1
1979	10318.3	19.8	0.2	—	0.0	0.0	

Source: Nigeria Trade Summary, December of relevant years to 1973 UN Yearbook of International Trade Statistics 1979, Vol. 1 for 1974-78.

UN African Statistical Yearbook 1976 Part 2: West Africa Central Bank of Nigeria Economic and Financial Review Vol. 18 No. 1 (June 1980) p. 86.

Central Bank of Nigeria Annual Report and Statement of Accounts 1979 p. 76.

ECA Foreign Trade Statistics for Africa Series C No. 2 1980.

Union. She organised one in Lagos late in 1971 and
another in 1974. Representatives of Soviet foreign
trade organisations were to be seen often in Lagos
while those of Nigerian firms frequented Moscow.
     Two reasons can be given for the decline and the
insignificance of trade. With respect to imports,
Nigerians are mostly interested in consumer goods of
which the Soviets have little to spare and what little
they have are generally regarded as inferior to Western
products by a Nigerian public that wants value for its
money. Durable goods, especially machinery which the
Soviets have, on which trade agreements concentrate,
are also regarded as inferior by Nigerians and in any
case often lack spare parts and after sales service
facilities. As for Nigerian exports, the primary commodity since the early 1970s has been petroleum; but
the Soviets have an abundance of this. Of the non-
petroleum products, groundnuts, groundnut oil, palm
oil, cotton and timber had disappeared from the export
list by 1974/75 while Nigeria has no manufactures of
interest to the Soviet bloc. Thus Soviet-Nigeria trade
has done little to reduce Nigeria's economic dependence
on the West.
     Prior to the announcement of a £50 million sterling
(N120 million) Soviet loan early in 1967 and the sending of seven experts to discuss the object of the
loan--the proposed Nigerian iron and steel complex,
--economic aid and technical assistance by the USSR had
been relatively small. A ceiling of N30 million in
credits at 2.5 percent interest had been offered in the
early 1960s. This, together with a Polish offer of N30
million in "industrial materials and technical skills"
and a Czechoslovakian loan of N10 million was the
extent of Soviet bloc economic to Nigeria before the
civil war. And there was some technical assistance,
principally in the form of scholarships and exchange of
experts.[25]   But as late as 1976 some eight years after
a formal agreement had been signed on the steel complex
and released the N120 million loan, Soviet technical
experts were still at the stage of holding talks to
finalise arrangements to start work. By this time
Nigeria no longer needed the loan as it was capable
(thanks to petroleum revenue) of financing the project
by itself. This, together with Nigeria's "drifting
back to Britain and America after the war," it has been
suggested, "was extremely frustrating for the Russians"
who thereafter employed tactics to delay the implemen-[26]
tation of the project.
     Public opinion mounted against the Russians over
the lagging project forcing the Federal Government to
make a public statement to clear the air. According to

the Government, the Russians were not at fault as extensive soil and other time-consuming investigations had to be conducted before a decision could be taken as to the exact location of the steel complex in the general area of Ajaokuta. That decision was taken in July 1975 and agreement for a detailed design of the complex signed the following month. Work was going according to schedule and the complex would go into operation in 1981 and the first phase would be fully operational by 1983.[27] Yet, by the latter date the complex was already in trouble, again.

Despite the continuous problem of the steel complex, the Soviet Union and the Soviet bloc countries have beeen willing to grant loans and credits in the decade 1970-80 as the oil glut forced the government to resort to massive borrowing from bilateral and multilateral sources. They have also been involved in huge service contracts and licencing agreements in the engineering industry as well as in massive technical assistance. Between 1970 and 1980 Soviet bloc loans and credits amounted to $228.6 million, but only $5.6 million of this is attributable to the USSR itself. Over the same period Soviet bloc countries accounted for $1,730 million in joint venture investments and contracts of which the USSR alone took $1,283 million.[28] The value of technical assistance is difficult to estimate, but it is no doubt very high. In sum, relations with the Soviet bloc in terms of economic programmes (if not in commercial activities) have continued to expand though increasingly more with the satellites than with the USSR itself.

c) **Diplomacy and Propaganda**

Before the civil war Nigerian-USSR diplomatic contacts were few and far between and limited to exchange of trade missions although exchanges with the satellites were a little more frequent. The war, Nigeria's need for Soviet arms to prosecute it, and the opportunity thereby created for the Soviets to establish a firm foothold--all raised high expectations of wider and closer post-war bilateral diplomatic contacts not only to symbolise the ascendancy of the Soviets in the management of Nigeria's affairs but also for its political and psychological effect on global diplomacy.[29] These expectations failed to materialise: there was no proliferation of Nigerian-USSR contacts, despite Nigeria's efforts (Table 2.3). Nigeria's sending of senior officials to Moscow was not generally reciprocated and when the Soviets did so, they sent what the

Nigerians considered to be low-level officials and felt slighted. Even President Podgorny excluded Nigeria from his March 1977 tour of the Front Line States; this "slight" reinforced Nigerian sensibilities given its close association with the FLS.

As for propaganda, the periodicals and similar publications that the Soviets employ as a resource have had neither wide circulation nor readership in Nigeria. This is in part because of the paucity of another propaganda resource--indigenous communist organisations or Nigerian-Soviet Friendship and Cultural Societies. While such societies proliferated during the war, by 1972 most had fizzled, just as the only political party founded "on the bedrock of the general truths and principles of Marxism-Leninism"--the Socialist Workers' and Farmers' Party (SWFP)--had petered out before it was formally proscribed along with other political parties by the military. In 1972, for example, Wahab Goodluck and Samuel Bassey, president and secretary-general respectively of the Nigerian Trade Union Congress (NTUC), an affiliate of the Soviet-dominated WFTU, were prevented from attending a Cairo conference of the OAU African Trades Union Federation for no apparent reason. A month later both men were put in detention. Soon thereafter, three other leftists--Jimmy Chijoke, the editor of the NTUC newspaper Advance; Dr. Tunji Otegbeye, leader of the SWFP; and one S.O. Martins, an official of the Nigerian-Soviet Cultural and Friendship Association--were also arrested and placed under detention.[30] Indeed, for more effective governmental control of the trade union movement, these were brought under one central organization--the Nigerian Labour Congress.

Another official propaganda resource--concrete undertakings in pursuant of cultural agreements --yielded few dividends. This was due in part to the paucity of cultural associations and in part to the alienation of the Nigerians who go to the Soviet Union under cultural exchange programmes. These Nigerians complain of round-the-clock regimentation and surveillance and of shoddy treatment as guests compared to the royal treatment the Soviets receive in Lagos.

In sum, then, while diplomatic exchanges at high levels, together with propaganda, trade and economic links as well as military assistance, are significant instruments of USSR policy, the men in the Kremlin have not extensively and effectively utilised these to attain their Nigerian objectives. As Africa Contemporary Record rightly points out: "Relations with

61

Table 2.3

Major Soviet Bloc – Nigerian Visits 1971–81

(to Soviet Bloc in bold type; from Soviet Bloc in light type)

Year	USSR	Poland	Hungary	Bulgaria	Rumania	Yugoslavia
1971						
Oct	**3 man delegation to USSR led by Wenika Briggs**	3 man delegation of Foreign Trade Ministry to Nigeria led by Ryszard Strezeleski				
Oct	Former Ambassador A.I. Romanov special mission from Kosygin					
1972						
June				Vice-Minister Trade, Ianko Chibukov		
1973						
Jan			New Ambassador Morton Szabo			

Table 2.3 (cont'd)

Year	USSR	Poland	Hungary	Bulgaria	Rumania	Yugoslavia
1973 May	V.P. Elutin, Minister of Higher & Specialized Secondary Education					
Nov			Presidential Advisor Losonezi			
1974 May	**General Gowon to USSR**					
July		A Director-General, Ministry of Trade				
Sept		Government delegation				
1975 Feb	7 agricultural experts					

63

Table 2.3 (cont'd)

Year	USSR	Poland	Hungary	Bulgaria	Rumania	Yugoslavia
1976 May	Commissioner for Industry Adeleye					
June	11 man delegation technical experts					
August	3 man delegation led by I.A. Mekyukov Deputy Minister of Assembly & Special-ized Construction				Vasile Patilinet Minister of Forest Economics	PM Dzemal Bijedi
Oct		Delegation led by Derzy Olszewski Minister of Foreign Trade & Shipping				

64

Table 2.3 (cont'd)

Year	USSR	Poland	Hungary	Bulgaria	Rumania	Yugoslavia
1977 March					President Ceausescu	
Nov	5 man military delegation led by General I.G. Pasvlosk Deputy Minister of Defence & Commander-in-Chief Soviet Land Forces					
1978 May				Commissioner for Economic Development Dr. Adewoye		
June		**General Obasanjo**			**General Obasanjo**	
Oct				President Todor Zhivkov		

Table 2.3 (cont'd)

Year	USSR	Poland	Hungary	Bulgaria	Rumania	Yugoslavia
1980 June						
1981 June		Parliamentary delegation				
June		Minister of Steel, Makele		Ognyan Secretary Central Committee of Communist Party		**President Shagari**

Source: Nigeria Bulletin on International Affairs and Africa Research Bulletin

the Soviet bloc--especially in economic and military programmes--continued to expand, but there was no sign of general Nigerian support for Moscow's approach to international affairs."[31]

iii) **Nigerian Responsiveness**

Limited success in realising Soviet objectives vis-a-vis Nigeria can be attributed to four inter-related factors. Some of these are simply unrealistic and there is incapacity or unwillingness to commit adequate resources to the instruments of policy. There is also a lack of skill (borne of inexperience in understanding and appreciating the Nigerian psyche) in applying these instruments to elicit the appropriate Nigerian response. The corollary of these explanations is Nigeria's own changing needs, its perception of the limitations on the Soviet's ability to satisfy those needs and its illusion of grandeur leading to exagge-rated self-importance in superpower relations and thus to the resentment of Soviet actions that in any way evinces ostentation or heavy-handedness.

As we have noted, the civil war and Soviet politi-cal, moral and material support had led to expectations of a solid foothold in the post-war years. But the war over, Nigeria again quickly embraced the "imperialists" both economically and diplomatically, a fact symbolised by Gowon's state visit to Britain (and official visit to the US) before visiting the USSR. For Moscow, a more permanent foundation for relations beside the one-way economic, military and diplomatic support seemed called for. A little surface ideological solidarity would do and henceforth Moscow insisted on this as a quid pro quo for relations approaching the closeness of the civil war years. This, of course, is unrealistic, given the centuries of Nigerian dependency on the imperialist global economy and its unabashed commitment to capitalism and liberal democracy (even if the latter has to be salvaged occasionally with military intervention).

Yet Nigeria, even during the war, had insisted not only on excluding ideology from its relations but also on maintaining its independence of action in interna-tional politics. In particular it insisted on its independence to relate with any friendly nation includ-ing those Moscow might regard as enemies; e.g. China. Moscow did not like this and was apparently alarmed at the ascendancy of China in Nigeria's political and dip-lomatic calculus. Nigeria had played a big role in China's admission into the UN and as early as 1972 had

67

exchanged high-level economic and trade delegations
which formed the foundation for subsequent cooperative
undertakings.[32] Among these were the 22-man technical
team sent on a two-year stint to the Nigerian Industrial Development Centre, Zaria ; the manufacture of
Nigerian-designed farming tools in China; the drilling
of boreholes to boost irrigation; and the agreement to
purchase Nigerian palm kernels, cocoa, cashew-nuts and
cotton.[33] And Nigeria continued to emphasize that
because both countries had similar economic problems
and both were developing and could therefore learn from
one another, there was wide scope for mutual cooperation and information exchange.

        Apparently, because the men in the Kremlin frown-
ed at these developments Lagos persistently had to
reiterate that economic cooperation was one of the best
ways to achieve international understanding; that
"trade goes on between nations irrespective of their
ideological leanings," and that "the same kind of
friendship which brings us here today   [Moscow, 21
May 1974] motivates us in our relations with all other
peace-loving peoples of the world without discrimination as to race, colour and creed, or as to political,
ideological and social orientation."[34] Nigeria was
clearly, if politely, rejecting a heavy-handed exercise
in arm-twisting. In March 1976 there was still some
politeness remaining when a government statement cryp-
tically said: "It ought to be made clear at this stage
that all the iron and steel projects being established
in this country are Nigerian projects. They are not
Russian projects, and cannot therefore form part of the
Russians' Five Year Programme. Nor should our projects
be confused with those of Pakistan or any other countries."[35] Three years later, politeness was thrown
overboard when, as we have noted, the Federal Government reduced the number of Soviet military advisers for
"inefficiency and their condescending attitude." The
Soviets have yet to learn how not to arouse Nigerian
sensitivities.

        The end of the civil war in favour of Nigeria and
the tremendous oil wealth that began to accrue to it
soon thereafter, boosted Nigeria's ego and provided a
material base for asserting long-coveted African
leadership. Suddenly, Nigeria "became the African
country most widely courted both by the West and the
East and it is continually looked to for support within
the OAU"[36] These developments changed, inter alia,
Nigeria's perception of its need for the Soviets. It
no longer needed "foreign aid," or so it thought until

the "oil glut" in the late 1970s and early 1980s shook
off the illusion; but by then the kind of aid it needed
could only be supplied by western consortia and
western-backed international financial institutions
(see previous and subsequent chapters). In 1978, for
instance, Nigeria raised a seven-year $1,000 million
Eurocurrency loan involving more than 79 banks in over
10 countries. And it planned "to raise $5,5000 million
abroad over the next three years from banks ($2,000
million), supplier credits (about $1, 5000 million),
the Euromarket ($1,900 million) and the World Bank
($1,000 million)."[37]

     Meanwhile, Nigeria felt it could pay for the ser-
vices it needed: what was essential, therefore, was
trade and more trade and, of course, the political
atmosphere to permit the sale of the sophisticated
technology it needed. This emphasis was reflected in
the Second National Development Plan and in the subsequent plans. Says the Second Plan document: the
country's external policy "will seek to maximise the
benefits which could accure from an expanding and more
diversified international trade and international
movements of capital and skills."[38] For the Soviets,
of course, trade and aid are weapons against imperialism and are therefore transacted with those ideologi-
cally opposed to capitalism, the father of imperialism.
Nigeria obviously was not one of these.

     As Nigeria-Soviet trade declined and general eco-
nomic relations failed to keep pace with the growth of
the economy, Nigeria came to the obvious conclusion
that the USSR either lacked the material basis for
beneficial bilateral relations or it lacked the will to
use it, or both. To depend on the USSR for the susten-
ance of any vital national institution (the performance
on the iron and steel complex had not been satisfactory
to the Nigerian public) was thus unacceptable. The
result was the diversification of the sources of supplies and training which, thanks to petronaira, was now
feasible. It is significant that by 1982 Nigeria was
signing agreements with India to train personnel from
the Ajaokuta Steel Company; an Austrian firm, Steyr
Daimler-Puch, won a N30 million--contract to build
armoured personnel carriers in Nigeria; and large arms
deals were being negotiated with six other West
European countries, the US and India. On the shopping
list were the Franco-German Alfa jets, West German
Leopard tanks, French corvettes, Jaguar fighter aircraft, frigates, missile systems and small arms and
ammunition.[39]

The Nigerians also came to perceive that Moscow lacked the political clout to help change events in Africa that they regarded as vital to their national interest. The key to the solution of the Zimbabwean, the Namibian and the South African questions lay in Washington and London not in Moscow. It was foolish, therefore, for any one to expect Nigeria to be in "a permanent state of confrontation with a country such as the United States just for the sake of confrontation or for the dubious virtue of appearing dynamic and progressive," just as it would be foolhardy to expect the country to be in a state of permanent alliance with any country."[40]

In any case there have been clear conflicts of interest with Moscow even in areas of seemingly convergent political/diplomatic activities such as Southern African and the Horn. Nigeria blamed the Soviet Union's "sad hardline" for the failure of External Affairs Commissioner Joe Garba's mission to bring warring Ethiopia and Somalia to the conference table in early 1978.[41] In Angola, Nigeria's initial preference and efforts to form a government of national unity not only conflicted with the USSR's position, the latter's arming of the MPLA also doomed the Nigerian effort ab initio. The lesson was clear: however beneficial they may be in the short-run, Soviet activities in Africa, and especially their role as the continent's foremost gun-runner, were dangerous in the long-run. The USSR was thus perceived as the new interloper whose expansionism (indicated where they over-stay their welcome) must be resisted. Suspicion of Soviet intentions continues.

It is significant that Nigeria's relations with satellite countries were relatively more successful. It is with these satellites that Nigeria has maintained more frequent diplomatic contacts at the highest levels. In particular, there have been increasingly close diplomatic and economic relations with Poland, Romania and Hungary (Table 2.3) Three main reasons account for this. First, there is no suspicion of these countries which are relatively weak and there are no real conflicts of interest with them in Africa. Second, these countries are less ideological and more pragmatic in their bilateral relations and they are willing to concede Nigeria's right of independent action just as they would want Nigeria to support their own right of independent action (which Moscow denies). This is why Nigeria's understandable silence on the Soviet invasion of Czechoslovakia in 1968 was so painful and has chilled Nigerian-Czechosolvakian relations ever since.

Finally, the satellite countries appear capable and willing to expend significant material resources in their relations with Nigeria. And they seem to use this capability effectively. Since the war Romania, among other things, has been involved in two large industrial complexes in wood processing and textiles in the Cross River State worth over N150 million and in wood processing in Ondo State worth over N15 million. Poland has mechanized the Enugu coal mines in a N20 million contract deal; has established Polamp (authorized share capital: N526,000) to manufacture electric bulbs; and has given over N20 million in loans to finance machinery and equipment for cement, textile and wood processing industries. Hungary, for its part, has invested heavily (over N70 million) in the cable and wireless industry and in glass factories at Badagry and in Kano State.[42] Commerce is also increasing with these countries. Not surprisingly, therefore, diplomatic contacts at the level of heads of state have been widespread.

Notes

1. Ali Mazrui, African International Relations
    (London: Heinemann, 1977), 2.

2. K. Brutents, "The Soviet Union and the
    Newly--Independent Countries" International
    Affairs (April 1979) 3-4 quoted by W. Raymond
    Duncan, "Soviet Power in Latin America: success
    or failure?" in Robert H. Donaldson, (ed) The
    Soviet Union in the Third Word: successes and
    failures (Boulder: Westview, 1981) 5.

3. Ibid.

4. Arthur Jay Klinghoffer, "The Soviet Union and
    Angola" in (ed) The Soviet Union in the Third
    World, 98.

5. Robert H. Donaldson, The Soviet-Indian Alignment:
    quest for influence (University of Denver
    Graduate School of International Studies, 1979),
    Monograph Series in World Affairs, Vol. 16, 5-6.

6. For details see Olatunde J. B. Ojo, "Nigerian-
    Soviet Relations: retrospect and prospect" Afri-
    can Studies Review 19 (3), (1976), 43-63 at 54.

7. A Soviet diplomat quoted in West Africa, 22 Feb-
    ruary 1969 and cited in E. A. Ajayi, "Nigeria-
    Soviet Aid Relations, 1960-69" Nigeria: Bulletin
    on Foreign Affairs 1, (January 1972), 8.

8. On these points, see Ojo "Nigerian--Soviet Rela-
    tions", 54-55.

9. Donaldson, The Soviet-Indian Alignment, 7.

10. For an analysis of the pre-civil war period, see
    Ojo, "Nigerian-Soviet Relations", 43-54.

11. Klinghoffer, "The Soviet Union and Angola",
    97-100.

12. On the role of the Soviet Union in the Nigerian
    civil war, see John de St. Jorre, The Nigerian
    Civil War (London: Hodder and Stoughton, 1972);
    Arthur J. Klinghoffer, "The USSR and Nigeria:
    why the Soviets chose sides" African Report 13
    (2), (February 1968), 9; F. O. Ogunbadejo, Civil
    Strife in International Relations: a case study
    of the Nigerian Civil War, 1967-1970 (unpublished
    University of London Ph.D thesis, 1974) Chapter
    7; and D.L. Morrison. "The USSR and the War in
    Nigeria" Mizan I (1), (1969), 21.

13. The clearest recent Nigerian government statement
    on its foreign policy objectives was that enuni-
    ciated by General Obansanjo on 29 June 1976.   It
    has since been repeated by other Nigerian leaders
    and can be said to summarise objectives that have
    been pursued since independence and are likely to
    be sought in the foreseeable future; see African
    Contemporary Record Volume 1976/77 p. B677-8 and
    Brigadier Joe Garba "Nigeria Re-affirms Stand on
    World Affairs Daily Times 11 February 1978, 24,
    26 and 28.

14. Nigeria: Bulletin on Foreign Affairs, 2 (1 & 2)
        (1972), 24.

15. For analysis of Nigerian strategic objectives and
    means see James H. Polhemus, "Nigeria and South-
    ern Africa: interest, policy and means" Canadian
    Journal of African Studies II, (1977), 43-66 and P.
    F. Wilmot, "Nigeria's Strategic Objectives in
    Southern Africa: a comparative analysis of the
    economic, political and military bases of strategy and
    counter-strategy of Nigeria and South Africa" Seminar
    Paper, Faculty of Social Sciences, University of Port
    Harcourt 25 May 1982.

16. Successive military regimes from 1966 have per-
    sistently declared that they would not impose any
    ideology on the country.

17. Quoted in Ajayi, "Nigeria-Soviet Aid Relations",
    7-8.

18. See Ojo, "Nigerian-Soviet Relations", 55.

19. United States Arms Control and Disarmament
    Agency, World Military Expenditures and Arms
    Transfers, 1969-1978.

20. Africa Contemporary Record Volume 1975/76, B 799.

21. Ray Ofoegbu, "Foreign Policy and Military Rule"
    in Oyeleye Oyediran (ed), Nigerian Government and
    Politics Under Military Rule 1966-79 (New York:
    St. Martin's, 1979), 124-149 at 139.

22. Africa Report November/December 1979.

23. B. Kozintsev and P. Kashelov, "Economic Coopera-
    tion of the USSR with the Countries of Tropical
    Africa", Foreign Trade (Moscow), 2 February 1978
    cited by Daniel S. Papp, "The Soviet Union and
    Southern Africa" in Donaldson (ed), The Soviet
    Union in the Third World, 83.

24. For text of the USSR agreement, see Nigeria:
    Bulletin on Foreign Affairs 1 (3), (1972) 33-35;
    also Federal Republic of Nigeria, Treaties in
    Force 2 (1970), 44-60.

25. For details, see Ojo, "Nigerian- Soviet
    Relations", 50-52.

26. Ofoegbu, "Foreign Policy and Military Rule,"
    138-139.

27. Nigeria: Bulletin on Foreign Affairs 6(3),(1976)
    34; and 6 (8), (1976), 61.

28. Computed from Africa Research Bulletin (1970-
    1980) taking care to avoid double counting.

29. See, for example Africa Diary, 26 November -
    2 December 1967, 3681; Africa Confidential (8
    June 1973), 7.

30. Ojo, "Nigerian-Soviet Relations", 59.

31. Africa Contemporary Record Volume 1976-77, B678.

32. cf. The four-man delegation led by the Commi-
    ssioner for Economic Development & Reconstruc-
    tion, Professor Adebayo Adedeji in August 1972
    and the ten-man Chinese delegation led by
    Fang-Yi, Minister of Economic Relations with
    Foreign Countries see Nigeria: Bulletin on
    Foreign Affairs, 2 (1 and 2), (1972), 24-25.

33. Ibid, 6, (2), (February 1976), 45; Africa
    Research Bulletin, 15 July - 14 August 1979,
    5221.

34.   Nigeria: Bulletin on Foreign Affairs 2 (1 & 2),
      (1972), 24; and 4 (1-4), (1974), 75.

35.   Ibid 6 (3), (March 1976), 34-35.

36.   Africa Contemporary Record Volume 1978-79, B741.

37.   Africa Research Bulletin, (15 January - 14
      February 1978), 4573.

38.   Federal Republic of Nigeria: Second National
      Development Plan 1970-74, 78.

39.   Africa Diary, (9-15 April 1982), 10934; and 29
      January - 4 February 1982.

40.   Joe Garba telling Nigerians and the Russians some
      home truths in an address, "Nigeria's Foreign
      Policy and the National Interest" at the Ahmadu
      Bello University, Zaria. See Daily Times, (11
      February 1978) 24-28.

41   Daily Times, (9 February 1978), 1.

42.   Africa Research Bulletin, (15 October - 14
      November 1971), 2198; (15 February - 14 March
      1974), 3046; (15 July - 14 August 1972), 2445;
      (15 February - 14 March 1972), 2308; (15 December
      - 14 January 1973), 2597; (15 June - 14 July
      1975), 3565; (15 June - 14 July 1976), 3945; (15
      February - 14 March 1977), 4209; (15 April - 14
      May 1979), 5110.

Chapter Three

Oil and Nigeria's Relations with the Great Powers:

the limits of oil diplomacy*

Akanmu Adebayo

In 1980 in New York, President Shehu Shagari
threatened that in the struggle against South Africa
and her Western supporters, Nigeria would not hesitate
to "use every method and if it is necessary to use
oil." In addition, while opening the Kaduna oil
refinery later in the year, the President made a similar open threat to use the power that derives from the
sale of barrels of oil.[1] This notion of the oil weapon
was brought-forward from the last military regime; for
it was claimed that General Obasanjo stiffened Carter's
back-bone in 1978 when he stated that Nigerian oil
might cease to flow across the Atlantic if the United
States lifted sanctions against Rhodesia.

Is the threat that Nigeria could effectively apply
oil diplomacy (or the oil weapon) against the great
powers one that could be carried out or is it merely a
foreign policy propaganda campaign? Did Nigeria in
fact apply oil diplomacy between 1975 and 1980?
Against which powers, with what degree of effectiveness, and what factors limited the effectiveness of
this application? These are some of the questions
which this chapter sets out to answer.

i) What is Oil Diplomacy?

There are three major participants in the oil
industry: the oil companies, the producer governments,
and the consumer governments.

---

*I wish to acknowledge the criticism and contribution
of earlier versions of this paper received from Doctors
S.O. Osoba and Toyin Falola; and Messrs Kayode
Soremekun and Funso Afolayan. The opinion and errors
are mine.

Each of these has been known to exert power and influence which at different points in the history of the development of the oil industry brought clashes and crises. This power play among the participants is what is regarded as oil diplomacy. In essence, oil diplomacy is a complex concept capable of being seen to operate at three main levels: corporate, producer and consumer levels.

The oil companies, especially the majors,[2] have a long history of dominating the industry. As oligopolistic multinational corporations, they have a long record of controlling the exploration, production, transportation, refining and marketing of oil. It has been asserted that their continued domination of the industry arises partly from the fact that they started the international search for oil when the major Third World producer governments exercised little control over their country's destinies; therefore, they gained significant concessions from colonial or semi-colonial governments[3] partly because they had the monopoly over the sophisticated technology of the industry. Their style of diplomacy consists in perpetuating this position of dominance in the face of economic and political nationalism, and keeping oil technology as far away from the producer governments as possible. For instance, C.C. Pocock, the Senior Managing Director of Royal Dutch/Shell, has expressed reluctance and pessimism about the transfer of oil technology to producer governments:

> I believe discussions on the transfer of technology in theory, as if it were a catalogue you could get from a shelf, are very dangerous because they lead us to ignore the real value of technological services.[4]

There are two categories of consumer governments: the industrialised nations (the great powers) who are also the 'parents' of the oil companies and the developing Third World nations. Both categories import oil which, until 1973, was very cheap. This situation began to change from the 1960s and by 1974 oil was neither cheap nor was its supply guaranteed. Generally, therefore, the diplomacy at this level is geared towards ensuring the availability of oil and at reasonably low prices. It is interesting to observe that recent events tend to show that consumer governments are succeeding: the glut which had engulfed the

oil market since 1982 eventually drove some OPEC members unilaterally to lower oil prices in February 1983.
It is also essential to note that the consumer governments and the oil companies are often on very good
terms diplomatically.[5] Except in the 1973-74 crisis
when the companies had to carry out embargoes against
their parent countries, their relations have been
cordial. This is partly because the ends sought by
both of them are often identical and partly because
they are both affected by the producer's oil diplomacy.

The producer governments occupy a marginal though
improving position in the industry. They have been
exposed to untold exploitation by the oil companies.
Until recently, they exercised no control over the
determination of the production and price levels, and
destination of their oil resources. Nevertheless, since
the end of World War II, and because of the intense
nationalist agitation that followed it, they have
started to assert their right to 'own' the oil industry
and use their oil resources selectively to affect
international politics. Diplomacy at this level, and
especially how successfully it can be employed against
a great power that imports a percentage of its oil
needs, is of central concern to this chapter. As such,
a contextual definition is essential.

Most of the current formulations on oil diplomacy
have one principal defect: that of holding oil diplomacy narrowly as synonymous with Arab use of oil in the
Middle East Wars. For instance, it has been defined as
"a three-pronged weapon which involved cutback in production, embargo on some countries known to be friendly
with Israel, and unilateral increase in prices."[6] This
would have been acceptable if one was describing an
incidence of the application of oil diplomacy. There
are however some commentators who avoid this conceptual
error. For instance, M.A. Olorunfemi defines the oil
weapon as:

> The use of oil as a means of scor-
> ing political goals through the
> ability of oil producers to pick
> and choose who can have access to
> their much needed commodity.[7]

Olorunfemi's formulation presupposes one element of
the diplomacy which is often not explicitly stated:
the "ability" of the producers to pick and choose.
This ability is a derivative of many developments,
including securing the control of the oil industry from

the companies and monitoring the marketing of oil by
regulating production and fixing prices. Many Third
World oil producers cannot do this, neither can they
withstand a lengthy production cut and lack of sales,
all aspects of the tools employed in oil diplomacy.

In short, oil diplomacy can be defined as the dual
operation of wresting the control of oil industry from
the oil majors and of manipulating the production and
marketing of, and wealth from, oil to affect international issues. This definition implies a double-
edged sword directed at, first, the oil companies for
gaining control of the industry and, second, the consumer governments for scoring political points either
by using the oil revenue to induce a group of consumers, or by denying oil to selected consumers.

ii)   **Nigeria, the Great Powers and Oil**

a)   **The Soviet Union**

It is clear that even assuming that Nigeria's oil
power was real, she could only hope to employ it
against a power that depends on her oil and that pursues a foreign policy clearly antagonistic to her
beliefs. The Soviets are the world's largest oil producer, apart from meeting all the needs of the Warsaw
Pact countries.[8] The Soviet Union is not one of
Nigeria's oil markets; therefore Nigeria has no degree
of oil leverage over it.

In addition, Soviet policies in Africa, at the time
that Nigeria was supposed to be wielding oil diplomacy
(i.e. 1975-1979), did not run counter to the latter's
interests. It is true that a point in her foreign
policy history (i.e. between 1960 and 1966), Nigeria,
inheriting the anti-communist views of the British
government, isolated herself as much as possible from
the Soviet Union. But with the civil war and with the
assistance which the FMG received from the Soviets in
arms shipments, Nigeria commenced a policy of closer
ties with the Soviet Union.

The major basis for antagonism between Nigeria and
the Soviet Union was ideology which is a basic component of Soviet foreign policy. But in her relationship
with Nigeria, it seemed that the Soviet Union de-
emphasised this component. In particular, in 1975 when

Nigerian foreign policy took an anti-imperialist turn, the Soviet Union and Nigeria were on the same sides in the Angolan and Zimbabwean crises.

In oil matters, Nigeria has received technical assistance from the Soviet Union. There were Russian instructors at the Warri Petroleum Institute and this has enabled Nigerians to gain knowledge about both Western and Soviet oil technology.[9] In addition, the contract for the construction of the giant iron and steel mill at Ajaokuta was won by the Soviet Union. This was appropriate as the Soviets produced more pig iron than any other country in the world. There were also trade agreements between Nigeria and the Soviet Union that allowed Soviet exports of various machines, equipment, building materials, electrical materials and consumer goods to Nigeria. The volume of this trade has been very low because the Soviet Union had no use for Nigeria's major foreign exchange earner--oil.

b) The United States of America

Nigeria's relations with the US have remained cool since the Nigerian civil war when the US refused to sell arms to the FMG and instead permitted the pro-pagation of a pro-Biafran campaign during and after the war. This cool relationship was worsened by the refusal of the US president to see General Gowon who was in New York to address the United Nations as the OAU Chairman.[10] Furthermore, in 1973 when the Sahelian drought struck a number of West African states including Nigeria, the FMG was angered by the US refusal to send 50 helicopters urgently needed to transport relief materials from Maiduguri to Chad and Niger.[11]

The first of the series of clashes that further strained the relationship occurred when Nigeria and the US disagreed on their South African policies, especially over the Angolan crisis. The Murtala regime brought in by the bloodless coup of July 1975 sided with the Soviet-aided MPLA (Popular Movement for the Liberation of Angola) and launched a "diplomatic blitzkrieg"[12] to win the recognition of other African states. The US, on the other hand, supported the South Africa-backed FNLA (National Front for the Liberation of Angola). The second clash was over the belief in Nigeria that the CIA was involved in the attempted coup of February 1976 and the assassination of General Murtala Mohammed. This belief may have had a substance of truth in it, as the popular, anti-imperialist, anti-

US stance of the Murtala regime undoubtedly disturbed the US.

The propaganda offensive launched in Nigeria between 1975 and 1976 was as if Nigeria was at war with the US. In July 1975, the Federal Government gave the US a quiet notice to vacate its embassy close to Dodan Barracks and occupy an alternative site at Okotie Eboh Street. When the US would not listen, the army forcefully occupied the premises, the government claiming that it was undesirable to allow the US to operate beside the country's Cabinet Office.[13] The New Nigerian in its editorial praised the government's move and added that "given the American obsession with tapes and bugs one wonders if the Cabinet Office has secrets any more."[14]

In January 1976, the FMG reacted sharply to what it termed as American "arm twisting" policy. Earlier, the Ford Administration had sent circular letters to all African heads of state, urging them to insist in the forthcoming OAU extraordinary meetings on Angola on the withdrawal of Soviet and Cuban military advisers as a quid pro quo for the withdrawal of racist South African occupation forces.[15] In its reaction, the Murtala regime totally repudiated the "false logic that equates the presence of Cuban and Soviet advisers in Angola with that of South African regular troops" and rejected the attempt by the Ford Administration to insult the intelligence of African nations through open and purposive teleguiding.[16] This "Statement on Angola" was carried by the Nigerian press with enthusiasm. The Daily Sketch captioned it "FMG blasts Ford" while the Daily Times titled it "Shut Up."[17]

Sequel to this incidence, the US Foreign Broadcast Information Service (FBIS) centre in Kaduna was ordered to close down. This action was again hailed by the Nigerian press.[18] The invitation originally extended to Henry Kissinger, US Secretary of State, was cancelled. This was also commended as a correct policy, especially as it repaid the US in its own coins.[19] In a lead story captioned "Kissinger, Stay Home," the Nigerian Herald stated that Kissinger was on a "Sunday school lecture tour to preach anti-freedom set theories."

The press sensations obviously could make one arrive at the simplistic conclusion, which was then prevalent, that Nigeria was now able to antagonise a major Western country on such fundamental African issues as equal rights, justice and independence. In fact, this was the image of Nigeria that the FMG intended to sell not only to Nigerians but also to Africans and the world at large: the image that Nigeria was now up-rightly assertive, and that the Murtala regime was radically purposive on matters concerning independence and majority rule in Southern Africa.

All available opportunities were exploited by the FMG between 1975 and 1979 to popularise this view of Nigeria's power and capability. The head of the Navy, Admiral Adelanwa, in 1978 stated <u>inter alia</u> that "we are growing from strength to strength and where it means direct involvement in the war against apartheid South Africa I would think we are up to the task."[20] He repeated this boast to newsmen abroad the NNS Nigeria, the country's biggest warship, that "the Navy as presently constituted is capable of quelling any external invasion."[21] In a television interview towards the end of 1978, General T.Y. Danjuma also made the assertion that Nigeria would match her South African policy statements with action and that the Nigerian army was capable of taking on South Africa, Cuban-style.[22] Speaking at the UN Security Council meeting earlier in March 1977, Brigadier Garba, Nigeria's Commissioner for External Affairs, threatened that foreign investors would have to choose between investing in Nigeria and dealing with South Africa because Nigeria would not hesitate to apply selectively the oil weapon against parent countries of erring multinational corporations.[23] It was believed that this was not an empty threat.

iii) **Beyond Power Assumptions and Assertions**

With the amount of publicity given to this claim by members of the Nigerian government, it is not surprising that some notable members of the academic world, especially those that had the ears of the government, began to peddle it about that Nigeria was now a "medium power."[24] The characteristics of this power were given as: (a) <u>an economy</u> which, though monocultural, has been well-managed and in which the proceeds from the oil sphere were directed into self-generating industrial fields; (b) <u>a huge population</u>--at least 40 million--whose literacy and technological content and proportion can be measured by the number of universities in the country and the qualitive aspects of education received; (c) <u>a stability</u> at the individual, government and system level; and (d) <u>the ability and willingness of the government to intervene in regional conflicts</u> and assume the leadership role on the continent.

It is obvious, even to the least informed, that the above formulations are not based on sound reasoning. When Adelanwa said that Nigeria could take on South Africa, he obviously must have been joking. As an analyst has put it,

> This Navy of ours has only one landing craft. Perhaps during an emergency we can commandeer our commercial ships for movement of soldiers from one point to another. But such ships will be highly vulnerable to enemy submarines and other anti-ship equipments. This Navy does not have a submarine; if there is one around our coast, it is not ours. It does not have an aircraft carrier, it does not even have ships capable of operating few defensive helicopters and other aircrafts.[25]

It takes little imagination to know that our Navy would crumble within a few hours under attack; and this is the Navy that would operate against South Africa!

As for Nigeria's assumption of the leadership of Africa, another analyst has suggested that this was a mere farce because of elements of internal ineptitude and total inability to manage the economy and to demonstrate to other African societies that Nigeria was capable of lynching from its own terrain the forces of monopoly capitalism.[26] Perhaps this is a radical view but it surely holds true as long as domestic ability results from a well-managed and diversified economy and a purposive political system.

In addition, a careful look at the country's economic (particularly oil) linkage with the US does not support the claim that Nigeria was a "new African power." Rather it proves, as events of 1977/78 attested, that Nigeria had more than the US to lose economically in a headlong, longdrawn collision. The US is an important single market for Nigeria's crude oil. As shown in Table 3.1, Nigeria's dependence on the US market in 1975/76 was an inconvenient 34.39 per cent. By 1978 Nigeria was the second largest exporter of crude oil to the US after Saudi Arabia.[27] In this period, also, oil revenue accounted for about 95% of Nigeria's total export earnings and 75% of the Federal Government revenues.[28] The serious consequences for the country of a disturbance in this oil trade cannot be overlooked as the quantity of oil involved was such that Nigeria could not expect to sell at the spot market.

What I am asserting here is that rational economic thinking was one of the factors which pervaded Nigeria's foreign policy making in 1977, during which time a new leaf was turned in the relationship between Nigeria and the US. The other factors responsible for this new turn have been given as: a) the Carter Administration's determination to treat Africa as a worthy place in the country's foreign policy; b) the appointment of a black Congressmen, Andrew Young, as the country's permanent representative at the UN, an appointment seen by Africans as representing the new administration's concern for Africa; c) the espousal by Carter and Young of the belief that African solutions should be adopted to African problems; and d) the popularisation of the view in the US that the Soviet Union should not be the only superpower perceived as supporting African aspirations.[29]

But the above factors are located concretely in the US; and the Nigerian side to the revived link seems to be the need to remedy whatever damage might have been done to Nigeria-US economic relations especially in oil matters, and further strengthen the economic ties between the two countries. This view is supported by the fact that in the ensuing rapprochment, Nigeria did not mind the facts that: a) the US did not recognise SWAPO as the authentic party of Namibia, and b) the Anglo-American proposals for the settlement of the Zimbabwean dispute were shoddy. In fact, the entente, which commenced on 10 October 1977 with the state visit of General Obasanjo to the US, was dominated more by talks on strengthening economic cooperation than by discussions on events in Southern Africa and the chances of Nigeria-US collaboration. The Nigerian Government took time to explain that in spite of the indigenisation and foreign exchange anti-sabotage decrees, enough room was still left for American investment in Nigeria.[30] On the basis of other talks given by the Nigerian delegation in Washington and New York, joint

Table 3.1

Africa, United States and Britain:

shares of Nigeria's oil trade

	1971/72	1972/73	1973/74
[1]Total Crude oil sold (barrels)	567,737,138 1.6 m.bpd	656,189,391 1.8 m.bpd	750,592,474 2.1 m.bpd
[2]Africa	10,428,591	9,317,760	12,455,876
[3]US	126,523,688	164,099,113	206,773,262
[4]Britain	103,268,532	105,651,959	116,163,275
[5]African purchases as percentage of total	1.83	1.42	1.66
[6]US purchases as percentage of total	22.29	25.01	27.55
[7]British purchases as percentage of total	18.18	16.1	15.5

Table 3.1 (continued)

	1974/75	1975/76	1976/77	1978
[1]	766,612,510 2.1 m.bpd	638,574,575 1.7 m.bpd	715,240,000 2.0 m.bpd	674,125,147 1.8 m.bpd
[2]	12,287,638	16,042,039	16,674,745	16,873,219
[3]	246,116,173	219,616,866	293,766,498	274,975,978
[4]	105,979,085	79,315,378	47,463,372	24,671,179
[5]	1.60	2.51	2.33	2.50
[6]	32.10	34.39	41.07	40.79
[7]	13.82	12.4	6.6	3.66

Sources: a) <u>Annual Reports</u>, NNOC for 1971/72 - 1976/77

b) <u>Annual Reports</u>, NNPC for 1977,1978.

committees were formed to discuss Agriculture, Education, Economic Development and Technical Assistance.[31] None was created to deal, for instance, with action against apartheid.

Commenting on the essential resilience of Nigeria-US relations, David Lamb, a writer for the <u>Los Angeles Times</u>, has rightly observed that even when diplomatic relations were on the rocks, as in 1976, "economic cooperation between the US and this capitalistic country of 80 million people moved ahead unimpeded."[32]

c) Great Britain

If there was a country that occupied a special place in Nigeria's foreign policy, and with whom Nigeria maintained close political and economic relations, it was Britain.[33] This is not surprising if we consider the years Nigeria spent under the colonial tutelage of Britain; the cultural affinity that resulted between Nigerians and the British, particularly in political matters; the tangible and intangible links left behind by Britain especially in economic spheres as aspects of her neo-colonial design on the country; and the enormity of British aid to Nigeria soon after independence.

Even though the British monopoly on Nigeria's foreign and economic policies had been shaken after the civil war, she still remained the largest single foreign investor in Nigeria, providing 40% of the total in 1978. Nigeria in 1978 took 28% of all British exports to OPEC countries.[34] In the oil sector, the Anglo-Dutch company, Shell-BP, laid the foundation of Nigeria's oil industry, a foundation which it exploited to the fullest. By 1979, Shell-BP was producing more than half of the country's total crude oil production. The government had, however, acquired 55% of its equity shares.

These details are necessary to an appreciation of Nigeria's economic relations with Britain, around which revolved the issue of Nigeria's use of diplomacy in dealing with Britain over the issues of independence and majority rule in Zimbabwe. Until 1975, Nigeria's Rhodesian policies lacked clarity and vigour. They were characterised by tacit support for the effete UN, OAU and Commonwealth policies and sanctions. But past efforts by these international organisations as well as British initiatives made prior to 1976 to occasion majority rule in Rhodesia were not concerted and often proved abortive.[35]

Nevertheless, certain changes began to occur: Portuguese rule in Mozambique and Angola collapsed in 1975; guerrilla warfare was stepped up in Zimbabwe; the Carter Administration was inaugurated in Washington and promised a new African policy; and in Nigeria the Murtala/Obasanjo regime entered the African scene with an anti-colonial, anti-White minority rule stance. The British negotiators therefore came under more concerted and intense pressure from both Africa and other parts

of the world. They therefore began to negotiate more
seriously with Ian Smith over the issue of majority
rule.

   The details of developments in Zimbabwe need not
detain us. The aspect of it that engages our attention
in this chapter is the Lusaka Commonwealth of August
1979, where pressure was brought to bear on Britain by
the African members so that at the end of the day a
"Plan for Zimbabwe" was adopted which recognised the
need for international support to make any resolution
on the Zimbabwe question a success.[36] On the basis of
this plan, constitutional talks were held between the
Patriotic Front, the Smith-Muzorewa coalition government, and the British negotiator at Lancaster House
late in 1979. On the basis of the agreements reached
there, a ceasefire was effected and the interim government of Lord Soames organised the elections held in
February 1980, which resulted in a victory by Robert
Mugabe's ZANU (PF).[37]

   Among the countries that applied pressure on
Britain at Lusaka was Nigeria: it used the oil weapon.
On the eve of the Conference, the FMG announced the
acquisition of all the 22.5% equity shares of the BP
marketing company.[38] In addition, the Government gave
the BP expatriate staff until the end of August to
leave the country, excluding only those retained on
contract by the NNPC, which acquired these shares on
behalf of the Government. The mood of many Nigerians,
as reflected in the press, was jubilant. The FMG was
praised by the Nigerian Herald in an editorial captioned "Action Against Apartheid" while the New Nigerian in
its editorial titled "Right Decision" wondered why the
FMG waited so long before nationalising a BP known to
have been keeping the racist machinery going.[39]

   The FMG stated that its reason for the nationalisation was to prevent Nigeria's oil from being shipped to
South Africa. (Margaret Thatcher had given formal
approval to BP to export North Sea and non-embargoed
oil to the racist enclave). It was also claimed that
the action was timed to coincide with the Lusaka Conference so as to pressure Britain into revising its
Rhodesian policy.[40] Nigerians and the world at large
were expected to see this as a clear indication of
Nigeria's ability and readiness to employ the oil
weapon, even single-handedly.

   The linkage between Nigeria's nationalisation of BP
and the subsequent British capitulation on the Rhode-

sian question is a controversial issue. It could be said, for instance, that, bearing in mind the temporising and reluctant attitude of Britain with regard to Zimbabwean independence since 1965, it is reasonable to surmise that Nigeria's nationalisation of BP assets was the decisive factor in Britain's move to adopt positive policies ensuring the territory's independence. It could also be claimed that it was the BP issue that hung over the Lusaka confabulation like a dark cloud and forced Britain to act; and that without it, Lusaka would have ended like other Commonwealth confabs, what with the foot-dragging progress made on Namibia and South Africa since then!

The position taken in this chapter is that the significance of the nationalisation on the Rhodesian issue should not be over-estimated unless one wants to arrive at a simplistic conclusion, such as that Nigeria's employment of oil diplomacy was the only major factor that ensured independence and majority rule for Zimbabwe. That Nigeria's pressure from the barrel of the oil was significant is not doubted. But the argument here is that this was just one of many factors that accounted for the success over the Zimbabwean issue. Other factors included the escalation of guerrilla warfare in Rhodesia itself without which no pressure would have been advocated; the decision of the rival groups of freedom fighters in Zimbabwe temporarily to bury their hatchet and work together under the umbrella of the Patriotic Front without which a state like Nigeria would not have been encouraged to apply pressure on Smith and Britain; the influence and activities of the Front Line States not only in providing sanctuaries for the freedom fighters and suffering indecent assaults from the Rhodesian and South African forces but also in making clarion calls to other African states to join in the struggle; and finally, the preparedness of the Smith-Muzorewa coalition government to negotiate after the failure of Smith's internal settlement, a preparedness without which no negotiating party would have succeeded. It is therefore logical to conclude that the Nigerian pressure from the nationalisation of the assets of the BP marketing company alone could not have compelled Britain to see the error in her Rhodesian policy and to change course. This position is supported by the following pair of reasons.

First, the nationalisation affected British investment in Nigeria only indirectly. It is true that BP is a multinational corporation which was at the time partly owned by the British Government and therefore that its nationalisation would automatically affect the interest of the parent government. But BP is traditionally "crude long," meaning that it always has more crude oil to sell than it has outlets for its marketing. At the end of the 1970s, BP sold to its customers among the oil consuming nations 100 million tons and sold another 24 million tons to other companies. It received from the Nigerian sources crude oil of about 12 million tons annually. The company, therefore, with the nationalisation, lost half of its third-party oil business.[41] This loss was estimated at £30 million which could be higher if the company were to purchase the equivalent quantity from non-OPEC sources or on the spot market.[42] This loss was not so disastrous to the company as the Nigerian government would have us believe, however. In fact, the marketing arm of the company constituted only a fraction of British investment in Nigeria. Other companies were not nationalised, nor was there a concerted threat that they would be. Therefore, I wonder where lay the potency of the "pressure"? Britain was conducting lucrative trade relations with Nigeria in machinery, equipments and consumer goods. In 1975 alone, she exported goods worth £512 million and recorded a trade balance of over £200 million in her favour. In 1976, she exported goods worth £774 million to Nigeria and took only £316 million worth of Nigeria's exports. In 1977, when she exported £1,068 million worth of goods to Nigeria she bought only £300 million worth of Nigerian goods.[43] It is easy to see that a company that fetched about £30 million was but small fry: the nationalisation of some other company also known to be dealing with apartheid South Africa would have caused Britain more inconvenience than the marketing arm of BP.

And second, North Sea oil and gas made Britain less dependent on Nigerian oil. As shown in Table 3.1, British oil imports from Nigeria progressively declined; and by 1978, she was purchasing just 3.66% of Nigeria's total marketed crude oil. As a result of the 1973/74 oil crisis, production in the North Sea was intensified. The proven reserves of the area were put between 1 billion and 4.5 billion tons. Britain was producing a modest 80 million tons per annum in 1979 and this made British demand from Nigeria very low indeed.[44] What was even more significant is that North Sea and Nigerian oil were of similarly low sulphur content. Britain would not have suffered seriously if Nigeria even went further than nationalising BP and placed an embargo on oil shipment to her. In fact, while Britain

was importing less and less oil from Nigeria, Nigeria
was importing more and more goods from Britain.

iv) Conclusion: limits of oil diplomacy

In the preceeding section, it was argued that
Nigeria had neither the capability nor the capacity to
unilaterally threaten any great power with either a
short or extended oil war. The Soviet Union does not
import oil; Great Britain imports a decreasing quantity
of oil from Nigeria, having become well served by the
North Sea oil and gas; and the US, which purchases over
40% of Nigeria's crude oil, could get the same quantity
of oil involved from other sources--OPEC, non-OPEC and
spot market. It seems, then, that an embargo on oil
exports to the US and her Western allies would be suicidal for Nigeria, for this group of countries together
purchases well over 80% of Nigeria's crude oil sales.

It is now opportune to indicate those factors whose
absence would make oil diplomacy a myth or a piece of
deceptive propaganda.[45] First, restrictive regulatory
measures have to be imposed by a group of major producers
acting in concert. This had been demonstrated in 1973
when the major Arab oil producers cut production, out-
lawed oil shipments to the US and increased prices.
They were able to achieve a condition akin to oil scarcity in the market; and to make the US and her Western
allies review, at least temporarily, their Middle Eastern policy. For a concerted effort such as this, the
issue for which oil diplomacy is employed has to be one
that concerns the major producers generally, or at
least one that receives their sympathy. It is wrong to
expect a unilateral action from one producer to be
successful given the availability of other OPEC and
non-OPEC sources. More concretely, Nigeria's crude oil
was in high demand in the 1973-74 crisis when oil
imports from the Middle East seemed uncertain. This is
an example of the transfer by the consumers of excess
demand to other suppliers. One can well imagine what
would happen if only a producer were acting alone in
the embargo: the impact of the measures would have
been unnoticeable.

Second, even assuming that the major oil producers
have agreed to an oil embargo, cutbacks in production,
a price hike etc., there has to be no glut in the market if efforts are not to prove abortive. A condition
of glut like the one we are experiencing now does not
allow for the employment of any restrictive measures

against a consumer whose demand would then be met from the excess of oil in the market. In addition, a period of glut is one that drags prices down; this would work against oil diplomacy which requires scarcity and high prices. In fact, this has been one of the reasons why oil diplomacy did work before 1973 as, throughout the period, oil was readily available and relatively cheap.

Third, even when there is no glut in the market, oil diplomacy would be in effective if the producer country's economy is not diversified enough to withstand a short or long drawn depletion in oil revenue. The majority of the oil producers and exporters in the developing countries, especially members of OPEC, are dependent on oil revenue for their programmes of social and economic development. Some of them, like Nigeria and Venezuela, are highly vulnerable to changes in the world oil market. A programme of efficient use of their oil revenues to develop the agricultural and industrial sectors of their economies has been embarked upon with only limited success. Their dependence on importation of manufactured goods, machinery and consumer items (even food!) often deplete their foreign reserves. A condition like this is not conducive to a prolonged oil war during which time very little oil is sold. In fact, a country like Nigeria, with an economy so closely intertwined with oil that the glut of 1978 and 1982 immediately put it in jeopardy, is not one that can afford an embargo cutback in production etc.

Fourth, the producer employing oil diplomacy should be able to control the oil companies. This is an aspect of the "ability to pick and choose," and is of central importance to oil diplomacy. An oil producing country that cannot determine the quantity to be produced, the destination of that quantity and the price chargeable on a barrel is not likely to be able to monitor effectively the compliance or unfriendliness of the companies to these rules. It is an established fact that Nigeria, even with the NNPC and its Inspectorate Division and when boasting of being the strongman of Africa, could not manage her oil industry or convincingly and accurately ascertain either the volume of oil lifted from her shores or its destinations. Worse still, in spite of her anti-apartheid stance and the claim of a powerful naval force, a South African tanker still had the audacity to enter Nigeria's territorial waters with the express intention of shipping home Nigerian crude oil. This inability to control the destination of oil through a firm and efficient regulation of the activities of the oil companies is

one that works against the effective functioning of oil
diplomacy.

And fifth, one final factor that works against the
effective application of oil diplomacy is the energy
policies of the industrialised nations. While there
are many alternative forms of energy in the world, oil
has become most acceptable because it is cheap when
compared with the cost of other forms. But Western
industrialised nations, especially after recovering
from the shock of 1973-74, have started to adopt policies that would insulate them against any future
occurrence. In fact, these energy policies are very
ambitious and include conservation of energy, development of alternative sources of energy with a view to
making them cheaper and workable, a programme of oil
sharing in emergencies, stock-piling of oil so that a
glut could be created to drive prices down, and
research and development. As a counterpoise to the
OPEC cartel, the Western consumer countries have formed
the International Energy Agency (IEA) which is charged
with the task of effecting aspects of these policies.
It is instructive to point out that the glut in the oil
market in recent times is in part a result of these
policies. The application of oil diplomacy by a single
nation like Nigeria is therefore unlikely to make
a   significant impact. Hence the need to re-
consider the salience of such diplomacy in the 1980s.

end

Notes

1. "The oil boomerang", West Africa, 3 November 1980.

2. According to Louis Turner, the oil majors are the eight oil companies today known as Exxon, Mobil, Gulf, Texaco, Socal, BP, Shell and CFP. See "Oil Majors in World Politics", International Affairs, 52, (3), July 1976, 368.

3. Ibid.

4. C.C. Pocock, "The Role of International Oil Companies", Proceedings of the OPEC Seminar on 'The present and future role of the national compaines', OPEC Headquarters, Vienna, October 1977, 199. For a similar view on transfer of technology, see "Interview with Managing Director of Boots", Financial Punch, 13 October 1982.

5. Some oil companies are known to court citizens of consuming countries in key posts. One Robert Caro reported that Lyndon Johnson, when he was Vice-President of the US, received ₦30,000 in sealed envelopes from one lobbyist for an oil company. See National Concord, 22 September 1981.

6. Olukayode Soremekun, The Role of OPEC in International Politics, M.Sc. Dissertation, Department of International Relations, University of Ife, 1979, 6.

7. M.A. Olorunfemi, "Oil as a Major Weapon in International Politics", Nigerian Ministry of External Affairs Lectures, July 1980, 1. See also Peter R. Odell, Oil and World Power (London: Penguin, 6th edition).

8. Galia Golan, op. cit., 143-151.

9. Renaissance, 19 July 1972

10. Jean Herskovits, "Democracy in Nigeria", Foreign Affairs, 58(2), 1979, 332.

11. Ibid.

12. A. Bolaji Akinyemi, "Murtala/Obasanjo Foreign Policy", in Oyeleye Oyediran (ed), <u>Nigerian Government and Politics Under Military Rule</u> (London: Macmillan, 1979), 155.

13. <u>Nigerian Standard</u>, 12 July 1975.

14. <u>New Nigerian</u>, 16 July 1975.

15. <u>Daily Times</u>, 8 January 1976.

16. Ministry of Information, "Statement on Angola", Late News Release No. 16, 6 January 1976.

17. <u>Daily Sketch</u> and <u>Daily Times</u>, 7 January 1976.

18. <u>Daily Times</u>, 27 January 1976 in its editorial titled "A Happy Riddance" further asked that the USIS be moved from the place near Dodan Barracks.

19. This refers to the earlier refusal of the US President to see General Gowon in 1973. See also <u>Daily Times</u>, 6 April 1978.

20. <u>Daily Star</u>, 18 April 1978.

21. <u>New Nigerian</u>, 16 March 1979.

22. T.Y. Danjuma, "Propaganda as African Liberation Weapon", <u>Nigerian Navy News Highlights</u>, 2 Otober 1978, 7.

23. Colin Legum, "Nigeria's Economic War Threat", <u>Observer</u>, 27 March 1977.

24. This is the view expressed by a participant at an exclusive seminar at the Nigerian Institute of International Affairs (NIIA) in 1979. See <u>Seminar on the Army, the Navy and the Air Force and Nigeria's Strategic Role in the World</u>, 19 March 1979 - 21 March 1979, Tape No. 1.

25. Olusegun Akindeji, "The Nigerian Navy: problems and prospects", <u>Nigerian Herald</u>, 14 June 1978.

26. <u>Seminar on the Army</u>, <u>op. cit.</u>, Tape No. 1.

27. Olu Akinmoladun, "Crude Oil: American's big bait in Nigeria", <u>Daily Times</u>, 19 April 1978.

28. Oye Ogunbadejo, "A New Turn in US-Nigeria Relations", The World Today, 53 (3), March 1979, 122.

29. See Ray Ofoegbu, "Foreign Policy and Military Rule" and A. Bolaji Akinyemi, op. cit., in Oyeleye Oyediran, op. cit.; See also Olajide Aluko, "Nigeria, the US and South Africa", African Affairs, 78(310), January 1979, 92-94.

30. Ministry of Information, "American Businessmen urged to invest in Nigeria", News Release No. 1838, 14 October 1977, being General Obasanjo's speech at a dinner party in New York with American businessmen.

31. Nigerian Tribune, 3 April 1978.

32. David Lamb, "After a Decade of Deterioration...", Daily Times, 6 April 1978.

33. Nigeria's foreign policy in the First Republic is the subject of many studies. The following contain relevant materials and information: Segun Osoba, Nigeria's Foreign Policy, Ph.D. Thesis, (Moscow 1967), A. Bolaji Akinyemi, Federalism and Foreign Policy (Ibadan: OUP, 1978); Gordon J. Idang, Internal Politics and Foreign Policy (Ibadan: OUP, 1979); Ray Ofoegbu, The Nigerian Foreign Policy (Enugu: Star Printing & Publishing Co., 1978).

34. The Guardian (UK), 23 September 1978.

35. Eliane Windrich, "The Anglo-American Initiative on Rhodesia: an interim assessment", The World Today, 35(7), July 1979.

36. Martyn Gregory, "The 1980 Rhodesian Elections--a first hand account and analysis", The World Today, 36(5), May 1980.

37. Ibid.

38. New Nigerian, 3 August 1979.

39. Nigerian Herald, 2 August 1979; New Nigerian, 3 August 1979.

40. New Nigerian, 13 August 1979.

41. The Guardian, 2 August 1979.

42. _Ibid_.

43. "British Exports to Nigeria May Grow Again",
    Daily Express, 20 May 1979.

44. See Judith Gurney, "North Sea Oil and Gas:
    implication for Western Europe", _The World Today_,
    31(10), October 1975; Lawrence Freedman, "British
    Oil: the myth of independence", _The World Today_,
    34(8), August 1978; Mark Webster, "Why Nigeria
    Went Gunning for BP", _The Financial Times_
    (London), 2 August 1979.

45. See Charles F. Doran, _Myth, Oil and Politics_ (New
    York: Free Press, 1977); Robert S. Pindyck,
    "OPEC's Threat to the West"; Fred S. Singer,
    "Limits of Arab Oil Power", _Foreign Policy_, 30,
    Spring 1978.

Chapter Four

Britain, Africa and International Order

James Mayall

Governments, it is widely held, have an obligation to defend the national interest, whatever that elusive aggregate is deemed to be. The governments of great powers often see themselves, in addition, as shouldering an extra obligation; namely to contribute to the balance of power and in other ways to underwrite the values and institutions of international society in the interest of stability. Of course, these values and institutions must operate to the advantage of the great powers themselves. But since they are regarded as public goods the benefits of which cannot be monopolised it is only fair, or at least inevitable, that he who plays the piper shall call the tune.

i) Introduction: national interests and international order

Such, very roughly, was the attitude of British government in their relations with the rest of the world during the period of British pre-eminence, say from the defeat of Napoleon to the end of the Second World War. Throughout this period, the latent tensions between a narrowly-defined conception of national interest--the maintenance of the British Empire on which British pre-eminence partly rested and the general practices and conventions of international society--may have been recognised by some of the more far-sighted politicians[1] but they were never publically acknowledged. The proposition that what was good for Britain was good for the Empire and good for the world was as firmly held (and with considerably less public embarrassment) as the notorious view of the American Secretary of State who held that what was good for General Motors was good for the United States. It provided the broad framework of a self-confident foreign policy. British pre-eminence, never in any case as secure as it can be made to look in the after-glow of nostalgia, has long departed the international scene and with it has gone the self-confidence and the framework of foreign policy. It was not a Marxist policy, but the late Ian MacLeod, one of the most percipient of post-war Conservatives, once noted that the attitudes

and policies of British pre-eminence had never been
self-sustaining: they rested on three material advantages: a) on the fact that the British had pioneered
industrial capitalism; b) on the existence of the
British Empire which had provided a large, open market
for British manufactures and had significantly augmented the country's diplomatic and military strength; and
c) on the British navy.

Overtaken by her industrial competitors, stripped,
albeit with a minimum of actual as opposed to rhetorical fuss, of her Empire by an alliance between nationalism abroad and liberalism at home, and with no permanent naval presence east of Suez since the late
1960s, the contemporary problem for British governments
in their relations with the non-European world can be
fairly accurately, if somewhat negatively, described as
damage limitation. In this regard Britain is arguably
not so different from the other industrial democracies:
they all wish to cooperate with Third World countries
in ways which will do as little as possible to undermine the existing distribution of power and influence
within international society. For British governments,
however, this general problem has a sharper utilitarian
focus which allows but does not guarantee a more positive outcome, namely how, in an uncomfortably competitive world, to transform the legacies of pre-eminence
and Empire from liabilities into assets.

In no part of the world has this general problem
presented British governments with greater difficulties
than in their relations with Africa. The broad strategy for effecting the transformation--decolonisation
within the Commonwealth--was announced to the world
with the granting of independence to Ghana in 1957.
But what exactly were the British up to? "If we want
things to stay as they are" Giuseppe di Lampedusa makes
one of his characters say in The Leopard, that marvel-
lous novel about the confrontation between the old
Sicilian order and Italian nationalism, "things will
have to change." Was this what Harold Macmillan meant
when in February 1960 he warned the South African parliament to adapt to the wind of change that was blowing
across the African continent? Nkrumah, the first
legatee of the old order south of the Sahara, certainly
feared so: neo-colonialism, he warned, with more
plausibility than usual, was the worst kind of imperialism because, unlike the real thing, it constituted
the exercise of power without responsibility.

But if that was their main purpose--to keep the old
imperial show on the road--at the time most British
ministers and officials untrained then as now in dialectical historicism, would probably have denied: they
were reacting, as always pragmatically and as they saw
it honourably, to the challenge of the moment. Thus
for some time they resisted the argument of General
Assembly Resolution 1514 which held that lack of preparation for self-government should not be used to
delay independence, but not so much out of opposition
to the principle, (principles have seldom been debated
in Britain in the abstract), as because the presence of
settler communities with entrenched political privi-
leges, as in central Africa, created practical obstacles to disengagement, or because the concept of an
independent state, dependent from its birth on budget-
ary assistance, was anathema to those trained in the
principles of sound administration and Treasury control.

By the middle 1960s, however, it was clear that any
such doubts had been brushed aside: the British
government (first under the Conservatives and then
Labour) had decided to seek the country's fortune in
Europe as and when the French would permit them to do
so. The Commonwealth sentimentalists on the Left and
far Right had been brushed aside, and what remained of
the Empire was to be scuttled as decently, but also as
quickly, as possible. The Central African Federation
was broken up in deference to the wishes of the United
Independence Party of Northern Rhodesia and the
Nyasaland Congress Party. Grants in aid were accepted
as a reasonable price for disengagement in Malawi,
Sierra Leone, the former High Commission Territories in
Southern Africa, and even Gambia was finally allowed to
acquire independence with no more than a theatrical nod
in the direction of an economically viable Senegambian
Federation. Only the anomolous constitutional status
of Rhodesia frustrated the strategy and constantly
interfered with attempts to create a network of low
key, but still special, relationships between Britain
and her former colonies. Fourteen years after Ian
Smith's Unilateral Declaration of Independence in 1965,
the military, economic and political constraints under
which the three major parties involved were operating
i.e. the Zimbabwe nationalists, Rhodesian whites and
the governments of the Front Line States, unexpectedly
provided a new conservative administration with the
diplomatic opportunity to secure the settlement that
had elluded its predecessors (see previous chapter).
With the implementation of the Lancaster House Agree-

101

ment, British sovereignty was finally removed from the
African continent. Whatever the future problems of
Anglo-African relations there are no residual imperial
commitments, such as those that exist in the Falkland
Islands and under the guarantee to the government of
Belize, which under any foreseeable circumstances seem
likely to lead to the projection into Africa of British
military power.

In the contemporary international order, with its
emphasis on territorial integrity and anti-colonial
self-determination, liquidation of imperial commitments
is certainly a necessary but not a sufficient step in
the transformation of liabilities into assets. Once
the major assumption of imperial pre-eminence--that
British and African interests were synonymous--had been
abandoned, the establishment of a framework for post-
colonial relations required, in addition, the identification of mutual interests between Britain and the
successor states.

In this chapter I shall concentrate on three broad
areas within which surely research has been conducted.
These are respectively: a) the organisation and
management of the international economy; b) bilateral
relations, primarily economic in character which occur
within this framework; and c) the overall political
organisation of international society. In the all
three areas, particularly the last, which is over-
shadowed by the unresolved conflicts of Southern
Africa, the legacies of British global pre-eminence and
imperial involvement have created both problems and
opportunities which distinguish Britain's African
policies from those of the other industrial powers:
the record of achievement, in other words, is mixed.

ii) **The Organisation of the International Economy**

The contrast between Britain and the other former
imperial powers is nowhere more evident than in the
field of macroeconomic organisation; the obvious
comparision is with France and Germany. During the
colonial period, all three countries hoped (sometimes
in vain) that their overseas possessions would contribute to their overall economic and political strength,
but the economic philosophies on which they based their
policies led them to pursue this common aim in different ways. As the initial industrial nation, Britain
was the first country to champion the doctrines of
economic liberalism as not only being in her own

interests but also in the interest of the international
community generally and of world peace.[3] Trade and
investment, of course, still followed or rather accompanied the flag but so long as she remained the work-
shop of the world, Britain was for the most part able
to rely on indirect methods for preserving imperial
markets and sources of supply.

At the time of the scramble for Africa the concept
had not been dreamt of, but had the Third World then
existed it would have begun on the Rhine. Germany
under Bismarck was the first country to insist on the
sovereign right of protection as an instrument of
development and as a means of closing the "gap" with
industrial Britain. It was not at this point the
liberal economy that Germany challenged so much as the
proposition that it knew no frontiers. In France, despite the importance of physiocrats and their successors
in the development of modern economic thought the mer-
cantalist tradition of economic statecraft and the
government's willingness to protect the economy for
political and cultural ends, had never been broken.
France, like Germany, also acquired her African empire
from a subordinate position in international society,
circumstances conducive at the best of times to protection rather than open markets. In any event, the
economies of France's African colonies were notoriously
bound to the metropole with hoops of iron: colonial
agricultural products were subsidised and provided with
a guaranteed market; France in turn monopolised the
colonial markets and guaranteed--i.e. controlled--the
CFA franc, a service which she still performs. When
France signed the EEC Treaty of Rome it was on condition that her partners share the cost of supporting
francophone Africa in return for the partial and largely theoretical opening up of their markets, i.e. to the
other five members of the EEC only. Nigeria, supported
by Britain and the other Commonwealth African states
challenged the legitimacy of Part IV of the Treaty
within the GATT on the grounds that the Agreement
permitted the creation of Customs' Unions but not the
creation of new preferences. Here, then, at the outset
of the post-colonial period was a significant converg-
ence of African and British interests: both stood to
lose from the creation of a privileged trading relationship between francophone Africa and the European
Six.

On this issue, however, the Afro-British alliance
was defeated. The Nigerian challenge to the association concept in the GATT failed and first the East

African countries and then Nigeria itself negotiated
their own agreements with the EEC to protect their own
interests.[4] Nevertheless, it is probably fair to claim
that in their general approach to the role of developing countries in the institutional structure of the
world economy, Britain and Commonwealth Africa remained
in agreement. Both sides were initially in favour of a
global regime to cover the relationship between the
industrial and developing worlds.[5] Only after her bid
to join the European Community was finally successful
did the British position on this issue finally change;
and even then, typically, the conversion was not to the
principle of special trading relationships.

On the contrary, left to itself no British government would have chosen to assert that the Euro-African
community of interests in which it was now involved was
intrinsically different and stronger than the mutual
interest shared with other parts of the new Commonwealth, in particular to the countries of South Asia.
British support for the Lomé Convention was for practical reasons: it provided a solution to the problem of
the residual Commonwealth preferences which, in the
absence of a convention, would have lapsed following
British accession. On the other side, Nigeria, whose
representatives played a leading part in the initial
negotiations, viewed them in a similarly pragmatic
light: they provided an opportunity for concerting
West Africa economic policies in parallel with the
ECOWAS project and more generally for exercising continental leadership.

But if at one level--that of dealing with consequences of the creation of the EEC and Britian's
subsequent accession to it--there has been a broad
conversion of British and African interests, on
another--that of dealing with African and Third World
demands for structural reform and a New International
Economic Order (NIEO)--there has been a significant
divergence. So long as it was a case of tinkering with
the liberal market system there was no real problem.
Indeed, to begin with, Britain tinkered with it itself
as a way of dealing with the costs which arose when she
yielded her position of pre-eminence to the United
States. From the signing of the Atlantic Charter
onwards, the Americans had sought the abolition of the
Commonwealth preference system and the sterling area.
The demands were resisted; preferences were frozen but
not abolished and for a time the sterling area was
actually strengthened, as the British attempted to deal
pragmatically with the post-war dollar shortage. But

these policies were tactical, essentially a means of
playing for time rather than a credible attempt to
influence the long-run structure of the international
economy; and in time they fell apart and were abandoned
in response to pressures from within Africa itself and
from outside.[6]

Thus, for example, the British not only developed
sectors of the East African economies to meet British
needs but developed also the system of common services
on which the East African Community was subsequently
based. British investors, particularly those in Kenya,
stood to gain from the regional integration of the economy; another example, it might be argued, of a smooth
transition from an imperial identity to a post-
colonial, some would say a neo-colonial mutuality of
interests. But as Eliowany Kisanga has shown, when new
and often more powerful multinational investors began
to compete with the British they often found it advant-
ageous to deal with national governments rather than
community institutions, thus reinforcing the already
impressive centrifugal forces within the region.[7]

The close monetary relations between Britain and
Commonwealth Africa similarly suffered with the demise
of the sterling area. Unlike France, Britain had in
any case never attempted to extend the control of the
Bank of England over Commonwealth African economies.
With the approach of independence, one after the other,
Britain's African colonies secured an independent central bank as one of the essential supports of sovereign
statehood.[8] And even before the final liquidation of
the sterling area, most of independent Africa had pru-
dently diversified their reserve holdings away from a
total dependence on the pound.

Such relatively gradual shifts in economic power
and diplomatic orientation--towards Europe in the
British case, away from Britain in the African--were in
a sense only to be expected within the open market
order. The British might regret a weakening of their
priviledged position in Africa, vis-a-vis their competitors, but they had no grounds on which to complain
about it. The Africans on the other hand had never
been consulted about the desirability of an open market
trading system. So they were free to complain.
Following the lead given by Algeria to the Group of 77
in 1974, they increasingly pressed for a radical
restructuring of the international economy to give them
a greater say in its management, to transfer resources
from rich to poor according to a criterion of need,

and to enhance the prices of raw materials, on which
most of them depended, through indexing and through the
creation of a financially independent and politically
powerful Common Fund for commodities.

As the least developed Group of 77, the Africans
were the most insistent on the creation of an institution which would not merely stabilise commodity prices
(a move which the British were more willing than some
to concede) but increase the flow or resources to them-
selves.⁹ In advancing these demands, Third World
governments were proposing a system of positive income
redistribution, analogous to that carried out by some
Western governments within their own societies since
1945. Indeed, President Nyerere has suggested that the
creation of such a global Keynesian system is essentially a matter of will, and that there is no essential
difference in this regard between the domestic and the
international context. There is, it should be noted, a
body of opinion in **Britain** as in the other industrial
countries, which endorses the re-distributive thesis of
the NIEO campaign--it forms, for example, the broad
orientation of the original Brandt Commission
report--but it is not a view which is shared by the
current British administration or by any of its predecessors. On the contrary, British governments have
repeatedly made it clear, in their actions if not in
ministerial speeches, that they believe the analogy
between the welfare state and the international community to be false.

In official British thinking on international economic affairs, there is a crucial distinction between
fair trading rules--i.e. those based on the typically
negative liberal principle of non-discrimination which
can be stretched to embrace the notion of preferential
access for developing countries but to to include a
collective mechanism for automatic income redistribu-
tion--and aid which is viewed as a discretionary matter
and, therefore, as an expression of a political relationship. Although the London-based Commonwealth
Secretariat has established for itself a useful role in
mediating between the two sides on North-South issues,
the British government itself does not stand out from
the other members of OECD as more accommodating to
African interests. In terms of the broad framework of
the international economy, Britain remains a status quo
power, despite the decline of its political and economic influence on the continent, while the African
Commonwealth countries are revisionists despite the
fact that many of them are ruled by a political class

which personally benefits from its association with
foreign capital and despite the growing economic dis-
parities between the Commonwealth African countries
themselves.

iii)   **Bilateral Relations**

        In their approach to bilateral relations with
African countries as much on the general issue of
multilateralism, the style of British and French post-
colonial policies stand in sharp contrast towards one
another. The special relationship between Paris and
the francophone African countries, although subject to
some dilution, continues to be guaranteed by a series
of bilateral political and military as well as economic
treaties. Since the abrogation of the British Nigerian
Defence Pact in 1962 and of the Simonstown basis of
agreement with South Africa two years later, there has
been no British equivalent. The Commonwealth represents an English language post-imperial association
but, although from its creation in 1966 Britain has
remained the largest contributor to the Secretariat,
the emphasis has been deliberately placed on the multilateral character of the Organisation; and, so far as
Africa and Asia are concerned, it has been most active,
and arguably effective, as an informal lobby on general
North-South issues, rather than a channel through which
Britain can maintain a priviledged postion in its
former colonies. In the past there has even on occasions been talk of Britain's withdrawal or explusion
from the Commonwealth. The present government, however, clearly values the organisation and has reason to
be grateful to Commonwealth countries for their support
in the Zimbabwe negotiations and at the time of the
Falklands War in April 1982. But even so, its commitments towards the Commonwealth are both less precise,
and almost certainly ultimately more dispensable, than
its commitments towards either the EEC or the Atlantic
Alliance.

        There is a further difference between Britain and
France which throws light on the British problem of
translating imperial liabilities into post-colonial
assets. France remains the centre of a powerful (even
if in a global sense a minority) culture area based on
the French language. It is not merely a question of
shared intellectual habits and life-style, although
both of these are important; it also provides France
with a comparative advantage in the securing of contracts as any analysis of the European Development Fund

will quickly demonstrate. By contrast Britain not only
surrendered its global pre-eminence but surrendered it
to another English-speaking nation whose traditional
anticolonialism was perfectly compatible with economic
and cultural competition with Britain to influence
Commonwealth Africa. Indeed, much of the recent his-
toriography of the post-war period suggests that it
positively required it.[10] Since at independence all
former British colonies set about diversifying their
external relations, and since the United States had
greater resources at its disposal, it quickly established in educational as well as economic and political matters a rival, and in some cases stronger,
magnetic field of attraction to the former metropolitan
power.

   Too much should not be made of Britain's decline
vis-a-vis the United States. In the overall conception
of the **Pax Americana**, Africa had low priority (see
Chapter One). Once the rigidities of the Cold War had
been established, the rulers of the new imperial republic were generally content to leave the 'policing' of
peripheral areas to their allies who were familiar with
the terrain. In the early years of American globalism,
Africa presented the Americans with no equivalent to
Dien Bien Phu, and as time went on they became positively anxious to share the burden wherever they could
with the former colonial powers.[11] Nevertheless,
except in matters which came before the Security
Council--which I will discuss in the final section of
this chapter--in its bilateral relations with African
countries, Britain increasingly returned to its original role as a nation of shopkeepers. Its primary concerns, in other words, were the protection of trade and
investment and the provision of aid both as an induce-
ment to African governments to stay within the liberal
market order and as a more direct buttress to British
exports.

   Let me first take the question of aid. In broad
terms the British aid record fairly accurately reflects
the country's economic standing amongst other members
of the OECD. Britain is the fourth largest donor
overall--after the United States, France, West Germany
and Japan--although when expressed as a percentage of
GNP (0.35% in 1980) the British performance is better
than that of the United States (0.27%) and Japan
(0.32%) but considerably worse than that of France
(0.64%) and Germany (0.44%).[12] About a third of
Britain's bilateral financial disbursements (£1.326m in
1980) have traditionally gone to Africa although when

technical assistance is included the continent accounts for about half the total aid effort.[13] In addition, about 30% of British aid--£526 million in 1980--is channeled through multilateral agencies, a significant proportion of which, of course, ultimately goes to Africa.

What criteria govern the British aid programme in Africa? Apart from saying that it is intended to maintain, and on occasions enhance, the area of interdependence and mutuality of interest--in other words to lubricate Anglo-African relations--it would be misleading to interpret its growth and pattern according to a deliberately pre-conceived economic or political strategy. On the contrary, as the merest glance at the pattern of disbursements will indicate, the programme continues to bear the imprint of particular problems which arose in the context of decolonisation. In 1975, for example, 82% of British aid still went to Commonwealth Africa, a proportion which has since been whittled away as a result of Britain's accession to the EEC and as a result of a deliberate government policy of diversification, but only marginally.

Within Commonwealth Africa, Southern and East African countries have obtained the lion's share of British aid transfers: in 1977 Southern African countries took £38.5m., East Africa £23.4m. and West Africa £13.5m. These figures reflect (or perhaps conceal) special circumstances. Kenya dominates the East African scene: between 1963-1979, Kenya was the second largest British aid recipient after India, receiving £180m, much of it to finance the Land Transfer Programme for buying-out British-owned farms in the country. In Southern Africa, the smaller countries--Malawi, Botswana and Lesotho--are not only major consumers of British technical assistance but also to begin with, (although no longer) recipients of grants in aid, while Zambia, also a major recipient of technical assistance (a consequence of the wildly-uneven development of skilled manpower under the Central African Federation) became a major recipient of financial aid after 1975 as a result of the collapse of copper prices and the Rhodesian crisis.[14] Since the independence of Zimbabwe, the pattern of concentration on Southern Africa has been reinforced as a result of reconstruction aid to that country and Britain's qualified support for SADCC. The relatively low aid figures of West Africa reflect on the one hand the fact that those countries which have been highly dependent on British assistance--for example the Gambia and Sierra Leone--had very small

budgets and on the other, the fact that Nigeria, the
African country which is most important to Britain,
decided after the quadrupling of oil prices in 1974
against seeking capital aid from the UK and other major
donors.[15] Of the African countries outside the Commonwealth which have attracted significant amounts of
British aid--aid to non-Commonwealth Africa and as a
whole represents about 10% of the total--the principle
recipients have been the Sudan and Egypt which were
once administered by Britain, although outside the
formal machinery of the Empire, and Ethiopia, the only
African country which escaped the European scramble.

    Within Britain itself, official opinion, and in the
end policy, has generally followed some way behind
changes of view and fashion within the professional
community of Western aid experts. Thus, for example,
under the Labour administration which held office between 1974 and 1979 there was conversion to the philosophy of basic needs which echoed a similar change of
orientation by the World Bank at the same time,[16] while
the present government--which has been in a vanguard of
the Western monetarist revolt has not only reduced aid
overall, in line with the general cutback of government
expenditures, but has also increased the Aid Trade Provision (ATP); i.e. that proportion of the aid budget
which is earmarked to meet specific requests for export
assistance by British industry which might otherwise
fall foul of GATT and OECD rules on export subsidies.[17]
Such changes of direction, however, are more a question
of degree than of kind. Although the British aid programme has never given rise to the degree of controversy within parliament as has customarily greeted the
American programme within Congress, its supporters have
always had to argue that it is not merely right to provide concessionary finance but that there are also
material returns to Britain from doing so. It was the
Labour government which accompanied its basic needs
strategy with the introduction of the ATP which its
Conservative successors, egged on by the Confederation
of British Industries (CBI), have sought to strengthen.

    In 1977 the overall proportion of aid which was
tied to the procurement of British goods and services
was estimated at 65.8%.[18] In a ministerial paper
written the following year, the then Minister of Overseas Development, Judith Hart, defended the programme
in terms which make clear the reasons for the bipar-
tisan support which it has generally enjoyed influential voices such as that of Professor Peter Bauer which
have from time to time been raised against it:

There are two basic ways in which
the aid programme helps British
industry. By helping foster income
creation and widely distributed
income growth in the developing
countries, it increases the overseas markets for British goods. In
the process it also provides opportunities for aid finance exports
both under bilateral and multilateral aid arrangement.[19]

On the first count, morever, even the British contribution to multilateral agencies, justified in the
last analysis as support for the system of liberal
multilateralism, also yields a more direct return. Of
all World Bank loans to developing countries in 1980,
the UK share of procurement was just over 6%, but in
East Africa it was 16.4% and in West Africa 9%. The
British share was even higher in soft loan credits
(IDA) to East Africa --17.5%--compared with an overall
share of procurement in developing countries generally
of 12%.[20] These figures suggest that Britain's comparative advantage in Commonwealth Africa has not been
completely eroded. In dealing with a nation of shopkeepers, it seems, there may be some circumstances in
which the familiar corner-shop still has the edge over
the more powerful but anonymous supermarket.

We should not be deceived, however, by such homely
analogies. It is the activities of the major industrial corporations, such as Lonrho, ICI, and the oil
companies, together with British banks and financial
institutions which dictate the pattern of trade and
investment. As with aid, this pattern is a product of
Britain's colonial involvement in Africa. Thus, despite a rapid growth in the immediate post-colonial
period, in the mid-1970s about 70% of private investment and about 60% of British trade with independent
Africa was still within the Commonwealth.[21] In this
case, however, the legacy of the past has revealed an
uncomfortable paradox: while government-to-government
aid relations[22] have given rise to relatively few political problems the steady expansion of private sector
links over which the government has only the most
indirect control (through Commonwealth and now EEC preferential arrangements, the support provided to British
export by the ECGD and through CDFC investment funds)
has increasingly exposed them to criticism from their
African trading partners.

111

The reason is well-known. Both aid and private
investment are heavily concentrated in two countries:
the Federation of Nigeria and the Republic of South
Africa. With its emergence as a major oil exporter, and
hence as a major importer of capital and manufactured
goods, Nigeria jumped to being Britain's twelfth
largest market in the world and its fifth outside
Europe.[23] Simultaneously, it became a more important
market than South Africa, which had traditionally
enjoyed pride of place in Britain's economic relations
with Africa, and thereby assured itself of British protection at the UN whenever, for example, the African
countries demanded the imposition of economic sanctions
in an effort to force the Republic to abandon its
policy of separate development. When Britain's stake
in the rest of the continent is added to its stake in
Nigeria, it is possible to argue that there has been a
massive shift in the balance of British interests and
that as a consequence the African countries, acting
under the leadership of Nigeria, are now in a position
to face Britain with the necessity of an historic
choice between white and black Africa.

That Britain has so far been able to avoid this
choice is also well-known. The explanation must be
sought in Africa as well as in Britain itself. Not
only is it as difficult in Africa as anywhere else to
persuade countries to engage in collective economic
sanctions when they would have to bear the cost of
imposing them themselves, but the African countries
generally need the industrial world more than they are
needed. For a time, Nigeria's oil wealth seemed to
exclude that country from this general rule, and indeed
gave a certain credibility to the idea of counter-
sanctions. But the world-wide recession and the development by Britain of North Sea oil, which is in direct
competition with the Nigerian product, suggests that
its exemption is more apparent than real. In any event,
while there have been token expropriations of British
interests--i.e. Barclays Bank and British
Petroleum--which have been defended as warnings to Britain over its Southern African policies, these have
been isolated incidents (for which there are also more
parochial explanations) and have made no serious impact
on Britain's £500m. investment in the Nigerian economy
(see previous chapter).

Within Britain there are well-organised pressure
groups, such as the Anti-Apartheid Movement and the
United Nations Association, which regularly campaign
for an embargo on British trade with South Africa, and

Liberal Parties and by the trade unions. No British government can afford to ignore such opinion completely, particularly now that is is possible to argue that Britain's historical entanglement with South Africa is putting at risk other, potentially more important, British interests. As a result of such pressure, indeed, the Government was persuaded in the mid-1970s to strengthen its alternative strategy of "positive engagement" by devising a code of conduct for British investors, the forerunner of the EEC code of conduct and the weaker set of principles which the Reverend Sullivan successfully persuaded a majority of US corporations with South African interests to adopt.

Pressure on successive governments for disengagement from South Africa has predictably engendered a counter-pressure in the form of the well-organised, and well-financed, activities of the United Kingdom-South Africa Trade Association (UKSATA). This Association which claims to have the backing of most of the "British companies with significant investment and trading interest in or commercial dealings with the Republic of South Africa and many of the medium and smaller British companies"[24] and is supported by a small but vocal group of MPs, regularly disseminates information on such matters as the value of British trade and investment (in 1982 £3,480m. and £11,000m. respectively); the impact on British employment from a policy of disengagement (an estimated addition of 250,000 to the employment figures); and the fact that "access to South African metals and minerals (i.e. platinum, chrome, vernadium and manganese) and since they must be paid for, to South African markets, is as necessary to the industrial West as access to Middle East oil." No British government can afford to ignore this pressure either, and indeed while Labour administrations have been generally more eager to disassociate themselves from South Africa politically and in sporting and cultural affairs[25]--for example, it was not until 1964 when Harold Wilson first became Prime Minister that the UK joined the US in imposing a unilateral arms embargo--they have been as adamant as their Conservative opponents in resisting both domestic and international pressure for the imposition of sanctions.

Since the economic as well as diplomatic isolation of South Africa is official OAU policy, it is inevitable, therefore, that South Africa should continue to cast a shadow over Britain's relations with the rest of the continent. Were it not for its South African en-

tanglement, it is at least conceivable that with the
surrender of all its sovereign claims the continent
would have been made safe for the descendents of the
Manchester school of economists who had been opposed to
colonial expansion from the beginning. As it is, however, it is largely because South Africa constitutes a
general problem for the international order in the outcome of which Britain has an historic interest (other
considerations apart, among the 40% of South African
whites who are of British descent, a substantial
although undisclosed proportion still hold British
passports) as well as the purely material interest
sketched above that Britain remains politically
embroiled in African affairs. It is to this final
problem of Afro-British relations that I now turn.

iv) **South Africa and International Order**

     In the period between 1945 and 1950, the political
map of the post-war international system was redrawn. It
was not to be altered in any fundamental way until the
early 1970s and much of it, indeed, survives to the
present day.[26] Among the governments of the Western
powers, two versions of this map circulated freely and
some of the most intractable contemporary international
problems--including the problem of South Africa--partly
arose from the inconsistencies between them.

     The first map, that of the United Nations, estab-
lished, so to say, the new constitutional order for
international society. As with the new economic order,
its form mirrored the values of its most powerful
members--the liberal democracies, and particularly
those of the United States. The major concession to
realism in the shape of the Security Council and the
power of veto which was granted to its five permanent
members ensured that the interests of the old imperial
powers could not be lightly brushed aside. But at the
same time, the commitment in the Charter to the right
of national self-determination and fundamental human
rights, when combined with the anti-colonialism of two
emergent great powers (they had not yet fulfilled de
Tocqueville's prophecy by being dubbed superpowers) was
sufficient to guarantee that the parliamentary procedures of the world body would be used to maintain
relentless pressure on the imperial powers to dismantle
their colonial systems and on their right to invoke
Article 2(7), which insulates domestic jurisdiction
from outside **interference, as** a defence against such
pressure.

Within this first constitutional map South Africa suffered from guilt by association. Only two kinds of states were envisaged: those which were already independent and whose domestic arrangements were constantly immune from scrutiny, and those which were to be created by decolonisation; the withdrawal of the Europeans back across the colour line to their own homelands. South Arica, an independent state since 1910, was not immune. However, its traditional policy of racial segregation, even before the National party reinforced it by the introduction of full-scale apartheid after 1948, was too blatantly at variance with the majoritarian principles under which first Asian and then African nationalists successfully demanded independence. As a result, from 1946, when the Indian government first raised the question of South African discrimination against the Asian community in Natal at the UN, South Africa's racial policies have been the subject of annual debate and censure. The simultaneous refusal by the South Africans to place the mandated territory of South West Africa under the UN Trusteeship Council created another issue of contention: not only was South Africa an anomalous state in the eyes of the new Afro-Asian bloc; it had committed the cardinal sin against the new constitutional order by refusing to prepare for independence those whose destiny had been placed in their hands by the mandate "as a sacred trust."

In the early post-war period, the British Labour government repeatedly refused to associate itself with this international campaign against South Africa, arguing that its racial policies were not a proper subject for UN debate and even questioning, on the advice of Foreign Office lawyers, the opinion of the International Court of Justice in 1950 that South Africa needed the permission of the UN before it could modify the status of South West Africa. The reasons for their attitude were complex, partly determined by their determination to have neither the principle nor the pace of decolonisation dictated from outside (except to a limited extent with the respect of the Trusteeship territories) but partly also by considerations of a more immediate strategic and political character.

By contrast to the first, the second map of the post-war world--that of the Cold War--determined the major international alignments from the late-1940s to the present day. But as I have already noted, initially the common Western stand against what was perceived as an imminent threat of Communist expansion concealed a more friendly rivalry between the United

States and the residual force of British imperialism. This placed the British government in a difficult position: in as much as it feared Soviet designs against its global interests, it needed to enlist American support beyond Europe as well as in the North Altantic area; but insofar as this would require the Americans to lend formal support to British imperial arrangements, proposals for an extension of the Western Alliance--e.g. into the South Atlantic--stood no chance of gaining Congressional support. As Ritchie Ovendale has been able to show in an article based on new material from the British archives, it was in this context that the Labour government formulated the basic policy towards South Africa which with relatively minor fluctuations has been followed ever since.[27]

The basic South African problem had three aspects. The first was <u>strategic</u>. So long as the Americans were unprepared to commit themselves to the defence of British and Western interests in the Middle East, the British would need all the support they could muster within the Commonwealth. As a professed anti-Communist power, South Africa stood ready and willing to help (despite its hostility to the UN it sent an air force unit to Korea). The fact that after 1948, the South African government contained men who were deeply hostile to Britain persuaded the Atlee government of the importance of doing nothing which would jeopardise the strategic relationship between the two countries. The second aspect was <u>economic</u>. Besides being the source of many of Britain's strategic raw materials, in the immediate post-war period South Africa was one of the few countries with which Britain had a favourable balance of trade, a consideration which gave it access to South African gold production to provide much-needed backing for sterling area reserves. The third aspect was <u>political</u>. It was deeply embarrassing for the government which had both initiated Britain's imperial withdrawal from India and introduced the welfare state at home to find itself bound by interest rather than sentiment to a government most of which policies it deeply abhorred.

The solution which the Labour party devised and which all British governments have adhered to ever since, was to make the best of a bad job. On the one hand there was no alternative to cooperation; on the other, any latent South African expansionism should be checked, in the first instance by refusing to incorporate the High Commission territories in the Union, as had originally been envisaged in 1910, and then by constructing a bloc of pro-British territories to the North. In presenting the paper which outlined this policy to the Cabinet, the Commonwealth Secretary, Patrick Gordon-Walker, explained it in the following way:

> Britain should be ready to develop those relations with the Union that bind her to us and make her unwilling to risk a break with us...these relations are also in our direct interest. Chief amongst them come cooperation in defence and in economic matters. Also important is to give the Union what help and guidance it decently can at the United Nations. Those who argue that because we dislike the Union's Native policy we should ostracise her and have nothing to do with her completely fail to understand the realities of the situation. Such a policy would not only gravely harm us in the defence and economic fields, it would also weaken our power to deter South Africa from foolhardly acts from fear of breaking with us. It would immediately and directly reduce our chances of holding the Territories, which form a vital part in any policy of containing and confining the Union's influence and territorial expansion in Southern Africa.[28]

It may seem far-fetched to claim that this policy has survived the events of the past thirty years, including the withdrawal of South Africa from the Commonwealth, the collapse of the Central African Federation, fourteen years of rebel government in Rhodesia, and the disintegration of the sterling area. Reflection, however, will I believe support its essential validity. The changes that have occurred in Southern Africa have been despite British policy rather than because of it. At the UN British governments have fought a long rearguard action against the African campaign to turn South Africa into a pariah state only joining the majority in criticising apartheid in the General Assembly once the British Empire itself had been effectively liquidated, and even then drawing a sharp distinction between criticism and action.

Whenever there is a demand for sanctions under Chapter 7 of the Charter, the British, along with the other Western powers, can be relied on to veto it, using whatever arguments are ready at hand to justify their action. It can be plausibly argued, of course, that it is the threat of sanctions rather than their imposition which is what matters, and that it is ultimate uncertainty about continued Western support which has persuaded the South African government to undertake even such cautious and half-hearted reforms as it has embarked upon. Maybe. On the other hand, the current stalemate in the Namibian negotiations suggests very strongly that, whatever the situation in the past, the South Africans now know that they have successfully called the West's bluff. It is true that Britain has now ceded leadership to the US in designing the containment policy but whatever differences there may be between the two governments over the line to be pursued within the Contact Group, it seems unlikely that they are fundamental.

Meanwhile, as in the past, the British government tries to have it both ways; i.e. to cooperate and contain simultaneously. Formal defence cooperation, it is true, has been abandoned (it is very doubtful whether this has been extended to the contract between the intelligence services). But economic cooperation remains as strong as ever and the British government continues to foster relations at all levels of South African society, for example, by sponsoring visits of verligte members of parliament to Britain and in other ways seeking to encourage domestic reform. It would be a brave person, however, who claimed that these efforts were accompanied by much hope. The collapse of the Federation was the biggest blow to the early containment policy but with the independence of Zimbabwe and the establishment of SADCC it has arguably been revised.

Whether in the face of African opposition to South Africa from within the country even more than from outside Britain can continue to have it both ways is uncertain. Probably in the long run it cannot. But for so long as the two maps of the international system cannot be reconciled, British governments are likely to conclude, as in the past, that the only option open to them is to make the best of a bad job. Their policy has never been popular in independent Africa but there are few signs of radical change.

Notes

1. For example, Disraeli speaking in 1852 about Britain's remaining colonial presence in North america: "These wretched colonies will all be independent in a few years and are a millstone round our neck."

2. Ian Macleod, "Reports of Britain's Death", Foreign Affairs, October 1966, 89-97.

3. Peter Cain, "Capitalism, War and Internationalism in the Thoughts of Richard Cobden", British Journal of International Studies, 5(3), October 1979, 229-47.

4. The Nigerian agreement was a victim of the Civil War and was never implemented largely, it has been claimed, because the French deliberately delayed ratification.

5. For example, the British supported the Commonwealth argument about non-reciprocity as the appropriate basis for North-South relations as opposed to the contrary position adopted under the first two Yaounde Agreements.

6. See Arthur Kilgore and James Mayall, "The Residual Lagatee: economic relations in the contemporary Commonwealth", in John Groom and Paul Taylor (eds), The Contemporary Commonwealth, (London: Macmillan, 1983).

7. Eliowany Kisanga: research in progress, London and Dar-es-Salaam.

8. Yusuf Bangura, Britain and Commonwealth Africa: the politics of economic relations 1951-1975, (Manchester: Manchester University Press, 1983).

9. See Geoffrey Goodwin and James Mayall (eds), A New International Commodity Regime, (London: Croom Helm, 1979).

10. For a fuller discussion of this point see James Mayall, Africa, the Cold War and After, (London: Elek, 1971).

11. Development Cooperation, 1982 Review, (Paris: OECD, 1982), 204-205.

12.   Guy Arnold, Aid in Africa, (London: Kegan Paul,
        1979), 39.

13.   Ibid, 40-43.

14.   Olajide Aluko, Essays in Nigerian Foreign Policy,
        (London: George Allen and Unwin, 1981), 62.

15.   The new British policy was set out in a White
        Paper published in 1975 under the title More Help
        for the Poorest. For a critical discussion of
        this policy, see Arnold, Aid in Africa, 45-50.

16.   Daniel Nelson, "Pounds of Flesh", Far Eastern
        Econimic Review, 19-25 November 1982.

17.   Arnold, Aid in Africa, 45.

18.   Ibid, 47.

19.   Vince Cable, "British Interests and Third World
        Development", in Robert Cassen, Richard Jolly,
        John Sewell and Robert Wood (eds), Rich Country
        Interest and Third World Development, (London:
        Croom Helm, 1983), 194.

20.   British Information Services, Central Office of
        Information, Britain and the Developing
        Countries, Africa, (London, January 1977), 7.

21.   Two exceptions were the disputes between the
        British and Tanzania governments in the mid-1960s
        over the latter's refusal to pay colonial Civil
        Service pensions and with Idi Amin's regime in
        Uganda over the mass explusion of Asians and
        abuse of fundamental human rights. Both disputes
        led to a suspension of British aid.

22.   See Alec Parrett, "Trade patterns, the Two-way
        Pull", Africa, 73, September 1977, 97-98.

23.   UKSATA, British Trade with South Africa: a
        question of national interest, (London: UKSATA,
        August 1982).

24.   The Annual Report of the MCC contains the follow-
        ing interesting report of the discussion which
        took place after the Test and Country Cricket
        Board had agreed to make ineligible for selection
        for England and group of players who had under-
        taken a private tour of South Africa in 1981: "A

member expressed concern as to whether the decision by the MCC Committee to support the ban was
truly representative of the views of members. He
also mentioned that the cricketers involved might
still take legal action. He informed the meeting
that of the ten resolutions passed by sporting
bodies in favour of breaking sporting links with
South Africa, eight had been proposed by the
Soviet Union." The minutes do not record the
political affiliation of the speaker but a Conservative MP is currently pressing the MCC to
conduct a referendum amongst its 18,000 members
to ascertain whether or not they support the ban
on representative cricket with South Africa.

25.   For a fuller discussion of this process, see
      "introduction" to James Mayall and Cornelia
      Navari (eds), The End of the Post-War Era:
      documents on great power relations, 1968-75,
      (Cambridge: Cambridge University Press, 1981).

26.   Ritchie Ovendale, "The South African Policy of
      the British Labour Government, 1947-51,",
      International Affairs, 59(1), Winter 1982/83,
      41-58.

27.   Quoted in ibid, 57.

Chapter Five

West Germany and Africa: what Africa can expect from the conservative government in Bonn

Rainer Tetzlaff

i) Introduction: economic interests of the FRG in the Third World

West Germany is a country which depends to a great extent on her exports of manufactured goods and on imports of raw materials; this has made her the second largest trading nation in the world. Therefore, the "development of a free world trade, the securing of the supply of raw materials and energy and of international traffic routes" lies in the "natural interest" of the Federal Republic of Germany (FRG).[1]

How deeply dependent and therefore vulnerable to possible disturbances of North-South relations is West Germany is shown in the following figures:

a) In 1979, 23% of all exports of the FRG went to developing countries;

b) nearly 30% of all exports of capital goods flowed in this direction;

c) one quarter of all German imports (that is circa 40 billion German Marks or 17 billion US Dollars) orginated from the Third World;

d) about 30% of the private investments are located there;

e) 23,000 German workers and employees work in developing countries (3,000 in the context of development projects, 20,000 as employees by private companies); and

f) the exports of manufactured products to the Third World created or secured about 700,000 jobs in the economy of West Germany; that is considerably more than the number of jobs Germany lost due to imports of manufactured goods such as textiles or light engineering products from developing countries (circa 100,000).[2]

123

Although one has to emphasize the great general importance of the Third World for economic prosperity in West Germany, one should not overlook the big and increasing gaps between different groups of developing countries. In a recent study the German Institute for Development Policy in West Berlin argued that out of 143 developing countries only 19 so-called "countries of crucial importance" ("Schwerpunktlander") possess oil resources, raw materials and big markets for manufactured goods to such an extent that the Western countries are relatively dependent on these countries as trading partners. Among these 19 privileged countries only three are African--Algeria, Egypt and Nigeria, and--as a special case--the Republic of South Africa.[3]

Looking at the present economic relations between the FRG and Africa, only eight or nine African countries are of any economic significance to West Germany. There are three oil-exporting countries: Nigeria, Libya and Algeria; then we have Liberia and Zaire as countries with important raw materials (iron ore and copper); then Kenya and the Ivory Coast as agriculture-based countries with good investment opportunities in industries; and finally there is South Africa, where some 600 German companies have invested money and which has some major importance as a supplier of uranium, chrome and other minerals.

The dilemma of German foreign policy towards the Third World originated from this rather strong dependence of her economy from the developing countries.[4] On the one hand, the FRG is dependent on a flourishing and smooth international division of labour between North and South, to reach her paramount aims--i.e. national security, economic growth, social welfare, and political stability within a democratic and pluralistic society. On the other hand, the most acute threats to the realisation of these aims come from some regions of the Third World, from countries most of which have suffered from this international division of labour, created in the Bretton Woods era, and which therefore today demand a new international economic order.

In the following chapter I want to confine myself to only some aspects of this problem of complex interdependence. I will discuss the question of what Africa can expect from the newly elected government in regard to two topics: a) to find solutions to the most pressing problems in Southern Africa and b) to contribute to a new and equal economic cooperation between North and South to the benefit of both.

124

ii) The Political Philosophy of the New Government

Since October 1982 West Germany has had a new government. A centre-right coalition of Christian Democrats and Liberals under Chancellor Helmut Kohl (CDU) replaced the coalition government under Chancellor Helmut Schmidt, who together with Willy Brandt led the Social Democratic Party (SPD) since the early seventies. With the fall of Schmidt, who, after eight years in power, fell victim to a parliamentary motion of 'no-confidence', an era of West German policy came to an end.

By conservatives and many other Germans who suffered from economic recession, inflation, unemployment and high interest rates the change of government was welcomed and praised as a "new era" of Bonn (in German: "wende"), as a turning-point of great political importance after thirteen years of coalition government between Social Democrats and Liberals.

Also the parliamentary elections of 6 March 1983, in which Kohl's party gained nearly 50 percent of all votes, confirmed the majority opinion of the West German electorate that the previous opposition party should be given a chance to form a new government and to solve the economic crisis. So the Christian Democrats--together with the Liberals again under the leadership of Hans-Dietrich Genscher, Minister of Foreign Affairs since 1974--announced a substantial reorientation of domestic policy.

And indeed, only a few weeks after the March elections the Kohl-Genscher government started legal initiatives to revive the economy and cut the network of social securities and subsidies, which the Social Democrats had taken pains to weave. Maybe there is no realistic alternative at the moment to fighting against the economic crisis--in any case there is a strong feeling, especially among the underdogs of the German labour force, that a conservative restoration is in full swing in the Federal Republic.

The new emphasis lies in encouragement of private enterprise as well as in belief in the curative powers of the free market system. One has to see if the new government in Bonn will have more success in struggling against stagnation and unemployment than similar economic strategies in Margaret Thatcher's UK or Ronald Reagan's USA.

But what about priorities in the foreign policy of the new West German government? What does "change", "turning point" or "wende in Bonn" mean in this regard? Should African peoples expect a different approach in Bonn towards the pressing problems of African societies? The new and old faces in Bonn--what do they think about the difficult process of granting independence to the people of Namibia; what do they think about international sanctions against the peace-disturbing policy of the aggressive apartheid-state in South Africa; and what about all the unsolved questions concerning a new international economic order?

To answer these questions it is first necessary to draw attention to the fact that since autumn 1982 there have been two rival concepts of German African policy in Bonn.

This conflict is not between the government and the opposition--as one might have expected--but between two parties within the ruling coalition government. While the previous and the new Minister of Foreign Affairs, the controversial Genscher, does not tire of assuring everyone that he himself guarantees the continuity and the calculability of foreign policy of the FRG, the Minister President of Bavaria and leader of the Christian Socialist Union, Franz-Joseph Straus, demands a complete reorientation, especially of policy towards Africa. This confusing competition over political influence on official foreign policy, which arose from a conflict of interest, is still going on. The problem is that foreign policy in Germany is seldom of one mould, because too many institutions have a stake in it. According to the Basic Law of the FRG (the "Grundgesetz"), the Chancellor (the "Bundeskanzler") alone "determines the guiding principles of policy and carries the responsibility for it." (Art. 65 of Grundgesetz). A Foreign Minister however--like all other ministers--directs his department independently with full responsibility, although within the general guiding-principles of the Chancellor, who also appoints the ministers. This competence for deciding the guiding principles of policy which the Basic Law grants to the Chancellor ("Richtlinienkompetenz") gives him in theory a strong power position. But in the concrete situation of forming a viable government after the March elections with the necessity of including Liberals as well as Christian Socialists (in other words the followers of Genscher and Straus), Chancellor Kohl had to find a fragile compromise between the two rivals.

126

This rather difficult situation which for an American or a French President would be quite unthinkable, found its outcome in the very vague declaration which Chancellor Kohl made on 4 May 1983 in the Bundestag, the German parliament.

In this government declaration, officially called "A progamme of renewal" ("Ein Programm der Erneuerung"), Helmut Kohl repeated the well-known principles of West Germany's "policy for peace" (Friedenspolitik):

> German foreign policy means in the first instance the preservation of freedom and the strengthening of peace in Europe and the world. For us an active peace policy is a political necessity and a moral obligation. We are a cosmopolitan country ("ein weltoffenes Land"), and we want to remain so. We want to be good neighbours in Europe. We do need partners and friends in the world. We have them and we wish to keep the friendship. We are able to do that because our policy is true to agreements made predictable ("vertragstreu") and reliable. Our friends can rely on us.[5]

Nowhere in his speech can one find much difference as far as political rhetoric of the East-West Conflict is concerned, between Kohl and the former Chancellor; Helmut Schmidt also regarded the national security of the FRG within the collective security system of NATO and the undisturbed development of West Germany as the second largest trading-nation of the world, as a unit. All efforts were made to come to an agreement with the Soviet Union and the other communist states in Eastern Europe, including the GDR, aimed at a policy of a balance of power, of a dialogue and cooperation. It was a guiding principle of Bonn foreign policy that no additional tensions should arise from German policy in its search for realising legitimate national interests in the world.

A close observer of the political arena in Bonn noticed that Schmidt's principles of foreign policy had to a certain extent influenced the international world

of thought and the language of the diplomats in Western
Europe. His political maxim has been:

> "Responsible policy not only in the
> German interest, but also in the
> consciousness of global mutual
> interdependence, presumes modesty
> and restraint while pursuing its
> own interests, the renunciation of
> predominance and of interference."[6]

The new government in Bonn will not have a great
deal of room to manoeuvre to change the established
policy of West Germany towards East and West dramatically. But it seems possible that the greatest changes
might be expected in its attitude towards the Third
World.

First of all it seems as if the new government
wants to reinforce links between development aid and
the political good conduct of the recipient countries.
The relevant passage of the May 1983 Declaration reads
as follows:

> The federal government will parti-
> cipate in the North-South dialogue
> in all its forms...Many developing
> countries rely on our assistance.
> For us, too, developing countries
> have been indispensable partners
> for many years. Many have proved
> to be good friends to us in diffi-
> cult times. They can expect that
> we help them in return as our
> friends...
> When we assist them (to satisfy the
> basic needs of the people, to esta-
> blish their own food production and
> to promote the supply of local
> energy), we also help ourselves,
> because we safeguard also jobs in
> our country.[7]

Further Chancellor Kohl postulated in the Declaration:

> The securing of peace is also one
> target of our foreign and develop-
> mental cooperation with the Third
> World--cooperation on the basis of
> partnership and mutual respect.
> The FRG supports genuine non-

alignment as much as regional cooperation as important elements of international stability.[8]

As far as the African continent is concerned the new political rhetoric has nothing new to say:

The federal government supports a genuine balance of interests ("Interessenausgleich") in Southern Africa. It advocates the overcoming of apartheid and the peaceful living together of all South Africans. Together with our partners in the West we argue for Namibian independence in due course.

And after these three meagre sentences on Africa (which resemble platitudes more than the guiding principles of a chief executive), the declaration turns to another subject, the obsession of Bonn's new North-South policy:

The Soviet troops have to withdraw from Afghanistan as much as the soldiers of Vietnam must withdraw from Cambodia. Both countries need a just solution, founded on the will of the population.[9]

It is not surprising that public opinion in West Germany was annoyed at empty promises and idle talk like this. Since 1969 the CDU/CSU had been in opposition and therefore had had time enough to prepare a solid, more concrete, and convincing strategy.

But at least one prominent political leader seemed to have a clear concept for an alternative African policy: Franz-Joseph Straus. In a secret policy paper of his party--the CSU--the Bavarian leader demands a[10] change of policy towards Southern Africa:

a) "German Africa policy must take into consideration that Moscow wants to bring the raw materials under its control, which are essential for Europe, and the sea routes to Europe round Southern Africa. The intention thereof is to subject Europe to political blackmail and make her submissive." (thesis 46)

129

b)   "An immediate end to the support of the pro-
     communist and terrorist SWAPO--...and influence on
     the European Community in this direction." (thesis
     48)

c)   "Distance from UN resolution 435 because elections
     are unrealistic as long as the Cuban mercenaries
     are in Angola." (thesis 49)

d)   "Reopening of the German consulate in Windhoek."
     (thesis 50)

And with regard to a reorientation of West German
development aid the paper demands:

e)   "The security interests of the West are not the
     only yardstick of our development aid. It should,
     however, not contradict our own essential interests
     or support forces hostile to us..." (thesis 37)

f)   "Development aid should not have the consequences
     as to subsidize extravagence, corruption or social-
     ist experiments." (thesis 38)

     Foreign Minister Genscher--the self-announced
guarantor of political continuity in the FRG--opposed
this relapse of thinking into cold war categories, of
course. In his subsequent address to African Ambassadors in Bonn (25 May 1983), he reconfirmed that there
will be no major change in Bonn's attitude towards the
problems of Southern Africa. At the same time he indicated some sympathy with Ronald Reagan's new Africa
policy! Moreover, when you bear in mind the fact that
in addition to the Ministry of Foreign Affairs and the
Office of the Chancellor there exist four party
foundations[11] which all pursue their own political
targets in Africa rather independently, then you can
imagine governments do not realise what the real
"African policy" of Bonn could mean.

iii)   A Renewed Policy of Containment?

     For African governments it is important to real-
ise that despite the "change in Bonn" there will be
more continuity than any drastic change in her foreign
policy towards developing countries, with the possible
exception of her South Africa policy (a topic I will
deal with later).

We live, however, in a new era of complex interdependence in which each nation is more vulnerable to events outside her control than ever before in history. No state can nowadays persue its own sovereign national foreign policy. Thus one has to distinguish between three external variables which determine to a high degree the possibilities and limits of the foreign policy of a nation-state.

First the political targets and economic interests of the main competing trading partners; second the tensions, contradictions and interest-conflicts in the international arena; these mean for the FRG mainly the oscillations of East-West policy between détente and confrontation; and third the development of the capitalist world economy, which at the moment faces one of its most severe depressions in this century.

The growing national protectionism in trade and commerce in the industrialized countries and the still increasing external debts of developing countries and socialist countries (which have reached the amount of ca. 800 billion dollars)--which catapulted the IMF into the very powerful position of the financial policeman of the Western world--are only two indications of the present crisis in the international economic system.
From the point of view of the freshly-elected government in Bonn the most dramatic change in the international power structure stems from the expansion of the Soviet Union in the Third World. Since the Soviet intervention in Afghanistan in December 1979, which was condemned by nearly all nonaligned countries, something like a renewed policy of containment of the Soviet influence in Africa, Asia and the Caribbean came into existence. All other political targets of a constructive South policy (like solving the conflicts in Southern Africa or finding viable solutions for the problems concerning fair prices of raw materials) are becoming more and more subordinated to the main task; i.e. to stop the increasing political influence of the Soviet Union in the Third World. The Soviet policy is interpreted by Bonn as an illegitimate and aggressive disturbance of long-established western interests.

Regarding the new slogans from the politicians in Bonn one gets the impression that this new concept of politicising German relations towards the Third World fits in with the global policy of the new US-Administration under Reagan. Thus it might not be just an accident that foreign minister Genscher published his new ideas in the US-magazine Foreign Policy. In a long contribution to the Fall 1982 issue with the title "Towards an Overall Western Strategy for Peace, Freedom and Progress", Mr. Genscher said:

> Assuming that the balance is secured in Europe, it is in Asia, Africa and Latin America that movements determing the global power relationship are to be expected. For this reason it is of paramount importance for the West to pursue a suitable policy as regards to the countries of the Third World and their desire for nonalignment...We for our part by no means want to transform parts of the Third World into Western zones of influence, and we demand from the Soviet Union only what we expect of ourselves: respect for the independence and self-determination of the countries of the Third World.[12]

For minister Genscher "détente" between East and West is not dead or useless; but he sees it as only one of the two pillars of a "dual strategy for peace." The first one, that of safeguarding equilibrium, is the foundation on which détente can be built and which is in fact indispensable for détente. Since World War II, the task for the West has remained the same, which is, according to Genscher: "that of curbing worldwide the expansion of Soviet power." Only the means to achieve this aim have to change always, according to the increasing military power of the Soviet Union:

> After the experience of the failure of a purely military policy of containment in Vietnam, this goal was now to be achieved primarily by a new method: the Soviet Union was to be integrated into a close-knit network of mutually beneficial cooperation and thus induced to subscribe to the principle of mutual political restraint and moderation on both sides in the field of armaments...

But the Soviet Union itself destroyed the foundations of the policy of <u>détente</u> and "peaceful co-
existence":

> Since the mid-1970s the Soviet
> Union has openly adopted a policy
> of indirect and direct military
> intervention in the Third World.
> Now, in the early 1980s, the
> Western democracies are therefore
> faced with a Soviet Union that has
> become a global superpower in mili-
> tary terms and is prepared--as
> demonstrated by the developments in
> countries ranging from Angola to
> Afghanistan--to make use of this
> newly acquired capacity for mili-
> tary intervention anywhere in the
> world.[13]

To understand the new foreign policy of the FRG
fully, it is necessary to analyse the "Weltbild" of
Genscher, i.e. his conception of the world and of the
causes of the big world conflicts.[14] In this view it
was the aggressive Soviet Union which established
<u>spheres of political-ideological influences</u> in Angola,
in Mozambique, in Ethiopia, Cuba, in Nicaragua and in
Afghanistan. Although nobody can seriously deny that
the military power of the Soviet Union and her influence in Third World countries has increased enormously
since the Cuban missile crisis of October 1962, one
cannot overlook the fact that Moscow has gained
influence--at least in Africa (the intervention in
Afghanistan is a different story, indeed the story of
an arrogant imperial occupation of a non-aligned
country) only in countries which the previously Western
policy of colonialism and exploitation led to long-
lasting wars for national liberation. Even the aristo-
cratic regime of Kaiser Haile Selassie in Ethiopia,
which suppressed its own people and proved to be incapable of internal social reforms, was supported by the
West unconditionally--like the government of the Shah
of Persia or other repressive regimes with a pro-
western orientation. Thus one must conclude that the
Soviet Union has acted as a shrewd, but cautious superpower, avoiding direct military confrontation with
Western powers, but whenever the occasion has arisen,
taking advantage of the weakness of the West by helping
socialist oriented governments to survive by providing
massive military equipment and advisers. So I do
believe that not a "grand design" determines the

African policy of the Soviet Union but one of <u>pragmatic</u>
<u>opportunism</u>.

Whether this defensive strategy of gradual and not
too risky <u>expansion</u> of the second superpower will be
for the <u>benefit of</u> independent Africa, I do not want to
discuss here (I do have strong doubts whether this
would be the case), but one thing is very clear: since
the Afghanistan intervention there is an objective
tendency in the antagonistic international system to
extend the East-West conflict to Africa, Asia and the
Caribbean. This happens mainly to the detriment of the
developing nations fighting for self-determination and
collective self-reliance. In spite of that one cannot
overlook that very often <u>local conflicts</u> in the Third
World invite the big powers for intervention.

The reaction of the Western powers to this new
"dangerous challenge" by the Soviet Union--as they see
it--is twofold: First, as much as even the American
device of the year 1977 is valid, namely that possible
military interventions of the Soviet Union should be
hampered, but without a direct military engagement.
This device is also valid for Germany, of course. But
that does not mean that the Western powers restrain
themselves from selling <u>weapons</u> to developing countries. Unfortunately, the German government decided in
1982 to change its previously rather restrictive policy, as far as supplies of weapons to countries outside
NATO are concerned. Previously it was forbidden by law
to supply arms to so-called "regions of tensions"
("Spannungsgebiete"), now this law is abolished and was
replaced by softer regulations. In 1979, West Germany
exported military equipment to some eighty states,
among them 71 developing countries. The five biggest
receivers of German military equipment in 1978 were the
following states:[15]

-   Iran: 959,8 Mil. DM,
-   Argentina: 433,9 Mil. DM,
-   Saudi-Arabia: 57,2 Mil. DM,
-   Nigeria: 56,2 Mil. DM and
-   Israel: 32,4 Mil. DM.

And second, the non-military reaction of the West to
the new Soviet challenge is to replace the Soviet Union
in its historic role as the "natural ally" of the Third
World. In the words of the West German Minister for
Foreign Affairs it sounds as follows:

134

We should not attempt to export our
own political, economic and social
models to the Third World. And we
must not allow ourselves to be mis-
used as protectors of outdated, un-
just structures. Our interests are
by no means endangered by the mere
fact that a developing country
calls its system socialist and its
economy a planned economy. The
important thing is that its government is able to act on its own, and
that it is not dependent on Moscow
for its existence and survival. As
a rule, the West will be able to
maintain fruitful relations with an
independent government, for it is
the West, with its affirmation of
the right to self-determination and
its willingness to provide economic
and effective trade ties and
technology, that is the natural
partner of the Third World, and not
the East.[16]

iv) **The EEC as the "Natural Partner" for Africa?**

One cannot deny that the economically strong and
democratic countries of the West which also have at
their disposal some unique cultural and educational
relations with Africa's "state classes" have good
opportunities to win this competition between East and
West to be the best and most helpful partner for all
for the Third World societies. One strong instrument
for keeping friendly relations with the former European
colonies and their new elites is the Lomé Convention
between the European Community and the so-called ACP
countries. This is regarded by many politicians and
scientists in West Germany as a "model" for a genuine
partnership between unequal states, as a real "breakthrough" in an otherwise blocked and fruitless North-
South dialogue. And especially diplomats of EEC-
countries self-consciously and self-confidently under-
line the fact that progressive countries like Ethiopia,
Zimbabwe and Guinea-Bissau have preferred to become
members of Lomé which has increased its number from 46
ACP states in the beginning to 63 states in 1983; that
even Angola and Mozambique are considering joining the

club is regarded as a further proof of the attractive-
ness of the Convention.[17]

As far as the assessment of Lomé by African
governments is concerned, I believe that many of them
have the attitude that a sparrow in the hand is better
than a pigeon on the roof, which means that belonging
to the club is better than getting nothing. In any
case the real impact of Lomé on the efforts of ACP
people to accelerate economic growth and to overcome
underdevelopment should not be over-estimated: trade
between both groups of countries did not significantly
increase, the amount of foreign investment in industries stayed far behind expectations, and the transfer
of real resources to the poorer countries could not be
increased as would have been necessary to meet the
basic needs of the people. I see only one innovative
and progressive element in the Lomé Convention; that is
the invention of Stabex. This is a collective system
of the European Community to stabilize the export
earnings of ACP countries, as far as their exports of
raw materials to the EEC--and only to the EEC--are
concerned. For this purpose the Community granted the
amount of 1375 m. DM for five years, a ridiculously
small amount which amounts to about two or three percent of the value of all the exports of the ACP-
countries. Although Stabex might be regarded as a
first step in the right direction of economic cooperation with a view to international burden-sharing between North and South, the real amount of transferred
resources from the West is by no means adequate to the
immense problems of unfair and fluctuating commodity
prices on the world market.

But it is noteworthy that the Stabex funds, which
are transferred to ACP governments in hard currency on
applications in special cases of emergency, are free
from strict control ("Verwendungskontrolle") by the
EEC. "Little presents strengthen friendship"-I
believe that is the political logic of the Stabex
system. Obviously, one can establish political zones
of influence in different ways!

Finally, I want to mention one further function of
the Lomé Convention. Created in 1974, when in face of
the successful OPEC-strategy some European governments
were afraid of the "chaos power" of the Third World
(eg. ex-Chancellor Schmidt), the progressive looking
Lomé Convention could be used as a consolation: it
should divert public opinion away from the frustrating
discussions of a New International Economic Order and

the demands of UNCTAD for a Common Fund to stabilise
the prices for raw materials ("Corea Plan") in all
countries.

In this respect the Conventions of 1974 and 1979
must have been very much in the interest of the Federal
Republic of Germany, because she was one of the hard-
liners in the North-South dialogue and had sometimes
got a very bad image as a wealthy and arrogant country
which was not willing to compromise. The fourth UNCTAD
Conference in Nairobi, Kenya in 1975 nearly failed
because Washington and Bonn tried to persuade the rest
of the world to apply only free market systems to cure
the economic evils of the developing countries. As
Rolf Hofmeier, the Director of the Africa Institute in
Hamburg, put it:[18]

> In respect to NIEO the FRG has
> always been in the camp of the
> hard-liners defending the economic
> self-interests of the industrial-
> ized Western countries. The over-
> all effect of the positive orien-
> tation of the aid policy and of the
> tough position taken on NIEO issues
> was a rather ambivalent one as seen
> from the perspective of the deve-
> loping countries. The economic
> argument, as expressed by the
> Brandt report (on problems of
> international development) of the
> stimulating effects for the
> Northern countries of more aid due
> to the intricate interdependence
> between North and South did not
> find much active support in the
> FRG. Although chaired by the
> former chancellor, work of the
> Brandt Commission generally has not
> had much substantial impact on the
> basic orientation of German Third
> World policy.

v) "Peace Politics" in Southern Africa?

Possibly the most important change of German
African policy has occurred in her attitude to the
conflicts in Southern Africa. As is well-known, West
Germany belongs to the so-called "Group of Five"--a
group of five Western countries, which has tried to

137

find a peaceful way to grant independence to the people of Namibia. In December 1976, the UN General Assembly approved--with 107 votes in favour and six votes against--the "armed struggle of the people of Namibia under the leadership of SWAPO for self-determination, freedom and national independence in a united Namibia."[19]

The five Western ambassadors on the UN Security Council at that time, who neither shared the majority vote of the UN, nor agreed with the plan of the South African government (to concede independence to Namibia at the end of 1978 on the Bantustan concept) founded the so-called "contact group of five." The ambassadors of the USA, UK, France, Canada and the FRG pledged themselves to find a peaceful solution by negotiation and in compliance with UN criteria.

Nobody can honestly deny that the "big five" made great diplomatic efforts to come to a practical agreement with the Vorster and Botha regimes. But it is also true a) that the Western powers completely failed to get any real concessions from the South African governments; b) that they never put pressure on the tough and relentless government in Pretoria (for example, by private investment); and c) that they finally lost any trustworthiness as "honest brokers" between South Africa, SWAPO and the so-called "Turnhalle" government under Dick Mudge. For example, when in January 1981 the South African government arbitrarily wrecked the Geneva conference about a ceasefire and the modalities for free elections in Namibia, there was no severe reaction from the West. Minister Genscher, it is true, blamed the South Africa delegation for the failure of the conference and for the fact that the plan to hold free elections in Namibia still in 1981 had thus to be dropped, but no deeds followed. After some weeks business went on as usual.[20]

Therefore, South Africa quickly learned that the Western countries are little more than "paper tigers"--and still have vested interest in the flourishing economy of South Africa. And despite all their rhetoric about the inhuman and intolerable apartheid system, they are not willing to give up or cut down their profitable business, although many experts argue that strategies of gradual withdrawal would be in the enlightened self-interest of the West. In West Germany the formula for legitimation of the present laissez-faire policy is called "Commerce and Politics--you should not link without real cause."

Furthermore, the apartheid regime learnt from the example of Israel how to deal with hostile neighbouring countries from a position of military strength: you do not negotiate with them, you attack, punish and humiliate them; that is as long as your superior military equipment, and the big powers involved, allow. Needless to emphasise, such power politics is very short-sighted if not suicidal.

That the South African army is nowadays very well equipped--with Impala fighters, tanks and modern transport facilities and so on--results mainly from its close economic and scientific cooperation with industrialised countries like Germany, France, Great Britain, the United States and Israel. And should South Africa have already developed its own capacity to construct atomic bombs--and many symptoms support this assumption--West Germany acted as a silent accomplice in South Africa's efforts in gaining this terrible means of threat and destruction.

From some secret documents of the German Embassy in Pretoria, which were stolen during a move and then published by Zdenek Cervenka and Barbara Rogers, it became known that above all some German natural scientists and businessmen, with the unadmitted support or at least toleration of government institutions, cooperated with South Africa to provide access to the necessary technical know-how.[21]

To summarise: the contribution of West Germany and the other four Western countries to solve the Namibian question led to the opposite of its original intention: the aggravation of the conflict. The five could not even prevent white South Africa from bombing towns and freedom-fighter camps in Angola and Mozambique--weak countries on friendly terms with the Soviet Union. What will be their predictible reactions? Moscow will send more and better arms to her allies, otherwise she might lose respect among her friends and allies in the world. That again could be used by Pretoria as a welcome pretext for asking for more sophisticated weapons from NATO-countries to contain and to combat "communism" in Africa. Here we face the dangerous scenario of a self-fulfilling prophecy.

What is the lesson of the failure of Western diplomacy in Namibia? It shows that a policy of peace-oriented negotiations is useless and even counterproductive when the actor in the case of failure is not prepared or willing to use alternative means, i.e. to

139

put noticeable pressure on the resisting, peace disturbing state.

The proclaimed "politics of peace" (Friedenspolitik)--
as West German diplomats like to call their comfortable
laissez-faire approach towards South Africa--looses any
credibility, above all among the Front Line States like
Tanzania, Zambia, Botswana and Zimbabwe, when the
government in Bonn is not even willing to do anything
concrete--except periodical sermons about the necessity
of "change by peaceful means"--against the permanent
violation of the human rights of other people. Bonn
has always refused to consider any form of international sanctions or boycotts against South Africa--a long-
standing demand not only by UN- and OAU- resolutions,
but also called for by many social scientists in West
Germany and elsewhere.

Unfortunately, there is no indication at the moment
that the new German government has learnt anything from
the failures of the past. Recently, one of the most
experienced and influential Christian Democrat politicians as far as foreign relations are concerned, Under-
Secretary Volkmar Kohler (in the Ministry of Economic
Cooperation), pledged himself to a policy of "peaceful
change" without recognizing SWAPO or the African
National Congress as true representatives of the
African people. Kohler stated:

> The geographic and economic posi-
> tion of Southern Africa and its
> deposit of raw materials make it
> imperative to counteract the Soviet
> Union's attempt to extend its
> influence to other states in
> Africa. A particular danger con-
> sists in the influence and the
> operations of other non-African
> communist states, the instigation
> of wars by proxy and the terrorist
> activities of organizations which,
> under the guise of freedom move-
> ments, are in reality pursuing
> totalitarian aims.[22]

And Kohler and his political friends regret that during
President Carter's term of office, many a critical
mistake was committed not only by the USA but also by
the FRG:[23]

> We include among these mistakes the
> Federal Government's decision to
> close its consulate in Windhoek.

140

In so doing, the Federal Government
was seen by the rest of the world
to bow to the demands of the
militant communist-dominated SWAPO
and to the pressure of its
sympathisers in Africa (i.e. the
"Front Line States").

You have to realise that this policy statement was
published nearly at the same time as our Minister for
Foreign Affairs Genscher openly declared to keep in
diplomatic contact with SWAPO Chief, Sam Nujoma, who
for the first time had been invited by Genscher to
official talks about a cease-fire and independence for
Namibia in 1981.

To conclude this sad chapter of German politics in
South Africa, I want to report the latest proposal of
German politicians towards a solution of the Namibian
conflict; this is the proposal by Straus and Kohler to
demand the withdrawal of the Cubans from Angola as a
precondition for holding free elections in Namibia. To
quote Under-Secretary Kohler once again:[24]

We accepted UN Resolution, 435,
even though it only opens up a
formal path leading to Namibia's
independence. But we also understood South Africa's misgivings
about the Security Council's
resolution on Walvis Bay and on the
question of SWAPO bases in
Namibia....We keenly welcome the
role played since January 1980 by
Dr. Chester Crocker, an old friend
of the Konrad Adenauer Foundation
(Crocker became Under-Secretary for
African Affairs in the Reagan-
Administration in 1982).
We support American efforts to
induce the Cubans to pull out of
Angola. Perhaps it would be
recommendable to replace Cuban
forces by an OAU force in order to
prevent Angola from sinking into
chaos when the Cubans leave Angola.

This statement indicates a change in the West
German approach towards the Namibia problem. The
attitude of the "honest broker," pursued by the "Group
of Five," has been abandoned unilaterally by the United

141

States, and the Germans--but not the French and the British--are likely to follow them without much hesitation. The idea of using the problem of the Cubans in Angola as leverage for a policy to solve in Namibia question orginated from global East-West considerations of the Reagan Administration, in which the political activities of the Cubans is ranked higher than the Namibians' right to freedom.

Thus the whole Western mission to promote peaceful change in Southern Africa proved to be a complete failure--a situation which the South African government used to start raids deep into the territories of Angola, Lesotho and Mozambique. The pleading for a strategy of "peaceful change" in view of a political regime based on brutal force and racial discrimination in reality means stabilising the political status quo, and that again means that the oppressed peoples have no alternative option than to use counter-force.

Notes

1. Günher van Well (Under-Secretary of State in the Ministry of Foreign Affairs), quoted in Rainer Tetzlaff, "Die Dritte-Welt-Politik der Bundesrepublik Deutschland Zwischen Friedensrtetorik und Realpolitik", Friedensanalysen, 15, (Frankfurt) 1982, 50.

2. Bundesministerium für Wirtschaftliche Zusammenarbeit (BMZ: Minister for Economic Cooperation), Vierter Bericht zur Entwicklungs- politik der Bundesregierung, (Bonn, 1980), 11-14.

3. Klaus Esser und Jürgen Wiemann (Deutsches Institut für Entwicklungspolitik, West Berlin), Schwerpinktlander in der Dritten Welt. Konsequenzen für die Südbeziehungen der Bundsrepublik Deutschland, (West Berlin, 1981), 29.

4. Tetzlaff, "Die Dritte-Welt-Politik", 50.

5. Bundeskanzler Helmut Kohl, "Ein Programm der Erneuerung" (Rede vor dem Bundestag), 4 May 1983, quoted in Frankfurter Rundschau, 6 May 1983, 12.

6. Kurt Becker, "Hemut Schmidts auBenpolitisches Vermächtnis", Die Zeit, 42, 15 October 1982, 3.

7. Kohl, "En programm der Erneuerung", quoted in Frankfurter Rundschau, 7 May 1983, 14.

8. Ibid.

9. Ibid.

10. "Entspannung muB untebrechbar sein". Ein internes Papier von CDU und CSU für die noch ausstehenden Koalitionsgespräche über die Künftige Orientierung der Deutschen AuBenpolitik: Frankfurter Rundschau, 30 March 1983, 10.

11. Konrad-Adenauer-Stiftung (CDU), Friedrich-Ebert-Stiftung (SPD), Friedrich-Naumann-Stiftung (FDP) and the Hanns-Seidel-Stiftung (CSU).

12. Hans-Dietrich Genscher, "Towards an Overall Western Strategy for Peace, Freedom and Progress", Foreign Affairs, 61(1), (Fall 1982), 59 and 61.

13. Ibid. 45.

14. Cf. Helmut Bley and Rainer Tetzlaff (eds), Afrika und Bonn: Versäumnisse und Zwänge deutscher Afrika Politik (Rowohlt, Reinbek bei Hamburg, 1978), 28f.

15. Tetzlaff, "Die Dritte-Welt-Politik", 87.

16. Genscher, "Towards an Overall Western Strategy", 60.

17. Klaus Meyer (Generaldirektor Entwicklung, EG-Komission), "Das zweite Abkomman von Lomé", Europa-Archiv, 1, 1980, 11-20 (special print).

18. Rolf Hofmeier and Siegfried Schultz, "German Development Aid Policy in Transition", Vierteljahresberichte der Friedrich-Ebert-Stiftung, 91, 91, March 1983, 477.

19. Cf. Helmut Bley, "Namibia, die Dundesreupblic und der Westen: 15 Jahre Kirsenverschärfung", Friedensanalysen (Frankfurt), 15: "Hilfe + Handel = Frieden ?. Die Bundesrepublik in der Dritten Welt", Redaktion Reiner Steinweg, 109-138.

20. Cf. Günther Jantzen (Institut für Afrika-Kunde), Kommentar Afrika, 8(2), 1983.

21. Zdenek Cervenka and Barbara Rogers, The Nuclear Axis: secret collaboration between West Germany and South Africa, (London: 1978).

22. Volkmar Köhler, "Europe's role in Africa: a German view", International Affairs Bulletin 6, 1982/3, 38.

23. Ibid., 42. Also important are Gerd Dieter Bossen: "Unberlegungen für eine neue deutsche AuBenpolitik in Richtung Afrika, Asien/Pazifik und Lateinamerika (Teil 2): Südliches Afrika, besonders Südafrika und Namibia", IIS-Auslands-Informationen, edited by the Konrad-Adenauer-Foundation, 6, 1983, 29 March 1983.

24. Köhler, "Europe's Role", 43.

Chapter Six

Japan and Africa: political economy and ambivalance

Michael Leifer

Geographical and historical distance have served Japan well in promoting a relationship with Africa. Geographical distance means that neither Japan nor the states of Africa are located within the other's strategic horizons thus avoiding tensions arising from possible conflicts of security interests. Historical distance is in part of a function of geography. Of supreme importance has been the absence of any legacy from the past similar to those of the former colonial powers. However, it is the industrial standing of Japan which serves as a countervailing factor which introduces tensions into relationships with the post-colonial states of Africa: in the main, Japan's relationships with the states of Africa are not those of equality because of the marked differences in levels of economic achievement expressed in the pattern of trade. Indeed, Japan's priorities have been essentially economic. Africa, has been contemplated as a rich store of natural resources and as a region of market opportunities which provide a valuable supplementary underpinning for an economy distinguished paradoxically by growth and vulnerability. In addition, within Africa, political priorities have interposed within the relationship. And, over the past decade in particular, Japan has been obliged to take increasing account of African political sensibilities and to deviate from a preferred apolitical non-alignment on issues which arouse strong feelings north and south of the Sahara. This degree of deviation has been expressed primarily in declaratory form so that a resource diplomacy precipitated by the Arab oil embargo in 1973 has not involved agonizing choices. Moreover, tensions have been contained at an acceptable cost and Japan appears to enjoy the best of both worlds in relationships with black and white Africa. The price paid, so far, has been a limited expression of black African grievance which has exacted no greater penalty than lack of support for Japan's candidature for a seat on the United Nation's Security Council. Japan, however, is not entirely without bargaining power of its own given its attraction as an economic partner which makes compromises necessary on the part of African governments.

145

Africa was not virgin territory to a Japan seeking
economic rehabilitation and development after the Second World War. Indeed, in 1983, the British Government had renounced the Anglo-Japanese Commercial Treaty
of 1911 in respect of its West African colonies in reaction to Japanese economic activity. Such inroads
were more evident in East Africa whose markets had
become dominated by Japanese products by the early
1930s. Britain, however, was unable to act in retalia-
tion in East Africa because of restrictions imposed by
the League of Nation's Mandates. The advent of world
war disrupted completely Japanese economic penetration
but after its conclusion, and with the onset of decolonization, Japanese businessmen and diplomats made
their way to Africa without the same sense of inhibi-
tion which marked their reentry to South-East Asia. On
the surface at least, the post-war relationship which
developed with an Africa in the throes of rejecting its
colonial shackles was free of the kinds of resentment
and bitterness experienced in South-East Asia where the
Japanese had been far more cruel colonial masters than
the Europeans whom they had dispossessed. In addition,
Japan still enjoyed a reputation for awakening coloured
nationalism through its resounding and historic victory
over Tsarist Russia at the turn of the century. As
well, despite the unsavory record of Japan's armies in
the Pacific War, the Japanese were regarded as coloured
victims of nuclear terror. Moreover, given the attendant constitutional consequences of Japan's defeat at
the hands of the Allies, its pacific international outlook meant that Japan could be regarded as being outside the context of resented and intrusive Cold War
rivalries. Although Japan was sheltered under America's nuclear umbrella and bound to the United States in
a mutual security treaty, its approach to an Africa of
independent states was not only free of colonial associations but also virtually free of political content
as well: political issues were carefully deleted from
the developing relationship.

Although Crown Prince Akihito and his wife paid a
visit to Ethiopia in 1960, it was not until after the
international energy crises precipitated by the Arab-
Israeli war in 1973 that a Japanese Foreign Minister,
Toshio Kimura, visited five African states (Ivory
Coast, Kenya, Nigeria, Senegal, and Tanzania) south of
the Sahara. It seemed that until an underlying vulnerability in raw materials was dramatically exposed by
the Arab oil embargo, Japan conducted itself in Africa
as a trading company.

Japan assumed a special attraction in post-colonial Africa because of its remarkable achievements in economic development; but it demonstrated initial political insensitivity by maintaining its trading links with South Africa and Portugal's African colonies and resisted African suggestions for applying sanctions against both South Africa and Portugal. In 1960, for example, the Japanese delegation to the United Nations voted against the Soviet proposal to establish a time limit for the abolition of all forms of colonialism, while in 1962 it abstained on resolutions to expel South Africa and Portugal from the Economic Commission for Africa. Indeed, one author writing in the mid-1960s concluded "It is apparent, therefore, that the Japanese are reluctant to say or do anything that might upset their Western friends."[1]

The position of the Japanese was protected somewhat by their own experience of and public opposition to racial discrimination. Indeed, it took time in Africa for it to be understood that the Japanese are themselves ambivalent about racial equality. Although the Japanese Government adopted a strong declaratory stand against the practice of apartheid within South Africa, it was unwilling to translate that stand into tangible measures of pressure against the South African Government. It is worth noting that in 1963, Japan exported US $83 million worth of goods to South Africa which then exported raw materials to Japan to the value of US $120 million. Indeed, in 1962, Ghana's United Nation's representative accused the government of Japan of making a deal with its South African counterpart to purchase more of its iron ore if South Africa would promise in turn not apply apartheid policies to Japanese nationals.

Any tensions arising from Japan's refusal to allow the political sensibilities of post-colonial Africa to influence its trading relationships did not, at least during the 1960s, have a notable affect on Japan's freedom of action. Newly independent African states faced with pressing problems of development expressed their displeasure but not beyond words. Indeed, in practical terms a more tangible issue was the growing trade gap in Japan's favour with post-colonial Africa; so much so that in 1963 Nigeria placed restrictions on purchases from Japan. In contention was Japan's restrictions imposed on the importation of agricultural produce to protect its own farming sector. An additional source of tension was the limited contribution Japan was then prepared to make to capital development

147

funds in Africa as a result of its reparations payments. Relations between Japan and Africa were limited before the early 1970s as illustrated in the Diplomatic Blue Book for 1969 which covered Japan's foreign relations in the period April 1967 to March 1968: there was no mention of Africa whatsoever. In successive years Africa was lumped together with Third World regions as suitable objects to secure an appropriate balance between Asia and the United States.

Africa, especially north of the Sahara, began to emerge as a area of importance to Japan as a result of the Arab-Israeli War in 1973. Significantly, the Diplomatic Blue Book for 1974 made specific reference to African countries as playing an increasingly important role in the international community and turning "more and more towards Japan in their hopes for the future." However, although Japan had recognised independent African states with each transfer of sovereignty and had established embassies in the more important capitals, Tokyo's immediate response to the Arab oil embargo was directed to the Arab world. Deputy Prime Minister Takeo Miki included Egypt in his tour of the Middle East in December 1973 and while in Cairo offered credits for widening the Suez Canal. Yasuhiro Nakasone then Minister for International Trade and Industry also visited Algeria, Morocco and the Sudan in January 1974. From this juncture, apart from responding to Arab political pressures in the form of compliance with boycott regulations against Israel, the Japanese government began to revise its position on a Middle East peace settlement which had been previously very much a function of its relationship with the United States. Unlike some African countries, Japan did not break off diplomatic relations with Israel. Israel's right to live in peace was upheld but Japan moved towards a position which favoured Palestinian statehood. Thus, although the Japanese government supported the Camp David Accords and the subsequent Peace Treaty concluded in 1979, the bilateral agreement between Israel and Egypt was depicted by Foreign Minister Sunao Sonoda as only the first step. Japan took the view that peace between Israel and its Arab neighbours should be based on the implementation of United Nation's Security Council resolutions 242 and 338 and on recognition of the legitimate rights of the Palestinians to seek an independent state. Moreover, it was maintained in Tokyo that the Palestine Liberation Organization's participation in negotiations was a prerequisite for peace.[2] A relationship with the PLO had been cultivated during 1976 and it opened an information office in Tokyo in February 1977. However, as indicated above, Japan did

not endorse Arab rejectionist sentiment over the Camp
David Accords. Although a firmer position on
Palestinian statehood was adopted by the European community, Japanese support for Camp David was demonstrated by membership in the World Bank sponsored consulta-
tive Group for Egypt. Japan's overall contribution
between 1973-80 amounted to some US $720 million which
constituted a material expression of support for
Egypt's position despite Tokyo's reluctance to be identified too closely with American policy. It has been
pointed out that "Egypt is the only country in the Arab
world which has been receiving a significant volume of
official Japanese aid unrelated to the size of its oil
exports." As well, "aid to Egypt is motivated by the
fact that Japanese businessmen see the country as a
promising base for the location of labour-intensive
industries."[3] Japan has contributed to major infrastructural and projects including water supply, tele-
communications and airport runways, while the government controlled Japan National Oil Corporation has
become a principal shareholder in the Egyptian Petroleum Development Company which produces around 10,000
barrels per day in the eastern desert. If President
Sadat's intention to vist Japan was unfulfilled, his
successor Husni Mubarak did so in April 1983. A joint
communiqué issued with Prime Minister Yashuhiro
Nakasone reflected Japan's position of balance towards
the central conflict in the Middle East. It endorsed
"a comprehensive settlement based on the principles and
guidelines incorporated in the Fez peace proposals and
President Reagan's peace plan." Recognition and respect for the right of Israel to exist was combined with
a corresponding demand that the "inalienable legitimate
right of the Palestinian people to self-determination,
under the UN Charter, must be recognized and respect-
ed."[4] Firm evidence of the continuation of Japan's
interest in Egypt's economic development took the form
of a yen loan equivalent to US $210 million.

Japan's attempt to square the circle in support for
the political fruits of Camp David, expressed in part
by economic benefaction towards Egypt while maintaining
a position on Palestinian statehood more in keeping
with its major suppliers of energy, constitutes a
characteristic aspect of its general resource diplomacy. That diplomacy conducted with reference to Egypt
and also to the states of the Mahgreb has been contemplated primarily with reference to issues of the Middle
East rather than those of Africa writ large. Such an
orientation has been reflected in bureaucratic arrangements within the Foreign Ministry in Tokyo where diplo-

matic relations with Africa north of the Sahara have
been handled by the First Middle Eastern Division.
When a measure of bureaucratic reorganisation took
place within the Foreign Ministry in 1980, responsibi-
lity for Africa north of the Sahara remained with the
First Middle Eastern Division while Africa South of the
Sahara remained within the overall ambit of the Middle
Eastern and African Affairs Bureau. Its single Africa
Division established in 1961 was divided into two: a
First Africa Division, dealing mainly with Francophone
states and other West African countries, and a Second
Africa Division dealing primarily with English speaking
states in eastern and southern Africa.

The measure of distinction between Africa north of
the Sahara as an extension of the Middle East and the
rest of Africa was pointed up after the Arab oil embargo of 1973. For example, in the Diplomatic Blue Book
for 1975, Africa was the last continent in the world to
receive mention and then only in very general terms
with reference to the problems of Southern Africa and
their central concern for African states. Indeed,
although Masayoshi Ohira, when Foreign Minister in
1974, told a conference of Japanese ambassadors
stationed in Africa that "we should acknowledge that
Japan's existence and prosperity can no longer be
viewed as something unrelated to that vast area that is
Africa," little substantive action followed. A measure
of response to African pressure over Japan's relationship with South Africa occurred in June 1974 when the
Japanese Government endorsed the United Nation's
General Assembly resolution which sought to prohibit
all cultural, sporting and educational exchanges with
South Africa. This minimal sanction, together with
declaratory support for an arms embargo, opposition to
direct investment and ritual denunciation of apartheid
did not then, or subsequently, have any practical
bearing on the longstanding flourishing economic association between Japan and South Africa. South Africa
ranks first among Japan's continental trading partners,
well ahead of Nigeria and Liberia whose third place
position is artificially made up of the construction
and sale of ships to Liberian registered companies.
Japan is a major exporter to South Africa of motor
vehicles, machinery, electrical goods and chemicals and
imports raw materials, mineral fuels and metals, hides
and skins as well as fruit and vegetables. In addition, Japan conducts a significant trade with Namibia
including the importation of uranium.

Table 6.1.1

Japan's Trade with Africa 1980
(Yen '000 with Yen 220 = US $1 approx.)

Country	Japan's Exports	Japan's Imports
Algeria	101,425,652	102,174,009
Angola	18,768,080	23,277,714
Benin	4,938,553	983,594
Botswana	93,995	104,936
Burundi	2,178,234	1,048,048
Cameroon	16,559,813	9,914,827
Canary Islands	39,951,507	45,025
Cape Verde	525,738	2,758
Central African Republic	652,147	2,162,743
Ceuta and Melilla	16,816,450	-
Chad	15,945	1,705,468
Comoros	96,537	12,163
Congo	3,890,184	3,153,829
Djibouti	5,346,983	-
Egypt	145,379,608	32,273,835
Equatorial Guinea	5,002	-
Ethiopia	14,196,421	6,538,954
Gabon	9,972,969	4,529,586
Gambia	1,074,837	6,516
Ghana	6,266,668	28,305,858
Guinea	724,366	11,143
Guinea Bissau	21,514	566
Indian Ocean Territories (BR)	38,597	5,463
Ivory Coast	27,435,572	10,336,063
Kenya	42,828,775	3,743,139
Lesotho	83,123	-
Liberia	317,694,863	76,578,528
Libya	118,878,625	80,962,984
Madagascar	8,380,928	13,316,296

Table 6.1.1 (continued)

Country	Japan's Exports	Japan's Imports
Malawi	4,759,565	994,389
Mali	1,547,163	2,027,855
Mauritania	655,601	6,678,514
Mauritius	7,192,609	20,766
Morocco	9,958,174	19,430,968
Mozambique	7,900,947	4,331,085
Namibia	415,775	11,603,666
Niger Republic	4,574,014	35,431
Nigeria	335,862,355	25,948,258
Reunion	4,880,923	4,704
Rwanda	6,471,881	455,530
St. Helena	14,242	-
Sao Tomé and Principe	549,296	-
Senegal	2,014,025	3,423,743
Seychelles	963,992	47,186
Sierra Leone	8,437,070	212,241
Somalia	1,164,991	-
South Africa	405,004,353	396,029,404
Sudan	15,133,152	12,853,510
Swaziland	1,250,651	4,754,098
Tanzania	25,446,665	5,381,951
Togo	5,483,520	208,266
Tunisia	15,048,975	227,325
Uganda	3,918,823	8,464,870
Upper Volta	2,282,928	3,820,945
Western Sahara	34,767	-
Zaire	10,186,775	30,744,428
Zambia	12,421,083	68,494,719
Zimbabwe	6,176,745	6,867,427

Exports from Japan are f.o.b., imports into Japan
c.i.f. Figures compiled by the Customs Bureau,
Ministry of Finance, Tokyo.

Reproduced in Japan and Africa. The Economic and Trade
Picture. The Anglo-Japanese Economic Institute,
London. Bulletin No. 169, May-June 1981, p. 5., and
Bulletin No. 197, June 1982, p. 5.

Table 6.1.2

Japan's Trade with Africa 1981
(Yen '000 with Yen 220 = US $1 approx.)

Country	Japan's Exports	Japan's Imports
Algeria	104,234,355	154,097,718
Angola	18,364,181	6,103,326
Benin	6,424,743	772,813
Botswana	142,166	77,877
Burundi	2,863,452	558,293
Cameroon	16,662,494	8,656,013
Canary Islands	30,422,210	566,234
Cape Verde	77,575	2,895
Central African Republic	534,037	1,663,280
Ceuta and Melilla	12,910,890	529
Chad	13,218	1,964,486
Comoros	351,402	96,662
Congo	5,398,107	3,831,416
Djibouti	5,634,207	711
Egypt	173,734,290	45,463,914
Equatorial Guinea	3,402	1,473
Ethiopia	14,599,551	6,726,136
Gabon	11,101,264	1,749,619
Gambia	723,701	-
Ghana	7,356,832	26,247,295
Guinea	800,347	8,946
Guinea Bissau	18,284	163
Indian Ocean Territories (BR)	502,262	-
Ivory Coast	18,951,071	11,239,160
Kenya	31,498,107	2,800,393
Lesotho	45,737	-
Liberia	374,770,151	68,830,595
Libya	235,721,142	78,581,077
Madagascar	3,472,492	10,301,787

Table 6.1.2 (continued)

Country	Japan's Exports	Japan's Imports
Malawi	3,346,582	2,439,475
Mali	1,458,277	2,206,786
Mauritania	2,876,891	11,604,025
Mauritius	4,060,092	27,880
Morocco	15,208,705	22,652,755
Mozambique	3,377,767	5,988,150
Namibia	319,138	5,601,437
Niger Republic	3,664,183	509,380
Nigeria	475,456,020	75,135,670
Reunion	3,555,021	17,788
Rwanda	6,001,540	151,101
St. Helena	635,999	14,932
Sao Tomé and Principe	106,309	1,091
Senegal	1,764,104	3,204,440
Seychelles	990,523	23,842
Sierra Leone	3,523,990	418,450
Somalia	1,229,913	20,792
South Africa	487,809,950	381,272,868
Sudan	22,099,861	12,572,839
Swaziland	1,376,391	1,831,738
Tanzania	20,755,797	4,062,434
Togo	5,995,476	652,430
Tunisia	20,554,238	193,049
Uganda	1,115,371	3,424,292
Upper Volta	2,243,698	2,719,175
Western Sahara	972	-
Zaire	17,693,660	15,730,782
Zambia	11,495,158	60,002,151
Zimbabwe	15,415,486	10,656,314

Exports from Japan are f.o.b., imports into Japan c.i.f. Figures compiled by the Customs Bureau, Ministry of Finance, Tokyo.

Reproduced in Japan and Africa. The Economic and Trade Picture. The Anglo-Japanese Economic Institute. London. Bulletin No. 169, May-June 1981, p. 5, and Bulletin No. 197, June 1982, p. 5.

Japan's relations with South Africa are conducted
on a practical basis without formal diplomatic representation. Representation is maintained at the level of
Consul-General. In South Africa, Japan's Consul-
General is treated as an ambassador. In Japan, South
Africa's Consul-General is always a diplomat of ambassadorial rank. Japanese businessmen rarely have problems securing residence visas for periods of up to five
years in South Africa. They are encouraged to bring
their wives with them for obvious reasons. Organized
parties of tourists as opposed to individual travellers
are welcomed. Japanese company representatives resident in South Africa, together with their families,
number approximately 500 and live mainly in
Johannesburg. They have their own club and school and
tend to remain among themselves. Most children return
to Japan for secondary education. Japanese residents
are accorded the status of 'honorary white' under the
race laws but the South African government has been
active to prevent the emergence of a settled group of
young Japanese able to claim South African nationality
on the grounds of birth. In addition, 'honorary white'
status does not permit marriage between Japanese and
South Africans. From the Japanese perspective, the
constraints of residence appear to be accepted. Indig-
nities are tolerated for material reward. The South
Africans, for their part, appreciate that black Africa
has come to enjoy a higher place in Japan's priorities
as a long-term source of national resources. However,
it has been argued within South Africa that:

> Japan cannot afford to make any
> substantive gestures against South
> Africa which is also becoming an
> increasingly important source of
> essential commodities. The only
> way out of this dilemma is to try
> to curry favour with Black Africa
> by making empty gestures (which
> will not goad South Africa to the
> point of acting against Japan's
> vital interests) while continuing
> to do business with South Africa.[5]

In virtually all respects, Japan's gestures have
been empty. For example, although cultural, sporting
and educational exchanges are prohibited, these forms
of prohibition can be overcome by the simple device of
a tourist visa. Japan appeared to comply with United
Nation's Security Council resolutions on Rhodesia
before the independence of Zimbabwe but commercial

links with South Africa were employed for the importation of Rhodesian chrome. South Africa's occupation
of Namibia has been denounced by the Japanese government as illegal and support proffered for its independence through United Nation's initiative. Indeed, Japan
has announced its intention of extending cooperation to
the civilian component of the United Nation's Transition Assistance Group (UNTAG) should it be despatched
for the purpose of assisting the independence of
Namibia. That said, Japan has not been inhibited in
conducting a significant trade with Namibia under South
African domination (see Table 6.1).

Japan's policy towards South Africa in particular
and Africa in general has been distinguished by a
quality of ambivalence which arises from the priorities
of resource diplomacy. Such diplomacy has been prac-
ticed in a way so as to permit full enjoyment of the
economic benefits of dealing on Japan's terms with both
black and white Africa with only minimal complaints
arising in the process. Occasionally, a measure of
protest is expressed which finds an outlet within
Japan. For example, a Nigerian academic writing in the
international edition of an English language weekly
published in Tokyo pointed out:

> Not surprisingly, Japan has not
> been forthcoming in support for
> Africa, either in the struggle for
> independence or against the evils
> of racism and apartheid or in the
> quest for economic development. To
> be sure, Japan often expresses
> understanding and sympathy for the
> African struggle for independence.
> But an examination of the speeches
> of Japanese delegates to the UN
> often reveals an attachment to, and
> interest in, vague expressions of
> support for Africa.[6]

However, despite an awareness of Japan's delinquen-
cy in terms of black African political priorities,
there has never been a serious attempt to confront
Japanese governments with a hard choice. Moreover,
although an incumbent Japanese Prime Minister has never
paid a visit to any African state, a good number of
African heads of government have responded to Japan's
"invitation diplomacy" including President Kaunda,
President Nyerere, Prime Minister Mugabe, President Moi
and President Mubarak. Japan's economic involvement

either as a partner in exploitation of raw materials destined for Japanese factories or as a partner in manufacturing joint ventures has served as the major motivation in the association which overides any objections to the evident measure of hypocrisy displayed in Japan's policies in Africa; policies, of course, which are not fundamentally different from those of other industrialized states.

In May 1979, Toshio Kimura, who made the first visit to Africa by a Japanese Foreign Minister, gave a lecture in Tokyo on the sixteenth anniversary of the inauguration of the Organisation of African Unity. Ths lecture was given under the joint auspices of the Japanese Federation of Economic Organisations (Keidamren) and the Africa Society of Japan. During the course of this lecture, he drew attention to the "almost unlimited" natural resources of the African continent. Because of issues of political sensitivity north and south of the Sahara, Japan cannot conduct its resource diplomacy solely on a material basis but is obliged to take some account of African political intents. But Japanese governments have not done so at the expense of their own economic interests. Correspondingly, in economic relations, with the exception of dealing with South Africa, the evident asymmetry consequent on Japan's remarkable growth rate has required greater attention to direct benefaction in order to mitigate charges of neo-colonialism. Thus in the Diplomatic Blue Book for 1981 it was stated that:

> Japan is of the view that it will
> ultimately contribute to Japan's
> own security for her to extend as
> much and as wide economic coopera-
> tion as possible to Black African
> countries with a view to helping
> their nation-building efforts.[7]

The volume of development aid allocated to African states has increased, while the number of volunteers dispatched by Japan's Overseas Cooperation Agency has been augmented. However, by and large, aid in the true sense tends to take the form of a large number of small projects. For example, a grant to Tanzania to purchase milk products, provision of food aid to Equatorial Guinea, grants to Cape Verde and Zambia to purchase Japanese rice and, finally, aid to Zimbabwe to import fertilizers from Japan. In total, bilateral official development assistance south of the Sahara (in terms of net disbursement) stood at U.S. $222.91 million in 1980

with grant aid at only U.S. $55.43 million.[8] Official
Development Assistance in 1981 extended under 'easier
terms' for all developing countries' economic and
social development projects amounted to U.S. $3.17
billion.[9] It would seem that there remains a significant gap between the form and substance of declared
concern by Japan for black Africa's economic condition.

Despite the measure of declared formal interest in
Africa by Japan expressed in terms of diplomatic missions, official visits and friendship societies, there
can be no doubting the accuracy of Dr. Agbi's observa-
tion that "In short, Africa ranks very low as a priority area for Japan."[10] Although conceived as a zone of
growing economic opportunity given the prospects of
resistance in more industrialized markets, Africa makes
a limited impact in Japan. In December 1982, the
Foreign Press Centre of the Japanese Foreign Ministry
released the findings of a <u>Public Opinion Survey on
Diplomacy</u>[11] which had been conducted on a sample basis
by the Prime Minister's Secretariat during the preceding June. The declared purpose of the survey was to
grasp the nation's awareness of diplomacy. Although
effective responses were secured from only 2,310
persons over the age of twenty among 3,000 men and
women approached, the results are not without significance. For instance, 37% of respondents indicated
that they were not interested at all in relations between Japan and foreign nations or in events in foreign
nations. Moreover only five respondents in all identified Africa as the region of the world in which they
were most interested, while in answer to the question,
with which country of the world do you wish to be most
friendly, no African state received mention. And in
response to the question, "do you think relations with
African countries are important," six percent of respondents answered "very important" and another thirty-
three percent said "fairly important." However, in
response to a question which asked, "what part of the
world should be considered important for Japan's future
economic cooperation," Africa was nominated by only two
percent of respondents. Asia attracted the special
interest of thirty-two percent and the Middle East
seventeen percent. Of course, such a sample survey is
not a precise indication of Japanese priorities but it
cannot be disregarded. Perhaps a more practical demon-
stration of Japanese interests in Africa is provided by
the actual number of Japanese journalists based in
Africa. Excluding thirteen correspondents based in
Cairo who are included under the Middle East, there are
only seven Japanese journalists in Africa. Five are

based in Kenya, one is in Zimbabwe and another is in
South Africa compared with 124 in North America, 133 in
Europe, including the Soviet Union, and 99 in Asia.
Only Australia is covered by the same number of Japan-
ese journalists based in Africa (excluding Egypt).[12]

If in many respects Africa is of marginal interest
to Japan (see Table 6. 2) that degree of marginality
has been transformed over the past decade as the Arab
oil embargo highlighted and reinforced an abiding sense
of national economic vulnerability and strengthened
emphasis on a resource diplomacy of strategic importance. The experience of the past decade has encouraged
a greater diversification of access on Japan's part in
order to obtain assured supplies of raw materials to
support a highly developed industrial base. However,
with a growing recognition of the important supplementary role of economic relations with Africa, north and
south of the Sahara, there arose a corresponding need
to respond to concrete demands for a more positive
political stand by Japan on issues central to African
interests and demands to play a more substantive role
in promoting economic development. In the event,
Japan's responses have been more declaratory and
symbolic than substantive and have been governed by a
determination not to prejudice economic relationships
enjoyed with any part of Africa as well as by the
growing demands on its surplus resources.
North of the Sahara, Japan has avoided confrontation through economic benefaction and involvement serving national interests and by formal support for
Palestinian statehood while endorsing at the same time
the Camp David Accords. South of the Sahara, Japan has
been less positive in terms of political commitment.
Solidarity against South Africa has been expressed
through minimal sanctions at no real risk to a bur-
geoning trade relationship. Indeed, Japan has refused
to be maneouvered into making choices which entail
tangible opportunity costs. Important in this exercise
has been the forebearance of African governments who
have not seen practical advantages in jeopardizing
their own economic associations with Japan for the sake
of political principle. In consequence, Japan, whose
attitude towards the continent of Africa is one of
studied ambivalence, continues both to enjoy the best
of black and white worlds and to spread its resource
risks in an age of uncertainty. If in form Japan has
modified the impression of being a proverbial political
fence-sitter, in substance little has been done to
indicate on which side of the political fence it is
situated. In reality, an abiding, apolitical, non-

Table 6.2.1

Japanese Overseas Direct Investment by Region
(Value US $Million)

	FY 1980			FY 1981		
	No. of Cases	Value	Share	No. of Cases	Value	Share
U.S.	966	1,484	31.6	896	2,329	26.2
Canada	40	112	2.4	65	167	1.9
North America	1,006	1,596	34.0	961	2,497	28.0
Brazil	38	170	3.6	53	316	3.5
Bahamas	113	222	4.7	225	614	6.9
Mexico	20	85	1.8	16	82	0.9
Peru	–	3	0.1	2	4	0.0
Latin America	247	588	12.5	353	1,181	13.3
Indonesia	96	529	11.3	88	2,434	27.3
Hong Kong	158	156	3.3	178	329	3.7
Republic of Korea	23	35	0.7	33	73	0.8
Singapore	132	140	3.0	164	266	3.0
Asia	646	1,186	25.3	712	3,338	37.5
Iran	–	71	1.5	–	0	0.0
Saudi Arabia	10	15	0.3	10	45	0.5
Middle & Near East	15	158	3.4	17	96	1.1
U.K.	127	186	4.0	49	110	1.2
W. Germany	57	110	2.3	55	116	1.3
Europe	364	578	12.3	229	798	9.0
Liberia	40	110	2.3	68	466	5.2
Africa	61	139	3.0	104	573	6.4

Table 6.2.1 (continued)

Australia	71	431	9.2	108	348	3.9
Oceania	103	448	9.5	187	424	4.8
TOTAL	2,442	4,693	100.0	2,563	8,906	100.0

Table 6.2.2

Japanese Overseas Direct Investment by Region
(Value US $Million)

	FY 1951-1981 Cummulative Total		
	No. of Cases	Value	Share
U.S.	9,136	11,207	24.7
Canada	547	1,087	2.4
North America	9,683	12,295	27.1
Brazil	1,184	3,224	7.1
Bahamas	804	1,301	2.9
Mexico	195	899	2.0
Peru	83	494	1.1
Latin America	3,058	7,349	16.2
Indonesia	1,064	6,858	15.1
Hong Kong	1,841	1,424	3.1
Republic of Korea	1,079	1,209	2.7
Singapore	1,219	1,202	2.6
Asia	8,675	13,168	29.0
Iran	108	1,002	2.2
Saudi Arabia	60	168	0.4
Middle & Near East	254	2,355	5.2

Table 6.2.2 (continued)

U.K.	765	2,119	4.7
W. Germany	528	613	1.4
Europe	2,751	5,270	11.6
Liberia	414	1,257	2.8
Africa	824	2,018	4.4
Australia	834	2,512	5.5
Oceania	1,266	2,949	6.5
TOTAL	26,511	45,403	100.0

Produced in Japan Review No. 77 of the Anglo-Japanese
Economic Institute

alignment, motivated by a consideration of economic
advantage, has not been modified beyond recognition.
The essence of Japan's policy towards Africa north and
south of the Sahara appears to convey the impression of
getting off the political fence without in practice
being obliged to take such an uncharacteristic step.
In terms of Japanese interests, such a policy makes
good sense as long as governments which would prefer
Japan to make hard choices are not themselves prepared
to accept the possible opportunity costs of forcing
such choices.

Notes

1. James R. Soukup, "Japanese-African Relations: problems and prospects", Asian Survey, Vol. 5(7), July 1965, 334.

2. See Valerie Yorke, "Japan's Resource Diplomacy", International Affairs, Vol. 57(3), Summer 1981, 442.

3. I.F. Klich, Japan and the Middle East Oil: Dependence and Foreign Policy. Research Report No. 20, Institute of Jewish Affairs, London, December 1980, 9.

4. Reproduced in BBC Summary of World Broadcasts Part III. The Far East. FE/7303/A4/1. 9 April 1983.

5. Martin C. Spring, "Japan-South African Relations", Newsletter, South African Institute of International Affairs. Vol. 6(4), 1974, 13.

6. S. Olu Agbi, "Africa: Japan's Continent-Sized Blind Spot", Japan Times Weekly, 19 June, 1982, 5.

7. Diplomatic Blue Book 1981, Ministry of Foreign Affairs. Foreign Press Center, Tokyo, 1981, 55.

8. Ibid., 56.

9. Japan and Africa: The Economic and Trade Picture. The Anglo-Japanese Economic Institute, Bulletin No. 180, (London) January-February 1983, 1.

10. Abgi, "Africa", 5.

11. Prime Minister's Secretariat, Public Opinion Survey on Diplomacy, (Japan: Foreign Press Centre, December 1982).

12. The Japanese Press 1982, Japan Newspaper Publishers and Editors Association, Tokyo, 1983, 36. NB: There is no record of any African journalist based in Japan (p. 102).

Chapter Seven

Canada and Africa in the 1980s

Douglas G. Anglin

The roots of Canadian policy towards Africa can
best be understood within the broader context of the
country's distinctive political culture and its forma-
tive experiences as an international actor during the
postwar years. A major national concern has long been
to identify and realize a recognizable and rewarding
role in world affairs, despite the steady relative
decline in Canada's international influence.[1] Whereas
in the immediate aftermath of World War II, Canadians
could aspire to the status of a "minor great power",
today the country ranks far down the scale in the global configuration of power. Although academic analysts
continue to proclaim Canada a "foremost nation" or a
"principal power,"[2] the government is acutely conscious of the very real limitations on its capacity to
act effectively--and, certainly, independently--in
foreign affairs. Its most consistent and constructive
contributions have been as a "linch-pin," a "helpful
fixer," a "peacekeeper," and an "organization maintain-
er," especially within the United Nations, the Commonwealth, and NATO.[3] The common thread linking these
roles has been a deep commitment to a functioning world
order, with a preoccupation with process taking precedence over the pursuit of substance. Yet, over the
years, the need, or at least the demand, for the services of a country with Canada's qualifications has
diminished.

While the exercise of friendly persuasion in the
course of quiet diplomacy has had its minor triumphs,
the outcomes from Canadian initiatives have rarely been
felt by the public to be fully successful or satisfy-
ing. Moreover, the attempt to live up to the requirements of a reliable, if quietly candid, ally has gene-
rated severe strains domestically. It has also created
problems for the international image as "good guys"
that Canadians crave for themselves, and have managed
to project abroad with surprisingly success. It has
not always proved easy to remain sympathetic and res-
ponsive to the entreaties of close friends and allies,
especially London and Washington, and, at the same
time, keep "good company" with like-minded Western

165

European democracies and Commonwealth states whose ideals Ottawa shares.

A striking structural feature of the Canadian political economy is the heavy dependence on external trade; exports represent nearly a quarter of GNP. Moreover, the country-concentration index is uncomfortably high, with over two-thirds of exports destined for a single market--the United States. In addition, Canada faces other formidable trade challenges: it remains outside every regional trading block, it suffers from declining industrial productivity, and it has to contend with a rising tide of protectionism as well as technological changes that threaten even its traditional markets. In present circumstances, therefore, it is scarcely surprising that the disincentives to disrupt existing trade patterns for political reasons are proving stronger than ever. Except in such cases as mandatory UN sanctions, the government has clung with unusual consistency to its policy of artificially divorcing the promotion of economic relations and the exercise of political influence. Its convictions have been strongly reinforced by its fierce nationalist resentment against the American practice of extending its legislative embargoes on trade, notably with China and Cuba, and extraterritorially to embrace Canadian subsidiaries of US companies. A corollary to this free trade philosophy is that Ottawa is much less disposed than is Washington to control or constrain the overseas operations of its multinationals.

A further constraint on progressive Canadian policies is the undoubted fact that significant sections of the public are distinctly less internationalist in their outlook than the government. With deepening recession, the inherent tendency of Canadians to turn inward has become even more marked. While an organized, active and enlightened "Africa constituency" exists--comprising principally of the mainline churches, a range of NGOs, a modest Black lobby and various radical fringe groups, mostly with interests focussed on Southern Africa--it is too weak in numbers and resources to make a serious impact on the ignorance or apathy of a majority of comfortable Canadians. Nor is it able to compete with the entrenched power of corporate interests whose concerns in Africa are considerable but, in the last analysis, profit-oriented.[4]

Finally, Canada boasts of being a bilingual and federal state. This is profoundly importantly in explaining Canada's concern to build bridges with fran-

cophone Africa, its predilection for peaceful evolutionary change in Africa, and its distrust of violent
revolution as well as its distinctive diplomatic style.
Despite the occasional yearning for the security of
defined principles and the exhilaration of slogans,
Canadians behave abroad much as they do at home.[5] As
one keen student has aptly observed, the "political
culture of Canadian foreign policy" is characterized
by:

> distrust of dogma and the doctri-
> naire, fear of extremes, suspicion
> of the rhetoric of grand designs,
> respect for diversity and for its
> power as the engine of politics,
> anticipation of conflict, belief in
> compromises, preoccupation with the
> limits of the possible, concern for
> process and for the orderly broker-
> age of interests, (and) dedication
> ultimately to the pragmatic.[6]

i)   Canadian Interests in Africa

In 1970, a comprehensive review of Canadian foreign
policy identified six "policy themes" which were said
to shape the conduct of the country's external relations. Two of these-Fostering Economic Growth (in
Canada) and Promoting Social Justice--are central to
the continuing debate on the Canadian perspective on
Africa.[7] A third objective--Working for Peace and
Security--is also relevant, though less so since the
African continent is not seen to have posed the same
threat to global security as other regions of the
world. Nevertheless, the years of independence have
proved increasingly turbulent and Canada, as committed
supporter of the United Nations and Commonwealth, has
not escaped involvement in the continent's affairs.
Over the past quarter of a century, successive governments in Ottawa have, with varying degrees of enthusiasm, accepted responsibilities for containing crises
and promoting stability in many corners of the continent. Direct interventions have included participation
in UNEF I in Egypt, in ONUC in Zaire, in the oil air-
lift to Zambia, in military training programmes in
Ghana and Tanzania, and in international observer teams
in Nigeria, Zimbabwe and Uganda. However, in only two
theatres of conflict does the potential exist for disputes to escalate into serious global confrontations.
In the case of the Horn, Ottawa has made a point of
staying studiously on the sidelines. Southern Africa,

167

on the other hand, has occasioned sustained agonizing
concern and controversy.

ii) **Fostering Economic Growth**

The impact of the world recession, the changing
international division of labour, and domestic stagnation have compelled the Canadian government to make
explicit what has become increasingly apparent in its
foreign policy in recent years; namely, the retreat
from Pearsonian internationalism into a frank pursuit
of policies which "directly serve our national
interests." In the current trendy terminology, the
balance is shifting from the traditional multilateral
approach to world affairs to a new emphasis on competitive "bilateralism" with "a select number of countries
of concentration," chosen principally on the basis of
their anticipated contribution to Canadian economic and
regional development. Ottawa's assertion of the primacy of economic imperatives over political concerns and
historical links does not imply the complete abandon-
ment of previous foreign policy objectives, notably
social justice. Nevertheless the clear intention is
that the thrust of policy abroad should now be directed
towards measures and targets which offer definite promise of commercial advantage. In the case of Africa,
Canadian decision makers are in the process of redraw-
ing perceptually their mental maps of the continent to
take account of the government's altered priorities.
In the past, Africa from an Ottawa perspective
was--like Canada--divided linguistically into French-
speaking and English-speaking territories, with the
Arab North considered an adjunct of the Middle East
(Table 7.1). Today the significant distinction is
increasingly between these countries with development
possibilities (and potential markets) and those whose
prospects are bleak (and can only be regarded as hard-
core welfare cases).

In the wake of the global crises of the 1970s, the
government enunciated a bold new economic strategy to
promote its priorities in the areas of regional and
industrial development within Canada. To complement
this domestic thrust, recognition was given to trade as
a primary objective of foreign policy, and steps were
taken to give effect to this decisive shift in focus by
introducing far-reaching organizational changes at both
the political and bureaucratic levels. In particular,
responsibility for all aspects of international economic policy was transferred to "a radically structured

168

Table 7.1

Development of Diplomatic Relations Between Canada and Africa, 1938 - 1983

	Resident Canadian Missions in Africa		Resident African Missions in Ottawa	
Year Est.	Anglophone Africa	Francophane Africa	North Africa	Southern Africa
1938				South Africa
1939				
1940				**South Africa**
1954			Egypt/ **Egypt**	
1955				
1956				
1957	**Ghana**			
1958				
1959				
1960	**Nigeria**			
1961	Ghana			
1962	**Tanzania**	**Zaire/Cameroon**		
1963				
1964				
1965				
1966	Tanzania/ Nigeria	**Senegal**/Zaire	**Ethiopia/ Tunisa**	
1967	**Kenya**	Cameroon	Ethiopia (to 1970)	
1969			Tunisia	
1970		**Ivory Coast**/ Rwanda	Algeria	
1971		**Niger***/ Niger/Gabon	**Algeria**	
1972			Morocco	Zambia
1973		Benin/Ivory Coast/Upper Volta		

Table 7.1 continued

Year Est.	Anglophone Africa	Francophane Africa	North Africa	Southern Africa
1974	Uganda	**Upper Volta*** Central African Repub- lic (to 1980)	**Morocco**	Zambia
1975	Lesotho	**Mali***/Benegal		
1976		Togo		
1977				
1978	Malawi	Mali	Sudan	
1979	Kenya	**Gabon**	Somali	
1980		Guinea/ Burundi		**Zimbabwe**
1981		**Rwanda***		
1982		**Guinea**		Zimbabwe
1983	Liberia			
	4 + 8	10 + 13	5 + 6	3 + 3

Resident Canadian Missions in Africa — Resident African Missions in Ottawa

*External Affairs (Development) Office
=Charge d'affaires

Department of External Affairs," headed by a troika of cabinet ministers (including, for the first time, a Minister for International Trade) and assigned "a fundamentally changed mandate" to "aggressively pursue international export markets." As Prime Minister Trudeau explained, the reconstructed Department was expected to be "very different from what exists now." Henceforth,

> Much greater weight will be attac-
> hed to economic factors in the
> design of foreign policy and the
> conduct of our foreign relations,
> to ensure they serve Canadian trade

objectives. Trade matters are becoming a more significant political
issue between governments. Canada
must therefore speak with a strong,
unified voice abroad.[8]

While superficially the incorporation of the trade
and marketing services into a revamped foreign office
might suggest that the diplomats had succeeded in
swallowing the salesmen, the suspicion exists that the
latter were expected to take over External Affairs
substantially in all but name. However resistance to
the recycling process among demoralized political
officers is considerable, and the ultimate success of
the reorganization plan is by no means assured.
Controversy continues even over the number and names of
countries of concentration.

Countries of Concentration

The original cabinet directive of December 1980
specified "relevance to our long-term domestic
development objectives" as the primary criterion in the
selection of "key economic partners" for "concentrated
attention." Nevertheless, it was recognized that

to avoid contradictions in our
relationships,...our
criteria...cannot be solely
economic. We shall have to take
into account a variety of political
factors such as the compatibility
of values, cultural links and
mutuality of interest in other
spheres.

Thus, although overwhelming weight was accorded to
economic indices, some attention was paid to immigra-
tion flows, opportunities for technical cooperation, a
country's human rights record, and political relations
generally. In the end, the list of 24 countries and
two regions which ultimately emerged included "both
long-established countries of concentration and relative newcomers," especially the NICs which were (at
least until the decline of oil prices and the deepening
debt crisis in the Third World) "among our best
potential partners." In the case of Africa, two
countries survived the selection process--Algeria and
Nigeria, both members of OPEC--and one regional
grouping: <u>La Francophonie</u>.[9]

171

Historically and politically, Canadian relations
with Nigeria have been more intimate than with Algeria.
Nevertheless, the latter has emerged (since 1976) as
Canada's best customer on the continent (as well as its
leading African supplier), whereas the former has
slipped from third place (in 1977) to seventh place (in
1982)--behind the five Mediterranean states and South
Africa (Table 7.2). However, Nigeria remains the
largest Canadian market in Black Africa, and potentially an even more profitable one in future; current
Nigerian imports from Canada constitute only a tiny
fraction of its total import trade.

Table 7.2

Canadian Trade with Africa, 1982
C$ Millions (and rank)

	Domestic Exports to Africa			Imports from Africa	
1.	Algeria	$496.3	1.	Algeria	$259.6
2.	Egypt	353.1	2.	South Africa	218.7
3.	South Africa	251.1	3.	Nigeria	64.7
4.	Libya	119.0	4.	Guinea	23.8
5.	Morocco	104.7	5.	Libya	22.7
6.	Tunisia	73.5	6.	Morocco	15.4
7.	Nigeria	61.6	7.	Zaire	14.8
8.	Mozambique	28.8	8.	Kenya	13.7
9.	Cameroon	28.3	9.	Ivory Coast	12.3
10.	Kenya	24.4	10.	Gabon	7.5
	TOTAL AFRICA	$1,653.7		TOTAL AFRICA	$686.8
	% TOTAL EXPORTS	2.02%		% TOTAL IMPORTS	1.02%

Source: Statistics Canada, Trade of Canada: Exports
by Countries and Trade of Canada: Imports by
Countries.

As the most populous country on the continent, a functioning democracy, and an acknowledged leader in Afri-

can affairs, Nigeria was an inevitable choice as a
state with which Canada would seek to develop a sound
long-term relationship. It was, in fact, the one
African country the Minister of External Affairs mentioned explicity in his initial short list of possible
countries of concentration. In any case, prudence suggested the inclusion of an anglophone country to balance a francophone one, especially as La Francophonie
was also singled out for special attention--again for
compelling domestic political reasons related to
Quebec's ambiguous status within the Canadian confederation, rather than for any economic justification.

There is still considerable confusion concerning
the precise implications of "bilateralism" for policy.
What is clear is that it was never envisaged that
Canada's relations should be restricted to countries of
concentration to the exclusion of all others. In fact,
in operational terms, the most promising long-term
markets for Canadian products, as perceived in Ottawa,
are principally:

a)   The oil exporting countries: Algeria, Gabon,
     Libyan, and Nigeria;

b)   Other middle-income countries: Congo, Egypt,
 -   Morocco, Tunisia, and Zimbabwe;

c)   Countries with comparatively well-managed or at
     least open economies: Cameroon, Ivory Coast and
     Kenya; and

d)   Countries with longer-term potential: Angola,
     Guinea, and Zaire.[10]

Already in 1982, these fifteen countries accounted for
three-quarters of Canadian exports to the continent,
with the four OPEC members alone responsible for over
two-fifths of the total.

The Canadian government is confident that its trade
can make further substantial inroads into new and
existing African markets, particularly in the case of
capital goods, equipment and expertise in the energy,
mining, transportation and communications sectors.
Certainly, the achievements to date in sales are
impressive. At a time of global recession and continental foreign exchange crisis, exports of goods to
Africa in 1982 reached nearly $1.7 billion (plus
another $600 million or more in services).[11] This

173

amounts to a near-doubling in value since 1979, and a tripling since 1977. Although part of this increase is attributable to inflation, it nevertheless represents a more rapid rate of growth than experienced in any other region of the world. Moreover, while Africa consumed only 2% of Canadian exports in 1982, it contributed 7%--almost a billion dollars--to the country's total trade surplus (Table 7.2). Nevertheless, two major constraints on continued significant penetration of the African market remain, in addition to competitive disadvantages. The first is the durability of Africa's established commercial connections with traditional trading partners. Equally important, however, is the limited interest, enterprise and persistence that many Canadian businessmen have shown in making the necessary effort to crack the admittedly difficult African markets.

iii) **Promoting Social Justice**

Development Assistance

Canadian trade opportunities in a majority of African countries appear limited at best (Table 7.2) as long as their economies remain at their present level of underdevelopment. Unfortunately, in many instances, the prospects for development in any meaningful sense are also far from promising. Despite this, throughout much of Africa, the administration of aid programmes represents the principal interest and activity of Canadian missions. This preoccupation has not gone unchallenged domestically. There is mounting evidence of disillusionment among the electorate at the inevitable failure of foreign aid efforts to meet the totally unrealistic popular expectations as to what could be accomplished in less than a generation. The chorus of criticism directed at the Canadian International Development Agency (CIDA) reflects the full spectrum of political opinion. At one end, the business lobby denounces CIDA's "overly philanthropic giveaway approach to aid" and, at the other, the radical academic critique stigmatizes the whole exercise as misguided, if not imperialistic.[12] Although some of the adverse verdicts are undoubtedly valid, there has also been much ill-informed fault-finding, especially in the media. As a result, CIDA has been forced onto the defensive and has become distinctly less willing to take necessary calculated risks for fear of failure.

Despite the deteriorating domestic climate of
opinion, the level of global funding continues to
increase annually and is currently approaching the $2
billion mark. After declining as a percentage of GNP
for several years, it is now, assisted by the recession, up to a modest 0.44% and is expected to reach 0.5%
by 1985 and 0.7% by 1990. At the same time, debate
within the government on CIDA's strategy and programme
in Africa rages on. Among the issues perenially under
scrutiny are:

a) The balance between bilateral and multilateral
    (untied) aid. Although Canada has been reasonably
    progressive by OECD standards in limiting the por-
    tion administered bilaterally to about 45%--rather
    than the minimum of 60% which business spokesmen
    have urged--the degree to which the bilateral pro-
    gramme is tied to Canadian goods and services (82%)
    is one of the highest of any donor.[13] This re-
    flects a frank recognition that otherwise few pur-
    chases would be made in Canada.

b) The proportion of bilateral aid allocated to Africa
    (47%). This is higher than that allocated to any
    other region in the world, especially on a per ca-
    pita basis. In addition, 43% of food aid and 56%
    of emergency relief goes to Africa.

c) The balance between Anglophone and Francophone
    Africa. For political reasons, a determined effort
    has been made to increase aid to French-speaking
    Africa to at least the level of Commonwealth
    Africa, where the programme has been in operation a
    decade longer. Although, in 1981-82 for technical
    reasons, the balance was temporarily upset with
    only 43% disbursed in Francophone Africa, in
    future, with the increasing difficulties many
    Anglophone African countries are experiencing in
    absorbing external assistance, the ratio is likely
    to be reversed.

d) The share allocated to the least-developed coun-
    tries (40%). As the poor countries are also
    generally those least responsive to development
    initiatives, there is a growing disposition to
    treat such support as more properly humanitarian
    relief rather than as genuine development assis-
    tance. Nevertheless, there is increasing concern
    for the neediest cases, with the result that

175

countries like Nigeria and Algeria are no longer
designated core countries for aid purposes.[14]

In the final analysis, the bottom line in development assistance in Africa is the formulation of an
appropriate and acceptable ideology and strategy of
change. While CIDA officials are considerably less
confident that they have discovered the key to success,
there is a growing conviction that the human factor
must be central and priority given to meeting basic
human needs. As the President of CIDA reported in
1981, in the past, "relatively too much emphasis" had
been put on "capital and physical resources, and too
little priority given to meeting basic human needs."[15]
Yet, admirable as this sentiment is, it has not been
easy to translate into projects. Inevitably, performance has fallen short of profession. Where success has
been achieved, it has most often been when working
through NGO channels at the grassroots level, essentially independently of the host government.

In addition to re-evaluating its approach to development, CIDA is once again reviewing its rules on
recipient eligibility. While these deliberations have
not yet been concluded, it seems likely that decisions
will be taken:

a) To restructure the present list of countries (Table
   7.3) into three new categories: first, countries
   capable of significant development (the primary
   targets of development assistance); second, basket
   cases requiring international humanitarian assistance to survive at a minimum level of existence;
   and, finally, countries offering export markets
   (where aid will be an adjunct to commercial penetration);

b) To restrict further (provided External Affairs
   resistance can be overcome) the number of core
   countries qualifying for more than token development funds;

c) To insist more firmly on the adoption of comple-
   mentary domestic politics--that is, "conditionality"--in such fields as population planning; and,

d) To accord substantial though not decisive weight to
   human rights considerations in determining the
   amount of aid, its form and the target groups it is
   designed to assist.[16]

176

Human Rights

These innovations, if confirmed, could significantly affect the political as well as the developmental impact of the Canadian aid programme in Africa. This is particularly true of the proposed upgrading of humanitarian concerns. Despite the major new thrust accorded trade in Canadian foreign policy, an articulate body of minority opinion exists within government, including the cabinet, determined to press for more energetic promotion of human rights as a significant, if inevitably subordinate, interest in Africa and elsewhere.[17]

Support for a more interventionist stance has found some expression in the administration of aid policy. Ottawa has traditionally been reluctant to cut-off aid to governments guilty of abusive practices, as this could result in the victims being "doubly penalized."[18] Nevertheless, it did suspend support to Uganda in response to Amin's excesses and curtailed the modest Burundi programme following the 1972 massacres. On the other hand, aid to the Chadians under Tombalbaye continued in view of the ravages of the Sahelian drought. More positively, Guinea has been elevated to a core country in part as a reward for recent improvements in its previous dismal human rights record. The same is true to a limited extent of Equatorial Guinea. Moreover, within the UN Commission on Human Rights, Canada has played a decisive role--in the absence of any other country willing to take the initiative--in seeking international action to restore basic rights to the long-suffering people of that unhappy land, even though it is a country with which Canada has had virtually no relations in the past.[19] Social justice considerations have also featured prominently in the recurring debates over Canadian involvement in South Africa, though this concern has been only occasionally and partially reflected in the policy outcomes.

Liberation

On South Africa, the Canadian government has struggled to reconcile its conflicting goals of Social Justice, Peace and Security, and Economic Growth. The result has inevitably been unsatisfactory compromise, full of contradictions and difficult to defend logically. Moreover, the fiercer and more forthright Canadian denunciations of the abomination of <u>apartheid</u>, the starker has been the contrast with the reality of

Table 7.3

Canadian Overseas Development Assistance to Africa, 1981-1988

	*Category I		*Category IIa	*Category IIb	*Category III	Total ODA 1981/82
	ODA 1981/82	IPF 1983/88	ODA 1981/82	ODA 1981/82	ODA 1981/82	
	Egypt $25.94	$107.00	Tunisia $9.22	Sudan $7.35	Libya $–	$
			Morocco 7.17			
			Algeria 1.07			
	$25.94	$107.0	$17.46	$7.35		$50.75
	Cameroon 18.34	145.02	Gabon 0.42	Benin 4.61	Mada-gascar 4.33	
	Zaire 14.49	85.07		Togo 0.07	Mauri-tania 2.24	
	Senegal 13.41	85.00			Congo 1.49	

*Category I (core countries of concentration),
IIa (export markets), IIb (transitional)
III (eligible for aid only on an <u>ad hoc</u> basis).

Table 7.3 (continued)

	*Category I		*Category II[a]	*Category II[b]	*Category III	
	ODA 1981/82	IPF 1983/88	ODA 1981/82	ODA 1981/82	ODA 1981/82	Total ODA 1981/82
	$	$	$	$	$	$
Sahel	11.98	n/a				
Mali	12.11	72.07				
Upper Volta	10.25	89.05				
Niger	5.26	88.09				
Rwanda	8.06	60.00				
Ivory Coast	5.27	73.8				
Guinea	0.34	47.1				
Burundi					0.35	
Chad					0.35	
Cape Verde					0.28	
Guinea-Bissau					0.17	
CAR					0.15	
Sao Tome					0.05	
Comoros					0.03	
Equatorial Guinea					0.03	
Regional					1.69	
	$99.51	$747.09	$0.42	$4.54	$11.16	$115.63

Table 7.3 (continued)

	*Category I		*Category II[a]	*Category II[b]	*Category III	Total
	ODA 1981/82	IPF 1983/88	ODA 1981/82	ODA 1981/82	ODA 1981/82	ODA 1981/82
	$	$	$	$	$	$
Kenya	46.04	170.00	Nigeria 0.13	Uganda 2.41	Ethio-pia 10.66	
Tanzania	25.66	175.00			Somalia 4.82	
Ghana	11.28	14.05			Mauritius 0.25	
					Gambia 0.22	
					Sierra Leone 0.14	
					Seychel-les 0.06	
					Djibouti 0.01	
					Liberia -	
					Regional 0.39	
	$82.98	$359.05	$0.13	$2.41	$16.55	$102.07

180

Table 7.3 (continued)

	*Category I		*Category II^a		*Category II^b		*Category III		Total
	ODA 1981/82	IPF 1983/88		ODA 1981/82		ODA 1981/82		ODA 1981/82	ODA 1981/82
	$	$		$		$		$	$
Zambia	10.93	99.03	Nigeria		Malawi	11.10	Mozam-bique	5.59	
Zimbabwe	7.06	60.00					Namibia	0.02	
(Lesotho	4.65	n/a					Angola	–	
(Botswana	3.81	62.08							
(Swazi- land	0.95	10.00							
(UBLS	0.72	n/a							
	$28.12	$232.01		$18.01		$11.10		$5.61	$44.83
TOTAL	18 $236.55	$1,446.05	5	$18.01	5	$25.40	23	$33.32	$313.28

Canadian policy, and the more hypocritical it has
appeared. Admittedly, in comparison with the much less
inhibited relationships other leading industrial
nations maintain with South Africa, Canada has undoubtedly been in the vanguard in giving substance to its
proclaimed detestation of the repressive racist regime.
Nevertheless, its record overall compares unfavourably
with that of the Scandinavian countries, and even with
that of Australia in recent years. Certainly, there is
more Ottawa could (and should) do to distance itself
further from Pretoria, even if the measures taken can
never in themselves be decisive.

What accounts for this persistent discrepancy
between word and deed? While it may be tempting to
seek an explanation in conspiratorial theories, the
truth would appear to be more complicated and mundane--
related as much to bureaucratic infighting, job preservation, electoral calculations and other immediate (but
irrelevant   preoccupations as it is to the intrusion of
corporate interests into the decision-making   process.
As a consequence, the coterie within the cabinet--led
by the prime minister but excluding the present foreign
minister--which feels passionately about the injustices
of apartheid has been compelled to fight every inch of
the way for even the meagre gains that have been
achieved. Equally instructive, however, in understanding Canadian action and inaction are a series of
assumptions which underlie and circumscribe government
policy. Although these maxims are rarely systematically articulated, few have gone unchallenged:

a) The present status quo in South Africa is in the
    interests of neither the white minority nor the
    West, including Canada;

b) Fundamental change is inevitable, and peaceful
    change both conceivable and desirable;

c) Apartheid is not a purely domestic matter; Canada
    and the world community are entitled to press for
    South African observance of internationally accept-
    able human rights standards, though not through the
    attempt to exercise extraterritorial jurisdiction
    in South Africa;

d) Canada has only a limited capacity to persuade or
    coerce the South African government to institute
    significant change, and no leverage at all acting
    unilaterally;

182

e) Politically-motivated economic pressure is politically undesirable on principle and politically
counter-productive in practice; and

f) Where the pursuit of democratization in South
Africa threatens to prejudice the cause of Namibian
independence, the latter must take precedence.

It is within these parameters, then, that the
Canadian strategy--if it can be so dignified--for fundamental change in South Africa has been formulated. Of
the options available to the Canadian government, only
a few are considered acceptable. To begin with, it is
not persuaded by South African-inspired claims that the
process of radical reform is already underway and
should not be disturbed. "What process? Where are the
changes?", the Canadian foreign minister asked rhe-
torically in 1980. "A minority of Whites still totally
dominates a majority of Blacks through repression,
force, and a society and system rooted in racist supre-
macy. This is not acceptable in any form and it never
will be." In fact, since 1977, the government has been
publicly pledged to the "destruction" of the apartheid
system and the introduction of "the principle of one
man, one vote."[21]

Armed Struggle

At the other end of the interventionist scale is
the question of direct Canadian support for the armed
struggle in Southern Africa. While Ottawa concedes
that a resort to violence is understandable, even
inevitable in the circumstances, it is still unable on
principle to condone or contribute to it. Its objections are more political than moral; both domestically
and internationally, Canada has long been committed to
the peaceful resolution of conflict. While this is the
ideal, it fails to recognize that, in South Africa,
military coercion may prove the one way to compel the
Pretoria regime to accept the need to negotiate a
"peaceful" settlement.

The most the Canadian government has been prepared
to contemplate in the way of military measures is an
arms embargo. This was first imposed on a voluntary
basis in 1963 and tightened in 1970, but it was not
until 1977 that the Western members of the Security
Council (including Canada) acquiesced in a mandatory UN
ban--and then only in the pre-emptive move to defuse
pressure for something "worse." For many years, the

government applied its regulations conscientiously.
More recently, however, its record on enforcement has
been far less creditable. One inexcusable display of
gross negligence, in particular, has gravely undermined
the government's credibility. This was its single
failure, despite ample grounds for suspicion concerning
Pretoria's hidden hand, to prevent the Space Research
Corporation developing, testing and then smuggling out
of the country to South Africa during 1977 and 1978
four illegal shipments of 155mm long-range artillery
shells. Other lesser sins of omission also call into
question the vigilance--or credulity or sincerity--of
the officials entrusted with enforcement.[21]

More positive have been the modest financial
efforts to bolster Southern African resistance to minority rule. In addition to contributions to UN funds
and the UN Institute for Namibia,[22] the Front Line
States have received assistance to enable them to
disengage from dependence on South Africa and thereby
lessen the present severe constraints on their freedom
of action. Ottawa has formally singled out the Southern African Development Co-ordination Conference
(SADCC) as an organization eligible for CIDA aid, thus
opening up the possibility of substantial Canadian
assistance to Mozambique and Angola, the only members
(apart from Malawi) not already designated core countries. The first grant under the SADCC umbrella is, in
fact, $15 million to rehabilitate the Nacala-Entrelagos
Railway in Mozambique.[23] Finally, in 1974, a programme
of humanitarian assistance to Southern Africa was
fought through Parliament following a stormy domestic
debate.[24] Although it has proved far less grandiose
than its critics feared, it has enabled small sums to
be filtered through mainly NGO channels to liberation
movements (including the South African ANC), political
refugees, trade union organizers, church activists,
women's cooperatives and adult education centres,
etc.[25] Much more money and courage will, however, be
needed if Canadian actions are to match Canadian words.

Negotiations

Confronted with the increasing embarrassment of
attempting to maintain convincing anti-apartheid credentials while resisting every military or economic
proposal to remedy the injustices, Canada along with
other Western powers was slowly and inexorably driven
to accept the necessity of devising a more constructive
response than reliance on its rather threadbare rhe-

toric. The outcome of this reappraisal was the decision in 1977 to offer Western good offices to promote a
negotiated settlement of the Namibian independence
issue. Over the past six years, the Western Contact
Group--quickly dubbed the "Gang of Five"--has struggled
valiantly but so far unsuccessfully within its restrictive terms of reference to coax the South African Defence Force to abandon Namibia. As the junior partner
on the team and the member Africans trusted most,
Canada's special role has been to sell each "final"
South African demand, first, to the Front Line presidents and then, through them, to the SWAPO leadership.

However, every concession has, with ritualistic
regularity, invited some fresh South African objection.
By cleverly "talking without negotiating", Pretoria has
succeeded brilliantly in extracting substantial SWAPO
compromises, in deflecting any further legal challenge
to its belligerent occupation of Namibia, in postponing
any independence settlement indefinitely, in taking the
political heat off South Africa itself, and in avoiding
a Western walkout or even an African boycott. The contact Group members have been compelled to submit to
this shameless manipulation only because they had ruled
out in advance any alternative strategy and lacked any
credible means of coercing Pretoria to negotiate in
good faith. To add to the crisis of Western credibility, the Contact Group is currently in cold storage
while Washington pursues its "linkage" policy bi-
laterally.

Economic Measures

Barring mandatory economic sanctions somehow escap-
ing a Western veto in the UN Security Council, there is
little hope of any serious Canadian political initiatives to restrict existing economic relations with that
country. Admittedly, the "South African connection" is
scarcely vital for either country. In 1982, Canadian
exports to South Africa represented only a quarter of
one percent of total Canadian exports and one percent
of South African imports. Similarly, imports from
South Africa amounted to a third of one percent of
total Canadian imports and one percent of South African
exports. In value terms, trade in 1982 declined compared with the 1981 peak--by 46% in the case of
imports. Canadian investments in South Africa are
equally marginal, constituting (in 1979) only one percent of direct "Canadian" foreign investment; even so,
60% of this is foreign-controlled.[26] Nevertheless,

South Africa is a more important trading partner and
investment field in certain sectors and industries,
especially manufacturing, than these global statistics
suggest. In any case, the major source of moral and
material support for the regime has been the substant-
ial--at least until recently--commercial loans Canadian
banks have liberally made available. While the current
level of loan transactions is difficult to ascertain,
the practice has not ceased, though it appears to have
been curtailed. As a result of public harassment, the
banks are now more cautious or circuitous in their
dealings.

The Canadian government has sought to dissociate
itself from any official economic involvement in South
Africa--without openly abandoning its liberal internationalist economic principles. Its policy, as enunciated in December 1977, may be summarized as "neither
encouragement nor discouragement", and, in particular,

a)   No direct government participation;

b)   No active promotion of trade or investment; and

c)   No interference with the freedom of Canadian entre-
     preneurs to pursue normal commercial relations with
     South Africa.

Underlying this third principle are two ideological
assertions. The first is, as one spokesman explained,
that "the type of relationship which exists in my
country between the state and private enterprise does
not permit government to impose bans on all activities
of Canadian companies in South Africa."[27] The second
is the contention that the mere existence of economic
relations with South Africa at a non-government level
in no way implies approval of its political policies,
let alone collaboration with apartheid. Much as Ottawa
would like to believe this, its claim is contradicted
by the abundant evidence that Pretoria attaches enormous economic and psychological significance to its
extensive open and clandestine commercial relations
with governments of every ideological persuasion around
the world.

As with most hard-fought compromises, the final
formulation of the 1977 cabinet directive lacked preci-
sion, and thus opened the door to renewed argument at
every state of its implementation. The response to the
rash of damaging media-reports on the employment practices of South African subsidaries of Canadian com-

panies is a case in point. From the outset, the government declined to press for disinvestment--except where it found itself a shareholder[28]--or to impose minimum standards of corporate behaviour. Instead, it promised a voluntary code of conduct. Yet, by the time it had concluded its consultations with interested businessman and bureaucrats, the document that emerged was the most innocuous of any devised in the West. In practice, it has proved an almost complete farce. Worse still, it has had the negative consequence of conferring legitimacy on the Canadian corporate presence in South Africa by giving official sanction to the pretence that foreign multinationals were contributing significantly to social change.[29] Although efforts are currently underway to regularize the reporting procedures and provide for a modicum of analysis and publicity, the substance of the code is apparently to remain unrevised and company reporting and compliance to continue on a voluntary basis.

In the trade sphere, three actions directed against South Africa have been taken. In 1978, the Canadian trade commissioners in Cape Town and Johannesburg were recalled and their offices closed. Then, in 1980, Commonwealth Preferences were belatedly withdrawn, after it was discovered that they affected three-quarters of imports from South Africa and only 2% of exports to that country.[30] Finally, in 1981, South African customers were formally denied access to Export Development Corporation (EDC) loan facilities.[31] However, Canadian suppliers continued to be eligible for EDC export insurance and guarantees as well as assistance under the Program for Export Market Development (PEMD) on the curious grounds that these programmes benefit Canada but not South Africa. The impact of these measures is difficult to gauge. Certainly, there has been no dramatic decline in trade. On the contrary, in some years, it has increased even in real terms. Nevertheless, trade officials argue that, if the same effort were expanded on promoting exports to South Africa as goes into the trade offensive elsewhere on the continent, the volume would quickly double.[32] This self-denial--to the extent that it exists--is one small distinction that sets Canada apart from other industrialized countries, notably France despite its socialist rhetoric, which are straining to increase their penetration of the South African market.

The Canadian government's alleged restraint in not fully exploiting its export opportunities in South Africa does not imply a willingness to endorse economic

187

sanctions, even though their cost would be minimal in comparison with what other trading nations would suffer.[33] Exceptional circumstances apart, it objects on principle to political interference with the free flow of goods among nations. Moreover, on the basis of past experience, including four ventures in the course of three years 1979-82,[34] Ottawa is highly skeptical of the utility of sanctions as an instrument to promote political reform. Certainly, for Canada to resort to them unilaterally could be regarded as a futile and costly gesture. "Cutting off trading relations by individual countries such as Canada," the foreign minister stated recently, "is unlikely to be effective unless part of a concerted international approach to the problem, and even then one can question its effectiveness."[35]

The practical problems undoubtedly associated with the application of sanctions do not account for Ottawa's shameful moral collapse in supporting unconditionally the standby credit portion of the $1.07 billion IMF loan to South Africa in November 1982.[36] While the argument against politicizing economic institutions has validity, this cannot excuse the abject failure to insist on the strict application of economic criteria in this case. Since Pretoria's balance of payments difficulties were a direct consequence of its apartheid policies, insisting on their abandonment would have been an entirely justifiable condition for the granting of the loan.

The one area in which the Canadian government has taken a firm, consistent and constructive stand in support of the international isolation of South Africa is that of sports contacts. Admittedly, Canadians experience fewer temptations than sports enthusiasts in countries where cricket and rugger are a national mania. Moreover, Ottawa was understandably anxious to avoid a repetition of the African boycott of the 1976 Montreal Olympics at the Edmonton Commonwealth Games in 1978. Nevertheless, the courageous leadership the cabinet has consistently shown on this issue, nationally and internationally, in the face of fierce criticism is in welcome contrast to its timid, compromising and disingenuous policy on economic disengagement.

iv) Interaction with Great Powers

Canadian interaction with the great powers in Africa has largely been confined to relations with the

West. Although it has sometimes been alleged--
principally by Western critics--that Canada has served
as the running dog of Western imperialism in Africa,
there have been few contacts and no real confrontations
with Soviet bloc countries in the course of their
various incursions into the continent, and no specific
Canadian interests endangered by their activities.
This is not to suggest that Canada is indifferent to
Soviet penetration, but it tends to take a more
phlegmatic approach to the problem than some of its
more alarmist allies. In particular, it is more
concerned with Soviet imperialism than with any
communist ideological threat, and does not equate every
manifestation of African nationalism with
Moscow-inspired Marxism. While Ottawa has no illusions
concerning the Kremlin's ambitions in Africa if given
the opportunity, it is skeptical of the existence of
any Soviet grand design and of the claim that Africa is
a priority target. The Russian's best hope of future
success is to capitalize on Western blunders in
Southern Africa.

In the case of China, there have been suggestions
that Beijing pressed for the termination of the Canadian military assistance programme in Tanzania in the
early 1970s, but otherwise relations have been correct,
even if somewhat distant.

Western Coalition

Canada is a full, active and loyal member of the
Western coalition of states, economically, politically
and militarily. As a middle-rank member, it is too
important to be ignored completely and yet not suffi-
ciently important to be really influential. If, as a
result, it is somewhat uncomfortable on occasion with
the international conduct of its major partners and
especially the United States, on the whole it shares
common interests and values with them. Admittedly, at
the United Nations, Canada likes to be seen voting in
the "good company" of the smaller, more progressive WEO
(Western Europe and Other) powers, especially Sweden,
the Netherlands and Australia. At the same time, it is
flattered to be invited to join the big boys in the
Western economic summits of seven leading industrial
states. This prestigious club has evolved into an
informal executive committee for the OECD and, to some
extent, NATO.

189

Although on African as well as other issues the
Canadian government prides itself on making up its own
mind, it almost invariably does so after close consultations with other Western governments. At times, it
may deliberately decide to defer to collective concerns
for the sake of Western unity, though the extent to
which Canadian interests are subordinated to rather
than simply convergent with the interests of trusted
friends and allies tends to be exaggerated. More
important are:

a) the annual bilateral exchanges at senior official
level with the United States, Britain and, perhaps
most comprehensively, France;

b) the biannual consultations in NATO's Committee on
.Africa, and its expert subcommittee; and

c) the almost daily diplomatic contacts in Western and
African capitals.

In addition, more specialized discussions take place:

d) within the Five-member Western Contact Group on
Namibia, which meets every few months at an official
level and periodically at ministerial level;

e) at meetings of the six-member CADA (Concerted
Action for Development in Africa) on aid policies;
and

f) in deliberations of the Paris Club on debt resched-
uling.

Finally, opportunities for formal or informal consultations on African issues come in many other forums,
including the UN General Assembly and the annual
Western economic summits.

While Canadian interaction with other Western
powers in Africa has been typically cooperative, conflicts have not been entirely excluded in the past and
cannot be precluded in future. The open breach with
Britain over Suez in 1958 was the most traumatic
instance, but less dramatic confrontations have occured
over NIBMAR in Rhodesia and British arms sales to South
Africa in 1970. However, the only sustained conflict
with an ally has been with France.

190

France

The issue at stake between Ottawa and Paris was no
less than the survival of Canada as a nation. Africa
had no direct interest in this Franco-Canadian contest,
except in the sense that President de Gaulle set out
systematically to destabilize all Commonwealth federa-
tions, including Nigeria. Nevertheless, many of the
fiercest cold war battles were fought on Africa soil,
with each side vying for the allegiance of francophone
African governments. As Paris began with most of these
governments firmly in its pocket, Ottawa was faced with
a bitter uphill struggle to wean them away.[37]

The central issue in contention concerned the
status of Quebec within the francophone community of
states, and especially the Agence de cooperation
culturelle et technique (ACCT) and La Francophonie.
France, in pursuing its policy of promoting Quebec
independence in connivance with provincial separatis-
tes, insisted that its government should be accorded
full and equal membership with Canada and other sovereign states. This strategy of subversion outlived de
Gaulle and persisted right up to the defeat of the
Giscard d'Estaing government in 1981, despite Canadian
consent to a compromise arrangement whereby Quebec (and
New Brunswick) could be admitted as "participating
governments"[38] in ACCT, though not in the more political La Francophonie. As late as 1980, Paris compelled
the cancellation of the proposed founding conference of
La Francophonie in Dakar in protest against rejection
of separate representation for Quebec. Once again, it
had succeeded in frustrating a personal ambition that
Prime Minister Trudeau shared with former President
Senghor of Senegal and President Bourguiba of Tunisia
to see the establishment of a French-speaking
communuate organique as a complement to the Commonwealth. While President Mitterrand has abandoned the
aggressive policies of his predecessors, La
Francophonie has still not come into existence.
Moreover, the Quebec issue will almost certainly be
revived by any successor Paris government.[39]

The initial Canadian response to French provocation
was to exercise what minimal diplomatic leverage the
government could muster. In 1968, it even severed
relations with Gabon after that country, in its capacity as surrogate for France, invited Quebec (but not
Canada) to an international conference of francophone
ministers of education in Libreville. Subsequently,
and more positively, Ottawa set out to buy francophone

African goodwill with aid offers. The courting of French-speaking Africa thus became perhaps the most dramatic new direction in foreign policy ever undertaken by a Canadian government. Beginning in the late 1960s, Canadian bilateral development assistance to Francophone Africa increased sharply from a few million dollars annually for technical assistance to more than $150 million in the current year. In addition, there are substantial subventions to a number of francophone institutions and emergency food and relief grants to drought-stricken areas. The political string firmly attached to this aid programme is the requirement that the recipients formally acknowledge their acceptance of the Canadian constitutional system.

Canada's foreign aid offensive throughout Francophone Africa saved the country without, however, solving the problem of normalizing relations with France. On the contrary, it aggravated them, as Paris resented a rival French-speaking presence intruding politically and commercially into its own "backyard." Consequently, Ottawa has been compelled to continue to nurse its far-flung francophone African constituency constantly and carefully. Indeed, since 1977, a cabinet minister has been specifically designated for this purpose. During those years, there have been 61 ministerial visits to Francophone Africa (compared to 22 to the rest of the continent) and 104 francophone ministerial missions to Canada (compared to 45 from elsewhere in Africa). Part of the discrepancy can be accounted for by the greater significance attached to ministerial exchanges in the development of trade ties in Francophone Africa than in Commonwealth Africa; but a substantial part of the explanation remains the political importance for Canada to continue to cultivate Francophone African sympathy and support. For similar reasons, with the exception of the recently inaugurated joint economic commission with Nigeria, all the bilateral commissions Canada has established in Africa are with francophone states.[40]

v) **African Reactions and Options**

Canada's success in loosening the strong bonds that bind French-speaking Africa to France--at least on the issue of its constitutional integrity--has been more than a matter of money. On aid, of course, Canada ranks fourth in the list of donors. Moreover, many of the diplomatic missions opened in Ottawa (Table 7.1) have been designed explicitly and almost exclusively as

aid lobbies and experience suggests that such investments have generally proved sound. However, Africans
have other incentives to strengthen their Canadian
connections. Two are particularly salient: the urge
to diversify their external dependence and the desire
to win a friend in the Western court. In both cases,
African states tend to hold high hopes and often quite
unrealistic expectations of what Canada is able and
willing to do to promote African interests.

For countries that are seeking to diversify their
traditional international contacts, Canada is an
obvious candidate. It is a middle power with no perceived colonial past, no current threat capabilities,
and a reputation for being quietly helpful. At the
same time, it has a developed economy with the industrial and technological competence and capacity that
developing countries seek. The recent establishment of
Petro-Canada International to assist African and other
Third World countries tackle their critical energy
problems has proved particularly appealing. For Francophone African countries seeking alternatives to
former metropoles, Canada is one of the very few possibilities with which it can communicate easily and confidently. The cordial and somewhat curious relationship that has developed between Canada and Guinea is
illustrative of this. For Sekou Toure, until his
death, Paris remained the symbol of neocolonialism and
Washington that of imperialism. Consequently, when he
decided on his "opening to the West," it was perhaps
inevitable, for political as well as economic reasons,
that he should turn to Canada. Guinea is also the
African country with the largest direct Canadian
investment: twice that in South Africa.

African states also look to Canada to exercise
leverage on their behalf in Washington and London
(though not in Paris). Their hopes in this respect,
though not entirely misplaced, appear excessively
optimistic. While Canada has on occasion interceded
with Western allies to espouse African causes, notably
on Rhodesia and on North-South questions, it has done
so more often in the interests of the survival of the
Commonwealth, the strengthening of the United Nations,
or the preservation of Western unity and integrity than
in solidarity with Africa. Ottawa recognizes that its
reservoir of influence in major capitals is limited,
and tends to husband its diplomatic credit for the
occasions that really count, few of which are direct
African concerns. In this respect, it is excessively
cautious. Just as Africans are inclined to inflate

Canadian powers of persuasion, so Ottawa characteristically underestimates them. Opportunities exist here for more realistic assessments of Canadian potentialities by both sides.

The real problem is the willingness of Canadians--the electorate even more than the government--to accord African issues higher priority. Here, the prognosis is not encouraging. On the contrary, if, as is widely predicted, a Conservative government is elected federally in 1984, it will be significantly to the right of even the shortlived Clark administration of 1979-80. Moreover, over the years, "Pretoria has assiduously and successfully cultivated prominent Conservate politicians."[41] The prospect, then, is that government policy in the future will be decidedly less progressive and vigorous than in the past in its pursuit of justice in Southern Africa and in North-South relations, including aid.

Notes

1. Peter C. Dobell, Canada's Search for New Roles: foreign policy in the Trudeau era (London: Oxford University Press, 1972), 4; Foreign Policy for Canadians (Ottawa: Queen's Printer, 1970), 8.

2. James Eayrs, "From Middle to Foremost Power: defining a new place for Canada in the hierarchy of world power", International Perspectives (Ottawa), May-June 1975, 15-24; Norman Hillmer and Garth Stevenson (eds), Foremost Nation: Canadian foreign policy in a changing world (Toronto: McClelland & Stewart, 1977); David Dewitt and John Kirton, Canada as a Principal Power (Toronto: John Wiley, 1983).

3. Peyton V. Lyon and Brian W. Tomlin, Canada as an International Actor (Toronto: Macmillan, 1979), 9-34; Dobell, Canada's Search for New Roles, 1-9.

4. Cranford Pratt, "Canadian Foreign Policy: bias to business", International Perspectives, November-December 1982, 3-6.

5. Denis Stairs, "The Political Culture of Canadian Foreign Policy", Canadian Journal of Political Science, 15 (4), December 1982, 685. In the original, the adjective "their" appears before each phrase. The Canadian commitment to "ad hocery" has, of course, been challenged by those who detect a consistent, underlying ideological bias in Canadian foreign policy.

6. Foreign Policy for Canadians, 14, 34-35. The government accorded "highest priorities to Economic Growth, Social Justice and Quality of Life Policies", while not neglecting Sovereignty and Independence, Peace and Security, and a Harmonious Natural Environment (p. 32).

7. Office of the Prime Minister, "Reorganization for Economic Development", Release, 12 January 1982, 2, 6. See also, Gordon Osbaldeston, "Reorganizing Canada's Department of External Affairs", International Journal, 37 (3), Summer 1982, 453-66.

8. External Affairs, "Address by the Secretary of State for External Affairs, Dr. Mark MacGuigan, to the Empire Club of Canada, Toronto, Ontario, 22 January 1981", 7-8; Jack Cahill, "Canada Seeks New Friends for the 80s", Toronto Daily Star, 12 April 1981, 84.

9. See M.A. Brault, "Canada's Advantage in Francophone Africa", Canadian Business Review 9 (2), Summer 1982, 13.

10. External Affairs, "Notes for an Address given by the Honourable Gerald Regan....at a seminar to promote market opportunities in Africa, Halifax, 15 December 1982", Statement, 6-7.

11. Strengthening Canada Abroad: final report of the export promotion review committee (Ottawa: Industry, Trade and Commerce, 30 November 1979), 35; Linda Freeman, "CIDA, Wheat, and Rural Development in Tanzania", Canadian Journal of African Studies, 16 (3), 1982, 479-83; Robert Carty and Virginia Smith, Perpetuating Poverty: the political economy of Canada's foreign aid (Toronto: Between the Lines, 1981).

12. Development Cooperation: Efforts and Policies of the Members of the Development Assistance committee: 1982 Review (Paris: OECD, 1982), 191 and 192; Strengthening Canada Abroad, 36. Overall 58.3% of Canadian aid in 1981 was tied. In 1983-84, CIDA's bilateral programme is expected to account for only 36% of total Official Development Assistance (ODA).

13. Canadians in the Third World: CIDA's Year in Review, 1981-82: statistical annex (Ottawa: CIDA,1982). Canada is committed to devoting 0.15% of its GNP, or about one-third of its current global programme to the least-developed countries.

14. Marcel Masse in Canadians in the Third World: CIDA's Year in Review, 1980-81, 2.

15. Rodolphe Morissetta, "L'aide de 'ACDI pourra etre' conditionnele", Le Devoir (Montreal), 20 Janvier 1983, 4.

16. This subjective assessment is not supported by a survey of a panel of External Affairs policy-makers in 1975-76, which ranked "Human rights and discrimination" the last of 15 Canadian foreign policy issues in terms of importance (Lyon and Tomlin, Canada as an International Actor, 41).

17. External Affairs, "Notes for remarks by the Secretary of State for External Affairs, Dr. Mark MacGuigan, to the Canadian Human Rights Foundation, Ottawa, March 267, 1981", Statement, 5-6.

18. External Affairs, "Notes for an Address by the Representative of Canada, Ambassador Yvon Beaulne, Geneva, 2 March 1983. Violations of Human Rights and Fundamental Freedoms in the World", UN Commission on Human Rights, 39th Session, Geneva, 1-2.

19. Dr. Mark MacGuigan, UN General Assembly, 22 September 1980, UN doc A/35/PV.4; Canada, House of Commons Debates, 19 December 1977, 2000.

20. "Space Research Corporation", (Montreal: Dossier CISO, Comite Quebec-Afrique, mars 1980); "Canadian Policy Towards Southern Africa" (Toronto: Taskforce on the Churches and Corporate Responsibility (TCCR), March 1983), mimeo, 17-25. On the involvement of a South African subsidiary of Massey-Ferguson (now partly Canadian government-owned) in a diesel engine contract for the South African military, see ibid., 11-14.

21. In 1982-83, Canada contributed $20,000 to the UN Trust Fund for Southern Africa, $200,000 to the UN Institute for Namibia and $350,000 to the UN Education and Training Programme for Southern Africa (UNETPSA). It also supports most other UN and Commonwealth bodies involved in projects in Southern Africa.

22. External Affairs, Communique, No. 12, 31 January 1983. In addition, another $100 million has been made available to SADCC members on a bilateral basis. For a critique of earlier Canadian programmes in the region, see Linda Freeman, "Canada and the Front Line States", in Douglas Anglin, Timothy Shaw and Carl Widstrand (eds.) Canada, Scandinavia and Southern Africa (Uppsala: Scandinavian Institute of African Studies, 1978), 69-84.

23. Paul Ladouceur, "Canadian Humanitarian Aid for Southern Africa", in Anglin, Shaw and Widstrand (eds.) Canada, Scandinavia and Southern Africa, 88-100.

24. Considerable public attention was drawn to this programme in South Africa as well as Canada when, following the the detention of Mark Caplan in November 1981, it was revealed that he and his Community Video Resource Association in Cape Town were partly CIDA--financed (Cape Argus, 26 November 1981).

25. Statistics Canada, Canada's International Investment Position 1979 (forthcoming). These figures may not be entirely reliable. See also, Guide to Canadian Collaboration with Apartheid (Toronto: SACTU Solidarity Community, 1982).

26. Yvon Beaulne, UN Human Rights Commission, 36th Session, Geneva, February 20, 1980 (translation).

27. TCCR, "Canadian Policy Towards Southern Africa", 7-8.

28. Ibid., 15-17; External Affairs, Communique No. 44, 28 April 1978.

29. External Affaris, Communique No. 60, 27 July 1979.

30. TCCR, "Canadian Policy Towards Southern Africa", 4-6. Eligibility for loans under the "Government Account" (which South Africa never used) ceased in December 1977, and under the "Corporate Account" (last used in 1976) ended in August 1981.

31. This opinion has not gone unchallenged (Ottawa Citizen), 20 March 1982, 9). In 1982, 9.5% of exports to South Africa were EDC insured, and 18.2% of exports to the rest of the continent.

32. Steven Langdon, "The Canadian Economy and Southern Africa", in Anglin, Shaw and Widstrand (eds) Canadian, Scandinavia and Southern Africa, 15-27.

33. John Kirton, "Economic Sanctions and Alliance Consultation: Canada, the United States and the strains of 1979-82", University of Toronto, March 1983, mimeo.

34. Allan J. MacEachen, Deputy Prime Minister and
    Secretary of State for External Affairs, Canadian
    Human Rights Foundation, Ottawa, April 22, 1983
    (text as delivered).

35. Centre for International Policy, Washington, Aid
    Memo, January 6, 1982. If Canada with 3.27% of the
    votes, had opposed the loans, support for it would
    have been reduced from 51.9% to 48.6%.

36. John P. Schlegal, The Deceptive Ash: bilingualism
    and Canadian policy in Africa: 1957-1971
    (Washington: University Press of America, 1978),
    189-219; Louis Sabourin, "Canada and Francophone
    Africa", in Peyton V. Lyon and Tareq Y. Ismael
    (eds.) Canada and the Third World (Toronto:
    Macmillan, 1976), 133-61; Michel Houndjaoue, "Essai
    sur l'etude de la cooperation bilaterale entre le
    Canada et l'Afrique francophone: 1961-1981",
    Etudes Internationales, 13 (2), Juin 1982, 263-81.

37. Africa Contemporary Record, 1971-72, 82.

38. Africa Contemporary Record, 1980-81, A175, B603;
    1981-81, A244; "Canada: new African strategy",
    Africa Confidential (London), 19 (16), 4 August
    1978), 305. Even Mitterrand appears to prefer the
    Franco-African Summit model (which excludes Canada)
    to a commonwealth of equal nations.

39. Three in North Africa (Tunisia, Algeria, Morocco),
    two in West Africa (Senegal, Ivory Coast) and three
    in Central Africa (Zaire, Gabon, Cameroon).

40. Andre McNicoll, "Public Relations South African-
    Style", CUSO Forum (Ottawa), Winter 1983, 15-19.

Chapter Eight

Israel and Africa in the 1980s:
the dilemmas of complexity and ambiguity

Naomi Chazan

The texture of the relationship between Israel and
Africa has altered substantially since the beginning of
the 1980s. The first phase of Afro-Israeli ties, span-
ning the 1960s, was marked by economic cooperation and
political entente. In stark contrast, the second,
which began in 1973 and continued until the end of the
decade, was characterized by a diplomatic stalemate
only somewhat mitigated by the elaboration of non-
formal economic links. The present, third, stage is
both more fluid and more amorphous than its predecessors. The components, the nature, and the direction
of the African-Israeli connection at this juncture lack
either clarity or coherence.

The purpose of this chapter is to scrutinize the
intricacies of the new Afro-Israeli association in an
effort to uncover the roots of its ambiguity. Specifically, it deals first with the conditions that enabled
a shift in modes on interaction; then with the substance of the evolving contacts in the separate spheres
of socio-economic, military, and diplomatic interchange; and finally with the consequences and implications of ongoing activities.

The main contention of this analysis is that an
admixture of pragmatism, utilitarianism and opportunism
has guided the multiplicity of Israeli-African exchanges in recent years. This overriding theme helps to
explain the resultant dualistic pattern of complexity
and disjunctiveness that underlies the present state of
the Israeli connection with Africa south of the Sahara.
Barring any major shifts in the structural conditions
informing policy options, this trend will in all like-
lihood continue along its multidirectional course in
the near future.

The close of the 1970s witnessed important changes
in the internal, continental and global frameworks that
had supported the Afro-Israeli deadlock of that decade.
Many African states were succumbing to a combination of
economic deterioration and political malaise. The
specter of severe food crises and concomitant security
threats inevitably necessitated a reevaluation of

internal priorities and hence of external alliances.
On the continental level, the solidarity of the early
1970s was breaking down. Divisions between African
states on Chad and the Western Sahara were compounded
by growing inequalities among the members of the OAU.
In the Third World range, the paucity of returns from
North-South dialogues and the limited benefits reaped
from exchanges among countries in the southern hemisphere evoked increasingly vocal reservations regarding
the continued utility of such contacts and of the
external militancy that lay at their foundation. The
international mood had also shifted. The intensification of great power rivalry, the effects of the global
recession, and the changes of government in western
Europe and the United States all demanded some re-
adjustment in African international orientations.

The impact on these mutations for Afro-Israeli
relations becomes apparent when related to specific
variables rooted in the Middle East context. The conclusion of the Camp David accords and the impending
Israeli withdrawal from the Sinai removed some of the
ostensible causes for the diplomatic rupture of 1973.
They also sowed discord in the Arab world. Consequently, the need to reassess the premises for the diplomatic ostracism of Israel was highlighted.[1]

This imperative was reinforced to a certain extent
by the accumulation of positive contacts with Israel
since 1973 in the economic, commercial and technical
spheres. Despite the absence of diplomatic relations,
trade had increased threefold, a variety of cultural
exchanges had been elaborated, and Israeli involvement
in infrastructure development had intensified. As a
result, the basis for a more equitable interchange,
predicated on mutual interests and reciprocity, had
been established.[2]

The combination of changing circumstances and
revised interests created an atmosphere in Africa at
once more amenable to exploring new opportunities and
more receptive to overtures emanating from Israeli
sources. The reconsideration of diplomatic contacts
was viewed as a potential means of promoting development and security priorities.[3]

Israel, for its part, was particularly anxious to
utilize the peace agreement with Egypt as a way of
breaking out of its international straitjacket. In
this revived quest for foreign partners, the role of
the third world, and particularly of Africa, was per-

ceived as central. Africa was not only seen (because of its proximity, history, and global weight) as the gateway to the reestablishment of an Israeli presence in other parts of the southern hemisphere; it was also considered to be the original trigger of Israel's global isolation.

Israel's new external assertiveness dictated that a more aggressive approach replace the heretofore reticent quality of Israel's operations on the continent. The primacy of political motives also determined a willingness to use all available tools (military as well as economic) to promote a diplomatic rapprochement, whose importance both in Africa and in the West was not to be belittled.[4]

The stage was therefore set for the commencement of a new era in Israeli-African relations. Despite pragmatism permeating the concerns of Israeli and African leaders, however, their priorities did not coincide. While Israeli policy highlighted economic and military contacts as vehicles for the resumption of diplomatic relations, the African perspective tended to emphasize diplomatic reappraisal, if at all, as a mechanism for the attainment of other benefits. The two threads of practicality on the one hand and interest divergence on the other were therefore apparent fom the outset of this period.

Israeli-African exchanges in economic and social spheres have expanded markedly in the past few years. The first, and among the most prominent, of this form of interaction has been in the commercial sphere. Israeli trade with Africa quadrupled in the eight years between 1973 and 1981. In 1980 and 1981 alone, Israeli exports to Africa increased by over sixty percent. The overall volume of trade in those two years grew by sixty-seven percent.[5] During this period the trade balance has tilted in Israel's favor, with Israel exporting over eight times as much as it has imported from Africa in 1981 (for full figures, see Table 8.1). Israel sells a variety of agricultural machines, fertilizers, chemicals, pharmaceuticals, industrial parts, and electronic equipment in exchange for agricultural products--primarily timber, coffee, cocoa, and cotton.[6] Although Israel now has trade relations with over thirty African states, key partners remain Nigeria (which alone accounts for fifty percent of Israel's trade with Africa), Kenya, Zaire, Tanzania, Zambia,[7] Ethiopia, the Ivory Coast and Ghana, in that order.

Table 8.1

Israel's Trade with Black Africa 1975-1981

Year	Exports	Imports	Volume (U.S. $ Million)
1975	78.8	27.5	66.3
1976	43.1	29.8	72.9
1977	57.1	24.5	81.6
1978	72.5	31.8	104.3
1979	75.4	19.3	94.7
1980	111.7	18.6	130.3
1981	124.0	15.3	139.3

Source: Israel Central Bureau of Statistics, Foreign Trade Statistics (Jerusalem, 1976-1982).

The bulk of Israeli commerce with Africa is conducted by several major semi-public firms, most notably Coor Trade (as well as its subsidiaries Dizengoff and Alda), and Motorola. Other private Israeli companies, such as Tadiran, Amcor and Teva pharmaceuticals, deal directly with African states. In the last several years, trade has also been promoted by a corp of Israeli businessmen, by some Jewish industrialists,[8] and to a minor extent, by multinational corporations.[9] The net result of the growing commercial exchanges between Israel and Africa has been to consolidate economic opportunities opened up in the past, and to establish a growing network of markets for Israeli products, which were expected to double in volume in 1983.[10]

Trade is only one element of economic linkages. A second, extremely lucrative, field of activity is in the service sector. The current value of contracts held by Israeli firms in black Africa is estimated at 1.5 to 3.0 billion dollars.[11] Israeli companies are engaged primarily in road construction, public housing projects, industrial development schemes, and large-scale sewage and irrigation projects. Some model agricultural projects (most notably President Mobutu's estate at N'sele and Felix Houphouet-Boigny's presidential farm near Yamassoukrou) have been constructed by Israeli experts.[12]

The lion's share of contractual activities has been preempted by Solel Boneh, Israel's largest construction company, which carries out major projects in Kenya, Nigeria, Cameroun, Ivory Coast, Togo, Zaire and Gabon. Its current operations include the construction of the cathedral in Abidjan, a series of road projects, hotels and factories in Nigeria, paving of the transAfrican highway betwen Ghana and the Ivory Coast, and several public buildings in Kenya.[13]

Other Israeli firms have also expanded operations in these countries. Among them are Ashtrom, Zaueim, Tahaf, (Water Resources Development International) Federman Construction Company, A.D. Bernowitz, Hiram-Zeevi and Zehariah Drucker. Much of the financing for their activities comes from their own resources; the remainder is subsidized by international banking and business concerns.

The companies engaged in contractual work in Africa employ between three thousand and four thousand Israelis. Africa has become, in the past two years, the major source of demand for Israeli engineers, construction workers and agricultural experts.[14] Particular emphasis has been placed on maintaining a low Israeli profile, while stressing efficiency and productivity. Despite the reversal in economic trends at this point, it was estimated that the increase in the turnover of these firms in 1982 would reach thirty-five per cent.[15] Thus, an intricate array of economic ventures has taken root in recent years, further solidifying Israeli's economic links with Africa.

A third, concomitant sphere, that of technical co-operation, is a carryover from the honeymoon period of the 1960s. During the 1970s, only a handful of Israeli experts served in Africa; but their numbers have grown with the renewal of diplomatic relations with Zaire and the establishment of interest offices elsewhere. Unlike Israeli experts in the field, usually dispatched only to countries that maintain full diplomatic relations with Israel, the quantity of trainees from Africa participating in short-term courses in Israel has jumped dramatically.[16] The Afro-Asian Institute of the Histradut, the Mount Carmel Center, the Foreign Training Department of the Ministry of Agriculture, the Settlement Studies Center of Rehovot, as well as academic institutions, have hosted hundreds of Africans from over thirty countries.[17] And contacts continue to expand indirectly as well, mostly through Scandinavian agencies and international bodies.

Despite the moderate upswing in technical assistance operations the budget of the Division of International Cooperation has been reduced drastically. It stood at only one million dollars in 1982. Holland and the Swedish International Development Agency have channelled additional monies to Israel to sustain some segments of its program. But the fact remains that the Israeli aid effort currently operates on a shoestring budget.[18] Severe limitations are therefore placed on the utilization of technical assistance as a tool to promote Israeli interests on the continent.

Other connections have followed the growth in economic ties. Tourism to and from Africa has shown modest growth rates in the past three years.[19] African pilgrimages to the Holy Land have increased, and the Nigerian government has granted subsidies for religious tours since 1980. The Jerusalem-based Interfaith Committee and the Tantur Institute for Advanced Ecumenical Studies continue to host clerics from the entire continent. Academic exchanges have proceeded apace. And most recently African athletes participated in the Hapoel games, and an Israeli dance troupe was scheduled to tour East and Central Africa.[20]

Afro-Israeli interactions in the economic and social sphere have evinced a variegation in scope and content, a measurable growth in quantity, and a not insignificant degree of mutuality. This balance has been facilitated by the reticence that has enveloped many of these contacts, and by the care devoted to avoid extensive publicity.

The response of African states to initiatives in these areas has been mostly favorable. Almost all African countries have some economic ties with Israel. The exception is a small group of states (including Mauritania, Somalia, Mali, Benin, Niger, Guinea-Bissau, Angola, Mozambique and Congo-Brazaville) who either possess an Islamic complexion or have ideologically-oriented regimes. Reservations on these links have been voiced in some multilateral gatherings, but they tend to proceed as long as they do not attract undue commentary.[21]

The bulk of exchanges has, however, been concentrated in a handful of states (Nigeria, Ivory Coast,

Kenya, Gabon, Zaire, and lately Zimbabwe) generally
considered to be among the continent's more prosperous
countries. Politically they cannot, nevertheless, be
cast into a common mold. Nor are they contiguous geo-
graphically. It appears, therefore, that what permits
them to engage in extensive contacts with Israel is
their pragmatism coupled with a willingness to diversify their external association in a way that would
best serve certain explicitly defined internal
interests.

The expansion of the economic facet of Israeli-
African relations during this phase reflects the utilitarian quality intrinsic to this form of interaction.
Rhetoric aside, the entrenchment of these interchanges
may be seen as an extension of mutually beneficial ties
fostered in previous years. They persist precisely
because of the tangible benefits that continue to
accrue to the partners involved.

The nature of military contacts between Israel and
Africa in the 1980s, unlike their economic counterparts, constitutes a departure from past patterns. The
emphasis in this period has shifted from training and
cooperation among security services to arm sales.
Israel's emergence as a major arms exporter was a by-
product of the expansion of the Israeli arms industry
in the 1970s. Israel today is the second largest non-
Western arms exporter (after Brazil), with estimated
sales of over one billion dollars in 1981.[22] The justification for engagement in arms transfers is couched
not only in economic parlance (military exports accounted for thirty-five percent of industrial exports in
1982), but also in political terms (the disbursement of
arms is seen as a major means of gaining diplomatic
recognition).[23] Since Israel is not the sole weapons
supplier of any state, Israeli policy-makers have also
rationalized the new military stress of their external
policy by claiming that if Israel did not supply certain items, other countries would surely fill the gap
to Israel's economic detriment.

The major purchasers of Israeli armaments in the
1970s were South Africa and certain Latin American and
Central American states. South Africa alone accounted
for thirty-five percent of Israeli arms exports in that
decade.[24] Since then, however, the bulk of Israeli
sales have been directed to Latin America, where
Israeli arms markets have expanded substantially.[25]

Arms sales to black Africa in the past few years have not been conducted as indiscriminately as in Latin America. Israeli military trade with Africa is used specifically as a tool to promote diplomatic ties. Care is therefore taken not only to avoid Israeli involvement in internal security operations, but also to confine military exchanges to support against external threats.[26] Inevitably, arms transfers go hand in hand with training and maintenance operations.

Although the military aspect of Israeli-African relations has been in evidence for some years, the impetus for the recent upsurge was provided by Ariel Sharon after his appointment as Minister of Defense in the summer of 1981. Sharon viewed the export of arms not only as a means of boosting Israel's munitions industries, but also as a crucial strategic tool. His interest in military contacts with Africa was an outgrowth of his efforts to create an anti-Soviet strategic belt stretching from Lebanon, via Egypt, the Central African Republic and Zaire, southward to South Africa.[27] To promote this concept Sharon pressed for a strategic Memorandum of Understanding with the United States, which included clauses outlining Israel's commitment to support American efforts to allay Soviet incursions in various parts of the third world. He also undertook a tour of four African states in the fall of 1981, in the course of which he signed military agreements with Gabon, the Central African Republic, and Zaire. To buttress the efforts to establish military links, Sharon employed a personal advisor on arms sales, and attempted to curb activities of private Israeli arms entrepreneurs.[28] The style associated with Sharon's activities in Africa is one of a bravado bordering on outright intervention. The demonstrative manner in which Israeli policy was conducted at this juncture evoked severe criticism both abroad and within Israel.

The Sharon mannerism may have been a passing episode which drew to a close with his resignation as Minister of Defense in February 1983. The substance of the contacts established at this point was hardly as ephemeral. During his tenure, ongoing Israeli military contacts with Kenya were cemented. Beyond the longstanding cooperation between the Israeli and Kenyan intelligence services (which came out in the open following the Entebbe raid in 1976),[29] some evidence has accumulated regarding arms transfers.[30] Israel's association with the intelligence services of Liberia, Ghana and Zaire has continued.[31] Military contacts

with the Central African Republic and Gabon, the
details of which are somewhat elusive, seem to have
expanded markedly. Israeli military training in
Swaziland has also been augmented.[32]   After a hiatus of
two years, Israel has resumed arms shipments to
Ethiopia and extended training facilities.[33]   The countries that have engaged in military contacts with
Israel have in common either their involvement in
interstate conflict, their anti-Soviet stance, their
strategic position, or a history of military exchanges
with Israel. They do not necessarily belong, however,
to that group of states with which Israel maintains
close economic ties.

The proliferation of Israeli military ventures in
Africa has not passed without comment. Outwardly, most
African states have strongly condemned the trend and
advised against military cooperation with Israel. The
reasons for this position are grounded in a deep dis-
taste for military intrusions of any sort into the continent; in a growing fear of superpower rivalry, both
directly and by proxy; in efforts to avert a split in
African unity because of divergent military alliances;
and in an antipathy towards any actions that would
highlight the military vulnerability of member
states.[34]

Despite the cohesiveness of this position, some
African states have not been averse to entering into
military agreements with Israel. These countries do
so, in all probability, because of pressing security
needs (both external and, regardless of Israeli protes-
tations to the contrary, internal) and because of respect for Israeli achievements in this sphere. Israel
is widely regarded, for better or for worse, as a small
state that has developed an awesome military apparatus.
Its experience and technological superiority provide
benefits not always associated with other arms suppliers. Moreover, Israeli military transfers are usually accompanied by much needed military training.[35]   For
these practical reasons, beyond those countries that
now maintain military ties, other states have approached Israel regarding the possibility of military
exchanges.

Israel's military operations do bring it close to
certain states in Africa to which it might not otherwise have access via economic channels. The price paid
for the stress on this type of linkage is the concomitant consolidation of an image of Israel as superpower and bully. Increased military contacts come hand

in hand with the growth of suspicions regarding Israeli
intentions and the prospects of its interference in
domestic affairs.[36] Regardless, however, of the political ramifications of these military exchanges, the
mutual utility of Israel and to certain African states
of such contacts will probably ensure their continuation if care is taken to avoid public scrutiny of these
sensitive topics. The significance of pragmatism, some
might claim opportunism, is consequently highlighted in
the military field.

The diplomatic arena furnishes the testing ground
of the two-pronged--economic and military--Israeli
effort to reestablish itself in Africa. In 1980,
Israel's diplomatic presence in black Africa was
sparse. Full diplomatic relations existed only with
Malawi, Lesotho, and Swaziland, countries heavily
dependent on South Africa. Interest offices were maintained in three capitals: Abidjan, Accra and Nairobi.
Despite manifold contacts in the preceding years,
attempts to cajole other African countries to break the
diplomatic stranglehold on Israel had not been crowned
with success.

The Israeli quest for diplomatic partners gathered
momentum after the success of the Begin coalition at
the polls in June 1981. At that point, the Foreign
Minister, Yitzhak Shamir, and the recently appointed
director-general of the Ministry, Dr. David Kimche,
launched a vigorous diplomatic campaign to woo African
leaders.[37] The importance attached to military matters
in Afro-Israeli ties induced these policy-markers to
enjoin the support of Ariel Sharon, the Defence Minister, in this effort. A joint committee of the Ministry
of Foreign Affairs and the Defense Ministry was established to coordinate activities in Africa.[38] On the
external front, contacts were made to mobilize the
assistance of the newly-elected Mitterand government in
France, and to harness support from the Reagan administration in Washington and Jewish groups in the United
States.[39]

The thrust of Israeli policy at this juncture was
to capitalize on economic and military contacts in
order to renew diplomatic ties. Preference was given
in foreign policy-making circles to that set of relatively strong African states--Nigeria, the Ivory Coast
and Kenya--with which Israel had developed flourishing
non-formal ties in the past. Some other states, known
for their pro-western predilections or for their fear
of Libyan intrusions, were also singled out for special

attention. But on the whole it was agreed that every
opportunity would be pursued to the fullest.

High level contacts commenced in the spring and
summer of 1981. Several countries, including Liberia,
the Central African Republic, the Ivory Coast, Ghana
and Gabon indicated some willingness to enter into
negotiations with Israel.[40] In late November, Ariel
Sharon paid his then secret visit to several states
including Zaire, Gabon and Central African Republic, at
which point cooperation accords were signed with these
countries.[41] Sharon, by this stage, had ostensibly
taken the lead in promoting Israeli interests in
Africa, thereby preempting, at least for a while, the
centrality of the Foreign Ministry in the process.[42]
In the aftermath of his visit, publicity was given to
the creation of Israeli interest offices in Kinshasa
and Libreville (these were accompanied by similar
interest sections in Lomé and Bangui).

A flurry of consultations ensued among various
African capitals, partly under French auspices. These
culminated in Mobutu Sese Seko's announcement in
Washington at the beginning of December of his intention to resume diplomatic relations;[43] a decision which
was relayed immediately to Ariel Sharon, then in
Washington putting the finishing touches on the strategic accords with the U.S.[44] Consultations between
Mobutu and other African heads of state took place
during the early months of 1982, with a view to achieving some consensus on a more extended renewal of diplomatic links. These discussions, prodded by several
visits of high ranking Israeli officials, did not bear
fruit, mostly because of the strong African reaction to
the annexation of the Golan Heights.[45]

In February and March 1982 further efforts were
made to change the African resolve in anticipation of
the final Israeli withdrawal from Sinai in April.[46] On
15 May 1982, Mobutu declared, somewhat unexpectedly,
that he was renewing full diplomatic relations with
Israel. The motives behind Mobutu's moves remain
ambiguous. While the official declaration on the
resumption of links stressed the government's belief
that since the original reasons for the cessation of
ties had been erased there were no longer any obstacles
to the reestablishment of direct contacts, clearly
other considerations intruded.[47] Zaire's economic
straits, magnified by a wasteful and inefficient
administration, made it a poor investment risk.[48]
Unable to attract much-needed capital from western

Europe or from a US Congress wary of its equivocal
human rights record, Zaire was anxious to find a new
source of support and a powerful lever with which to
pressure Washington. The attraction of Israel, under
the circumstances, was not insignificant.[49] Diplomatic
ties with Israel could help to alleviate economic and
security strains, and could possibly be parlayed into
influence elsewhere. Zaire, unlike many other African
states, viewed diplomatic relations with Israel at this
point as practically worthwhile.

Although Israel might have preferred that its reentry into Africa be initiated by a country less isolated than Zaire, since May 1982 Israeli exchanges have
expanded. In the wake of visits by Zairois and Israeli
emissaries the new Israeli ambassador to Kinshasa,
Michael, presented his credentials in late June, as did
his counterpart in Tel-Aviv in July. There followed a
period of official visits in preparation of a scheduled
tour by Prime Minister Begin.[50] Afer several delays,
it was finally decided that Foreign Minister Shamir
would go in Begin's stead.[51] Shamir left for Zaire in
late-November, accompanied by a large entourage which
included industrial, agricultural and defense experts.
During the course of his visit, two separate agreements
were ratified, one on technical and agricultural cooperation, and one on international cooperation.[52]
Shamir's visit was followed by an equally demonstrative
one by Ariel Sharon in January 1983. During his stay,
Sharon signed several accords on military affairs with
his hosts.[53] These were later clarified by the Zairois
Minister of Defense, who visited Israel just prior to
Sharon's resignation.

The military cooperation treaty concluded in January summarizes a series of intense discussions which
began in late-October with the visit of an army delegation led by General Avraham Tamir. During Shamir's
stay, defense sources revealed a plan to revamp the
structure of the Zaire army, but this was considered
overambitious.[54] The January pact did commit Israel to
a five-year plan for reorganizing all those sections of
the Zaire army which did not already receive foreign
aid. Israel was given primary responsibility for
restructuring the 12,000 man Kamanyola division, based
in Shaba. It also provided for the expansion of the
Special Presidential Brigade, for Israeli support in
the establishment of a new artillery batallion, and for
naval training.[55] Within this framework, Zaire agreed
to buy military hardware from Israel,[56] some of which
was Soviet booty captured from the Syrians in the

Lebanese war. The sources for the financing of these purchases by Zaire, and of the military aid package in general, have yet to be divulged, although the January agreement calls for a fifty-fifty division in the cost of the program.[57]

In the agricultural and technical spheres Israel agreed to expand agricultural aid, increase the number of training courses in the field of rural development, and help in the planning of regional development schemes in several provinces in Zaire. Israel also undertook to encourage the expansion of private investment in Zaire.[58] Most recently, an air transport supplement was added to these economic provisions. To underwrite the technical assistance obligations, Israel allocated a special budget of half a million dollars, and has sought to raise additional subsidies for these schemes.

The results to date of these exchanges with Zaire are far from clear. Israeli attempts to promote Zairois interests in Washington failed twice: first in the Senate Foreign Relations Committee in June 1982, and then again in the House in March 1983.[59] The Israeli economic presence in Zaire is not of major significance and the military accords have run into funding problems. The concrete benefits accruing to Zaire from the normalization of relations with Israel have yet to materialize.

From the Israeli perspective as well, it is difficult to assess the consequences of the Zaire entente. On the one hand, it now appears that the Zaire initiative has assumed the trappings of a solitary event lacking that ripple effect it was expected to generate. Some governments have stated categorically that they would not resume ties with Isreal; even those who have avoided such explicit declarations have not come forth to follow in Zaire's footsteps. Israeli critics claim that this process proves that the government's policy of putting all its eggs in the doubtful Zaire basket has backfired. On the other hand, African leaders did not rush to condemn Mobutu's decision. They did not substantially revise their relations with Zaire, nor did they cease all communication with Israel. To the contrary, there is ample evidence that the Israeli-African dialogue has proceeded unabated, both directly and via intermediaries.[60] Relations with certain countries have improved noticeably[61] and calls for a reconsideration of connections with Israel continue to be debated throughout the continent. Thus if Israel

213

has not been able to maximise on the Zaire reversal, it has not suffered a diplomatic setback as a result. The pragmatic value of utilitarian ties can neither be corroborated nor refuted at this conjucture. Under the circumstances it is difficult to avoid the conclusion that the outcome so far of Israel's latest diplomatic offensive in Africa is nothing short of ambiguous.

African responses to the Zaire move in particular and to the Israeli bid to repair ties in general have therefore been mostly ambivalent. Some of these reactions may be linked to the demonstrative manner and the military style with which Israeli relations with Zaire have been conducted. Others may be an outgrowth of the lack of influence of Zaire in African circles. By not seeking consultation prior to his announcement on the resumption of diplomatic relations, Mobutu alienated other African leaders and accentuated his regional isolation. And still other hesitations may be attributed to the fact that the military overtones of the new Israeli presence in Africa have made some African statesmen especially wary. While sympathetic perhaps to the developmental needs and security problems of Zaire, they are unwilling to sanction yet another foreign military intrusion into the continent. However compelling these caveats, they cannot alone begin to account for the current fluidity in the Israeli-African association.

One set of explanations for this pattern hinges on the linkage of current flows to the behavior of other external actors. Some commentators have tied the reluctance to resume relations with Israel to the close coordination between Israel and American maneuvers on the continent. In this view Israeli--US cooperation in Africa signals a new imperialist threat to African integrity. By spearheading US interests in Africa, it has been suggested that Israel, in this line of reasoning, is tantamount to submission to American designs. African resistance to Israeli overtures thus bears witness to the concerted determination not to compromise the vital concerns of African independence.[62]

Ample evidence has been brought forth to buttress this type of analysis. Reference is made to the western orientation of Israel's main allies in Africa, to the inclusion of Africa in US agreements with Israel, and to the possible financial backing granted by the US to support Israeli activities in Africa. What this mode of explanation cannot illuminate is Israel's strong ties with pro-Soviet countries such as

Ethiopia,[63] or Israel's association with France, whose
interest in Africa hardly overlaps with that of the
United States. Nor can this factor shed light on the
renewed search of many African states for western
allies, or on Israel's failure to gain US support to
help fulfil its obligations to Zaire. Israeli activities in Africa may indeed frequently parallel western
interests, but the proponents of this thesis would be
hard-pressed to prove that Israel has operated in
recent years explicitly at the behest of the administration in Washington.

Another externally-derived series of explanations,
one much favored by Israeli sources, attributes the
current diplomatic stalemate to the ubiquitous Arab
influence in Africa. Since 1973, Afro-Arab relations
have expanded along a variety of axes. Not only have
Arab states extended over $7.5 billion dollars in aid
during this period, but a web of joint institutions has
been established on the economic and diplomatic
fronts.[64] The Arab Bank for the Economic Development
of Africa (BADEA) has become a major funnel for the
dissemination of aid funds. The Afro-Arab summit,
despite its shaky start, has continued to provide a
forum for political interchange.[65] OPEC includes some
African members. Arab states have diversified their
interests on the continent. Their early concern with
Islamic bodies has expanded to include a heavy involvement in infrastructural development, in educational
ventures, in cultural exchanges, and in commercial
ties. This variegation has found expression in
increased Arab diplomatic representation in Africa, and
in the concomitant augmentation of African missions,
especially to the moderate Arab states of Saudi Arabia
and the Persian Gulf.

In this perspective, the Arab expansion in Africa
has paralleled, both in substance and orientation, patterns familar to the Israeli experience of the past
decade. But it has superseded Israel in quantity and
scope. If Arab monies were influential in the original
decision to sever relations with Israel, their impact
was purported to be all the more profound a decade
later.[66] Indeed, Arab reactions to Zaire's declaration
on the resumption were swift and ruthless. Some
states, led by Kuwait, Saudi Arabia, Libya, Iran,
Bangladesh, the United Arab Emirates, Iraq, Tunisia,
and Algeria, suspended diplomatic ties with Zaire. The
Arab League announced that Mobutu's initiative was in
direct contravention of the principles of the Afro-Arab
summit of 1977.[67] And the PLO went out of its way to

decry the move. All aid to Zaire through BADEA, OPEC, the Saudi Fund for Development, and other Arab agencies was cut off.

The harshness of these responses was meant to serve as a warning to other African states contemplating similar steps. To some degree, such pressures were effective. Senegal, Mali, Nigeria, Zambia, Benin and Guinea announced that they would not follow in Zaire's wake.[68] But even if some African states asserted their affinity with the Arab position African responses were hardly gratifying to the Arab states. With the exception of Congo and Mauritius, no African state condemned Mobutu. The silence of African countries was a serious setback for Arab diplomacy.[69] It questioned, rather than reinforced, the extent of Arab influence in contemporary Africa.

In fact, the Zaire move highlighted the degree of African discontent with major elements of Afro-Arab cooperation in the past few years.[70] Reservations emanated partly from disenchantment with economic links. The extent of Arab concern with African economic growth was debated openly, as was the issue of whether the benefits gained outweighed the negative repercussions of skyrocketing oil prices and widespread inflation.[71] Hesitations were also voiced regarding the muted Arab commitment to the decolonization process in Southern Africa and the divergence between African and Arab interests in the Horn of Africa.[72]

Certain specific occurrences of this time also undermine the validity of elements of this argument. The first African head of state to visit Zaire after the May 15 pronouncement was Libya's Ghaddafi. Moreover, it is still not clear that the Arab donor bodies have indeed ceased all disbursements to Zaire.[73] If anything, Mobutu may have shown that it is possible to defy the splintered Arab world without suffering a major reversal.

It appears, therefore, that the attempt to connect African ambivalence towards diplomatic contacts with Israel to the continuing Arab influence is problematic at best. Such an analysis misses the subtleties inherent in Afro-Arab relations today and disregards the crucial fact that Israel and the Arabs no longer present a mutually exclusive alternative for African leaders.[74]

216

Thus externally rooted explanations for the fluidity of Afro-Israeli ties in the diplomatic sphere,
while containing a kernel of truth, suffer from an
oversimplistic bias which tends to overlook the autonomy of the actors involved. While these explications
cannot be dismissed, when employed on their own they
carry insufficient explanatory weight.

A second tier of explanation focuses less on the
external context and more on regional matters. African
political interests in the Middle East, which in 1973
centered mostly on the plight of Egypt, have shifted in
the past decade. Three key issues have moved to the
forefront. The first is the preoccupation with the
Israeli seizure of territories by force, which has been
coupled by a consistent demand for a full withdrawal of
Israel from lands occupied since the Six-Day War.[75]
Israel's intransigence on this subject has been condemned repeatedly by African organs.[76] A second subject of concern to Africans is the specific issue of
Jerusalem. The Israeli unification of the city, and the
subsequent declaration of Jerusalem as the eternal
capital of Israel, has been viewed almost unanimously
in Africa as a violation of the religious sensitivities
of millions of Christians and Muslims throughout the
continent.[77] But perhaps at the apex of recent African
concerns in the Middle East has been the question of
Palestinian self-determination. The plight of the
Palestinians and their quest for political expression
have provided a rallying point for African leaders
still engaged in the struggle for the total liberation
of their continent.[78] African analyses of the Middle
East conflict have sought to make the problem of the
future of Palestinians the crux of any effort to resolve the crisis.[79]

The salience of these positions was magnified in
the course of 1982. The annexation of the Golan
heights, the Israeli invasion of Lebanon, the expulsion
of the PLO from Beirut, and the massacres in the
refugee camps of Sabra and Shatila provoked an outcry
from African capitals. Almost uniformly, African
leaders decried the aggressiveness of Israeli policies
and called for the immediate removal of Israeli troops
from Lebanon.[80]

African attitudes towards the Middle East have
undergone a process of clarification and redefinition
in recent years. The importance attached to these
positions, and to the principles they represent, cannot
be underestimated. The relationship, however, between

these stances and the present state of Afro-Israeli
links is by no means self-evident. If these policies
accounted for African behavior, then it would stand to
reason that no ties with Israel could be entertained.
Not only is this not the case, but African policy-
makers have taken care to moderate their responses to
recent events,[81] and have gone out of their way to
differentiate between their deprecation of Israeli
policies and their acceptance of the existence of
Israel.

Israeli efforts to obtain recognition in Africa
coincided with a particularly volatile and problematic
period in Middle East politics. From an Israeli viewpoint, the timing of the Zaire move has proved to be
unpropitious. By underlining African opposition to
some essential facets of the Begin government's policies, it might have precluded further initiatives in
Africa. As a deciding factor in comprehending African
ambivalence to diplomatic ties with Israel, this set of
concerns nevertheless remains somewhat unconvincing.

Some observers have suggested that African continental concerns supply the missing link in the
analysis of present trends in Afro-Israeli relations.
During the past decade, the perception of Israel as a
serious obstacle to African unity has grown.[82] Since
the 1973 rupture was not only of itself a mark of continental unity but was also embodied in repeated OAU
resolutions, the prospect of an Israeli return to
Africa has been viewed as contradictory to the Pan-
African vision.

Concern over the Israeli relationship with South
Africa has exacerbated these fears. Since 1974, when
Israel upgraded its diplomatic representation in
Pretoria to ambassadorial level, Israel's links with
South Africa have proliferated on virtually every
front. Economic cooperation has expanded, tourism has
increased, and South African investments in Israel have
risen. Military cooperation has become extensive.
Israel has sold sophisticated hardware to South Africa,
has trained counterinsurgency units of the South
African Army, and has collaborated in South Africa's
nuclear development program.[83] Although small in
quantity and unequal in quality, Israel's alliance with
South Africa has blossomed at precisely the same time
that relations with Black Africa have ebbed.[84]

The nature of this relationship has touched upon
African sensitivities on a number of crucial points.

218

First, Israel's policy is viewed as a sign of acquiescence with the prime purveyors of racism. Despite official declarations regarding Israel's abhorence of apartheid, the cynicism with which Israel has pursued its ties with South Africa has been received as a sign of its moral bankruptcy.[85] Second, ties with South Africa have been interpreted as Israeli support for settler colonialism. They have also frequently invited comparison between Israel and South Africa on that score.[86] Third, by flaunting their association with the number one enemy of Africa, Israeli leaders have come to be seen as traitors to the African cause.[87] This position was expressed forcefully by ex-President Shagari in a recent interview:

> We acted as Africans because of
> Israel's continued cooperation with
> racist South Africa. Israel has
> further intensified this coopera-
> tion with South Africa. We have
> continued to be horrified by this
> attitude. So it is not just the
> question of Israel's quarrel with
> the Arabs; it has another quarrel
> with Africa as well. We just can-
> not ignore Israel's continued
> strong and growing friendship with
> an enemy.[88]

African condemnation of Israel because of its South African connection is both vehement and understandable. By singling Israel out for particular opprobrium (frequently at the expense of other alliances of a much more extensive sort),[89] this criticism has proven to be liability for Israel. A reservoir of ill-feeling has developed around this topic. But whether this connection is a reason or an excuse for Israel's ambiguous position in Africa is still very much open to debate.

The correlation between Israel's South African contacts and threat to African unity is, however, generally accepted. For this reason Zaire's decision to reopen diplomatic channels of communication was decried, and Mobutu's move was censured as antithetical to the interests of continental unity.[90] Zaire, however, did not suffer unduly for its action. Although a decision on its application for membership in SADCC was delayed, its standing in major African forums has not been affected. Splits in the ranks of the OAU may have induced Zaire's initiative as much as this move may have influenced divisions in Africa.

The attribution of the diplomatic ambivalence towards Israel to pan-African and Middle Eastern concerns, however, reflective of prevailing stances on these issues, renders explanations of existing trends incomplete. The consistency of African positions on major elements of the issues involved in each of these areas is at odds with the fluidity that characterizes their contacts with Israel.

These circles of concern only make sense when placed in the context of the specific pragmatic considerations of individual African states. The tendency to experiment with contacts with Israel is an outgrowth of the different weight allotted to local needs as opposed to continental and global considerations in the foreign policies of each of the countries in the region. When African leaders broke diplomatic relations with Israel, they did so to a large extent in concert with Third World currents and in support of other African states. The present reevaluation of this decision seems to be guided primarily by domestic and bilateral factors.[91] In conditions of economic and political disequilibrium, pragmatic interests play an overriding role. The unevenness and diversity of responses to Israel's efforts to gain recognition in Africa today highlight the distinctive interests and priorities of each of the states on the continent.[92]

The predominant focus of ongoing reassessments in individual African capitals centers, first and foremost, on how to forward substantive concerns. This process has commenced with separate evaluations of internal priorities and national interests. Economic needs, security problems, religious affinities, ideological predilections, development strategies, and external alliances, differ from country to country.[93] So too does the relative stress placed on issues of African unity, African liberation, and decolonization. Involvement in and concern over the ongoing conflict in the Middle East also varies. Fears of superpower rivalry play divergent roles in the process of policy formulation in given regimes, as do evaluations of the importance of continued contacts with the Arab world.[94]

The specific mixes of each of these elements has led to the adoption of different tactical approaches to the question of the resumption of diplomatic ties with Israel. Some countries and leaders have suggested that the only way to promote domestic and African interests and to affect the peace process in the Middle East is to stop the boycott of Israel (once an opportune moment

is found,[95] and to engage in discussions with its
leaders. Others claim that the best means to pursue
declared goals, both locally and internationally, is by
continued ostracism of Israel and by enhancing its
international isolation.[96]

Differences of opinion on content and approach have
triggered widespread debates on the subject of Afro-
Israeli relations. The most prominent and thorough of
these is the one taking place in Nigeria, whose roots
go beyond the parliamentary motion calling on the Nigerian government to reestablish diplomatic relations.[97]
Similar discussions have been aired publicly in Ghana,
the Ivory Coast, and Kenya, and in official circles
elsewhere.

The outcome of these multiple reconsiderations has
been of a dual nature. On the one hand, no country has
taken the diplomatic step of renewal of ties with
Israel; on the other, economic and military ties have
not been terminated. This ambivalence reflects a
serious process of reevaluation which has still to
reach its proper conclusion. It also is an indication
of the fact that many policy makers have not yet decided whether formal ties with Israel will proffer greater
economic, military, or political returns than those
reaped by maintaining ongoing nonformal links. They
have also not defined what they can offer Israel in
exchange.[98] Thus a revived interest in Israel exists;
its lack of diplomatic expression mirrors an uncertainty regarding the benefits of such official gestures.
The dissolution of the original reasons for the rupture
could justify a diplomatic breakthrough; the injection
of new issues can explain any reluctance to proceed in
that direction. In the interim, many African attitudes
towards Israel retain their intrinsic amorphousness.

Pragmatism permeates Israeli and African perspectives on their mode of diplomatic interaction. But the
interests of the parties concerned are not always
aligned. Israeli political objectives diverge, often
markedly, from those of their African counterparts.
There is a disjunctiveness in means and ends, and in an
understanding of how these can be accomplished. Diplomatic ties, unlike economic and military exchanges, are
more pragmatic than utilitarian. As long as the pragmatic worth of existing utilitarian connections remain
hazy, ambiguity will prevail in the diplomatic domain
of Israeli-African interactions.

The Afro-Israeli relationship has commanded undue attention since its inception over twenty-five years ago.
This intriguing quality may be due to that fact that
these links encapsulate the fears and the hopes, the
interests and the desires, the dislikes and the
attractions, of the entities involved. Fascination
with this topic persists into the third, and much more
nebulous, phase of African contacts with Israel.

In this current stage new emphases have emerged,
new points to contacts have developed, and political
dimensions have assumed a new urgency. The differences
between Israel and Africa have been highlighted, but so
have some commonalities in global dependency. The
human component has also changed: gone are the pioneer
and the supplicant; they have been replaced by the
businessman and the technocrat, the soldier and the
scholar, the official and the representative of multinational concerns. Israel no longer deals with all the
states on the continent, but its contacts are also not
confined to a mere handful of relatively prosperous
countries. The style of Israeli-African ties, once
conducted surreptitiously, veers towards the demonstrative. Israel and Africa are still engaged in exploring
the normalization of their interrelationship; a quest
which seeks to inject existing contents with a mutually acceptable form.

In the meantime complexities proliferate, amibigui-
ties abound and contradictions persist. The gap between principles and opportunism, between non-alignment
and dependency, between an atmosphere of change and the
absence of movement, continues. This dualism and con-
vergence and their disjunctive and reciprocal by-
products are a function of the mobility of structural
conditions and a sign of the present indeterminacy of
the African, Middle Eastern, and global situations.

In these circumstances, the dilemmas of policy-
makers are manifold. Two main options for action have
been presented. The first, predicated on the assumption that existing links are a reflection not of one's
own interests but of those of the other side, calls
essentially for inaction. In this approach no further
steps can be taken since prevailing links are beyond
the purview of each government. Many Israelis are con-
vinced that they cannot control Africans concerns or
opinion; and many Africans claim that policies must
change before they can engage in dialogue with Israel.
In this strategy, Israelis and Africans are absolved of
keeping abreast of realities in each other's environ-

ment in anticipation of changes not dependent on their own initiatives.[100]

The second option presumes that mutual awareness of the concerns of both Israel and African states may bring about changes in the structure of their interaction. On the Israeli side, this approach requires a serious review of some major contradictions that have arisen in the past few years. On the substantive level, Israel has based its reentry into Africa on the green line of agriculture and economics and on the red line of military cooperation. These two methods attract different interests in Africa and often conflict. It is doubtful whether they can or should be employed in tandem indiscriminately. Israel's selection of partners has also been problematic. By extending undue support to Mobutu, its leaders have not distinguished clearly between links with a state and support of a (in this case repressive) regime.[101] They sought to make Zaire a linchpin of their African policy, when they knew full well that Israel's interests lie more clearly with other African states. Israel has also continued to deal openly with South Africa while courting African leaders. It may be necessary to make a clearer choice. Israeli policymakers may need to resolve the contradiction between their contention of acting autonomously in Africa and their undue association with US interests. In a similar vein, Israel cannot expect French support in Africa if its actions continue to further American interests alone.

Many of these dilemmas emanate from a lack of clarity regarding the organization of Israel's Africa policy. The open rivalry between the Foreign Ministry and the Defense Ministry has been counterproductive. The reassertion of the primacy of the Foreign Office in policy matters may go a long way towards rectifying the distortions of the Sharon era. It may also reduce the strident style that raises expectations and invites disappointment. Changes in these spheres should not, however, overshadow the need to review Israel's African posture. This means coming to terms with African concerns and sensitivities and recognizing the fact that Israel is not, and should not be presented as, a major power in the continent. The quest for normalization is dependent upon a willingness to probe areas of mutual interest and to reduce expectations to levels which conform to Israel's size and capabilities. Such a reassessment demands careful planning, evaluation, and policy formulation.

On the African side, too, similar issues arise. It might be important to reconcile requests for military assistance with condemnation of such aid. Concern for the Palestinian cause may need to be viewed in light of Arab inactivity on their behalf. Sympathy for Arab positions may have to be balanced with a greater under-standing of Israel's security needs. Charges of proxy activity by Israel may have to be brought into line with efforts to use Israel as a channel of communica-tion with the west. In this second option, the need to argue basic points of contention, to lay bare differ-ences, to grapple with paradoxes, and to determine policy measures on the basis of greater understanding, is accentuated.[102] The third policy option based on the perception of Israeli-African relations as a func-tion of shifting structural circumstances calls for active measures aimed at redesigning internal condi-tions in order to create an environment more amenable to mutual exchange.

None of these possibilities is mutually exclusive. In the interim, it is reasonable to suggest that the present pattern of complexity, dualism, fluidity, and ambiguity that characterizes Israeli-African exchanges will continue and perhaps even intensify. The combina-tion of utilitarianism and pragmatism that lies at the core of this relationship underlines both the conver-gence and divergence of present interests and the pros-pect of reciprocity which inform the Afro-Israeli rela-tionship of the 1980s.

Notes

The author would like to thank Irene Eber for her thoughtful suggestions, Katya Azulay for her research assistance, and the Harry S. Truman Institute for the Advancement of Peace of the Hebrew University of Jerusalem for support which made research on this paper possible.

1. The significance of this factor has been mentioned in numerous Israeli and African sources. For one example see: Brooke Unger, "Israel, Out of Sinai, Looks to Renew Lost Ties to Africa", The Interdependent, Vol. 8,(3), April-May 1982.

2. For an overview of this period: Naomi Chazan, "Israel in Africa", Jerusalem Quarterly, No. 18, Winter 1981, 29-44.

3. For one example see: Femi Aribisala, "Thought-Piece on the Question of Nigerian-Israeli Rapprochment", Nigerian Forum, Vol. 2(4 & 5), 1982, 525-526.

4. This assessment is based on a series of interviews with Israeli Foreign Ministry officials, conducted at various points during 1981-1983.

5. Extrapolation from figures appearing in: Israel Central Bureau of Statistics, Foreign Trade Statistics (Jerusalem: 1980-1982), passim. For earlier figures see: Ethan A. Nadelman, "Israel and Black Africa: a rapprochement?" Journal of Modern African Studies, Vol. 19(2), 1981, 191, who relies on the same source.

6. The list of items traded is extensive, covering literally hundreds of commodities. Consult ibid, for details.

7. Ibid., and African Business, April 1983, 16-17.

8. One example is Nissim Gaon, who is considered to be the king of the peanut trade. Afrique-Asie, No. 281, 25 October - 7 November 1982, 16.

9. This is not a widespread phenomenon. See the controversy over Lonrho's attempt in this connection: The Times (Business News), 3 May 1982, 54.

10. *Jeune Afrique*, No. 1149, 12 January 1983, 26.

11. David Blumberg, "Bilateral Relations in the Absence of Diplomatic Ties: Africa and Israel in the Post-1973 Era", B.A. Thesis, Department of Government, Harvard University, March 1981, ii.

12. *Haaretz*, 15 June 1982 and *Maariv*, 21 February 1982.

13. Culled from the Israeli press, 1981-1983.

14, Results of Manpower Israel Survey, reported in *Maariv*, 21 April 1982.

15. *African Economic Digest*, 4 June 1982, 6.

16. Emmanueal Lotem, "Israeli-African Relations in the Eyes of the Press", *International Problems*, Vol. 14 (3 and 4), Fall 1975, 39, attacks the rationale behind this policy, which still persists.

17. For a look at one part of this program: Gershon Fradkin, "FTD: Trainees Revisited", *Fidma: Israel Journal of Development*, Vol. 6(2), 1981, 16-22.

18. Evidence by Eliashiv Ben-Horin before the Knesset Foreign Affairs Committee, reported in the *Jerusalem Post*, 14 December 1982. Foreign Minister Shamir announced recently that he hoped that American Jews would contribute to Israel's technical cooperation program: *Maariv*, 1 December 1982.

19. Blumberg, "Bilateral Relations", p. 50, cites a growth figure of 37% during the years 1976 - 1979.

20. The latter was accompanied by a major controversy because of insensitive press releases. See *Haaretz*, 5 May 1983.

21 This brought about the loss of Solel Boneh's contract to construct the UN Environmental Programme's headquarters in Nairobi, *African Economic Digest*, Vol. 3 (15), January 1982, 2. It also led to the placement of Kenya's Kocol company on the Arab boycott list, *African Economic Development*, Vol. 8 (7), February 1983, 9.

226

22. *Christian Science Monitor*, 4 January 1983. The figure on arms exports is quoted variously at between $1 billion and $2.5 billion per annum in the past two years.

23. Leslie H. Gelb, "Israel Increasing Military Training and Arms Sales in Latin America", *International Herald Tribune*, 18 -19 December 1982.

24. Stockholm International Peace Research Institute, *World Armament and Disarmament: SIPRI Yearbook 1981* (London: Taylor and Francis, 1981), 188. For an overview see: "Israel: Marchand de Mort", *Afrique-Asie*, No. 1013, April 1982, 26-28.

25. Interview with Bishara Bahbah, who has now completed a Ph.D. dissertation at Harvard University on this subject.

26. Israel's military involvement in Africa is far more confined than in Latin America. Benny Morris, "Arms at any Price", *Jerusalem Post*, 4 June 1982, highlights this distinction. Israel has also generally avoided supporting resistance and opposition movements, as it did in the Southern Sudan in the 1960s. For example, it flatly rejected a request for aid from Ugandan rebels. *Haaretz*, 2 July 1982. There is, however, some rumour of Israeli activity among UNITA rebels in Angola, *Jerusalem Post*, 16 January 1983 (which cites Angolan sources).

27. This conceptualization has been confirmed by some official sources.

28. *Maariv*, 23 December 1981.

29. Planning sessions apparently took place in Israel, *Haaretz*, 24 January 1983.

30. Blumberg, "Bilateral Relations", 36, citing *SIPRI, 1980 Yearbook*, 1980 Yearbook, 148.

31. Martin Bailey, "Israeli Spies in Africa", *Africa*, No. 130, June 1982, 37-38. Also see *Jeune Afrique*, No. 1102, 17 February 1982, 210-211.

32 *Africa*, No. 126, February 1982.

33. *Jeune Afrique*, No. 1139, 3 November 1982, 33.
     There have also been some speculations regarding
     Israeli involvement in Chad after Hissene Habre's
     takeover in 1982.

34. Some of these points are debated in Adeoye A.
     Akinsanya, "The Entebbe Rescue Mission: A Case
     of Aggression?" *Journal of African Studies*, Vol.
     9, No. 2, 1982, 46-57; and in U.O. Umozurike,
     "The Israelis in Entebbe--Rescue or Aggression",
     Nigerian Journal of International Affairs, Vol.
     5, Nos. 1 and 2, 1979, 46-58.

35. Some of these points are underlined in "Israel's
     Omnipotence", *Afriscope*, Vol. 12, No. 9,
     September 1982, 7.

36. In this context, the recent charge of Israeli
     collusion in an attempted coup in Ghana is
     indicative. See report in *Haaretz*, 19 April
     1983.

37. For some background on Kimche: *The Times*, 19
     August 1982.

38. Mentioned in an article in *Maariv*, 9 December
     1981.

39. Early contacts were made with Guy Penne in Paris.
     Elements of the French involvement at the outset
     were discussed in *Jeune Afrique*, No. 1094, 23
     December 1981, 13, *Le Monde*, 8 December 1981.
     Ignacio Klich, "Israel's Return to Africa",
     Middle East International, 4 June 1982, 11-12,
     elaborates on these contacts. Richard L. Sklar,
     "Africa and the Middle East: What Blacks and
     Jews Owe to Each Other", paper presented at the
     8th Annual Spring Symposium of the Afro-American
     Studies Program, University of Pennsylvania,
     March 1982, 17-18, deals with meetings held bet-
     ween African and American Jewish leaders.

40. At that point, it seemed that the Central African
     Republic would be the first to renew diplomatic
     relations, but the overthrow of David Dacko in
     August 1981 preempted that possibility.

41. For more details consult the *Jerusalem Post*, 24
     November 1981, and *Maariv*, 27 November 1981.

42. Sharon took along some private advisers, including Arye Ganger: _Haaretz_, 4 December 1981.

43. _New York Times_, 3 December 1981. This announcement was widely covered in the press at the time.

44. The fact is that these two visits, despite much publicity to the contrary (see _Jerusalem Post_, 4 December 1981), were purely coincidental.

45 Only a number of African states abstained in General Assembly on the vote to impose sanctions on Israel after the Golan annexation (including Gabon, Liberia, Malawi, Swaziland, the Central African Republic, and Zaire). The majority voted for the resolution. _Maariv_, 7 February 1982.

47. _Quotidien de l'Agence Zaire Presse_, No. 596, 15 May 1982. The statement also suggested that the move was an act of independence on the part of Zaire, and that it did not imply the cessation of Zaire's recognition of the PLO. These points were reiterated in _Actualite Nationale Zaire_, 21 May 1982, 1-2.

48. For general background see Crawford Young, "Politics of Penury: Zaire", _SAIS Review_, Vol. 3, No. 1, 1983, 115-130.

49. This point was raised in _Le Monde_, 29 May 1982, and in all the Israeli press throughout May, 1982. For an African viewpoint see _West Africa_, No. 3412, 3 January 1982.

50. This was delayed several times because of the war in Lebanon, and some (diplomatic) illnesses. _Le Monde_, 4 August 1982 and _West Africa_, No. 3392, 9 August 1982, 2028.

51. _West Africa_, No. 3405, 8 November 1982, 2929.

52. _Jerusalem Post_, 29 November 1982. The visit was covered by numerous Israeli journalists attached to the entourage, and hence reported extensively in the Israeli press.

53. This tour was also given major coverage in the Israeli press.

54. *Jeune Afrique*, No. 1145, 15 December 1982.
    Foreign Ministry sources in Israel claimed that
    the timing of the announcement was designed to
    divert the limelight from Shamir. See *Haaretz*,
    17 December 1982.

55. These details culled from *Haaretz*, 20 January
    1983, *Jerusalem Post*, 21 January 1983, *The Times*,
    24 January 1983, and *New African*, January 1983,
    4.

56. Variously quoted as ranging from $8 million (*West
    Africa*, No. 3410, 13 December 1982, 3241), to $12
    million (*Haaretz*, 17 December 1982), to $18
    million (*The Times*, 3 December 1982).

57. *African Business*, No. 55, March 1983, 25-26
    states that the arms sales were carried out on a
    purely cash basis.

58. *Zaire: a special supplement of the Israel Econo-
    mist*, November 1982, was one effort in this
    direction.

59. *International Herald Tribune*, 11 March, 1983.

60. A meeting between Shamir and Felix Houphouet-
    Boigny was reported in *Haaretz*, 2 November 1982.
    A meeting between Shamir and Daniel Arap Moi was
    reported in the *Jerusalem Post*, 13 December 1982.
    African diplomats at the UN met with an official
    of the World Jewish Congress, *Jerusalem Post*, 20
    March 1983. Israeli emissaries visited twenty
    African states in early 1983.

61. This is especially true of Ethiopia. See report
    in the *Jerusalem Post*, 4 March 1983. Israeli
    interest in Ethiopia is not only of strategic
    importance, but also of Jewish interest because
    of the Falasha Jewish community there. The
    entire ambivalence highlighted in Robert Einav,
    "Looking Clearly at Africa", *Jerusalem Post*, 30
    May 1982.

62. This thesis has been propounded in many sources.
    For some examples see: *West Africa*, 25 October
    1982, 2735; Benjamin Beit-Hallahmi, "Israel's
    Global Ambitions", *New York Times*, 6 January
    1983; "The Israel African Connection", *Africa*,
    No. 68, April 1977, 41-43. For a Soviet view,
    see: V. Sidenko, "Israel's African Ambitions",

Arab-Palestine Resistance, February 1971, 71-79.
The roots of this approach may be gleaned from
Africa Research Group, "Israel's Imperialist
Mission in Africa", <u>Arab-Palestine Resistance</u>,
May 1970, 42-54.

63   For some background see Peter Schwab, "Israel's
     Weakened Position on the Horn of Africa", <u>New
     Outlook</u>, Vol. 21, No. 2, 1978, 21-25 and Shlomo
     Slonim, "New Scramble for Africa", <u>Midstream</u>,
     Vol. 23, No. 9, 1977, 30-35.

64. "Political Tensions Cloud Arab-African Coopera-
     tion", <u>Middle East Economic Digest</u>, 4 June 1982,
     24-25. By far the best background to date is to
     be found in Hartmut Neitzel and Renate Notzel,
     <u>Africa and the Arab States: Documentation on the
     Development of Political and Economic Relations
     since 1973</u> (Hamburg: Institute of African
     Studies, 1979).

65. For a review see "Le Chaud et le Froid", <u>Jeune
     Afrique</u>, No. 114, 12 May 1982, 25.

66. In all probability the attribution of the rupture
     of diplomatic relations to Arab pressures was
     misplaced. Highlighted in: J. van der Meulen,
     "Israel's Relations with Africa", <u>Kroniek van
     Afrika</u>, No. 2, 1974, 166-184; Elliot P. Skinner,
     "African States and Israel: Uneasy Relations in
     a World of Crisis", <u>Journal of African Studies</u>,
     Vol. 2, No. 1, 1975, 19; and Arye Oded, "Africa
     Between Israel and the Arabs", <u>Hamizrach
     Hahadash</u>, Vol. 25, No. 3, 1975, 184-209.

67. <u>FBIS Daily Report</u>, Middle East and North Africa,
     Vol. 96, No. 18, May 1982 and paid advertisement
     in the <u>Weekly Review</u>, 28 May 1982, 2.

68. <u>Afrique-Asie</u>, 7 June 1982, 20.

69. Klich, "Israel Returns to Africa", p. 41; and
     "Political Tension", 24.

70. Godfrey Rabat, "Afro-Arab Solidarity in Need of
     Repair", <u>The Times</u>, 3 June 1982, 6 and <u>New
     African</u>, No. 177, July 1982, 38-39.

71. Olusola Ojo, "Afro-Arab Financial Cooperation",
     paper presented at the 24th Annual Meeting of the
     African Studies Association, Bloomington, October

1981; and Kunirum Osia, "Afro-Arab Relations: Elastic or Fragile?" Paper presented at the 25th Annual Meeting of the African Studies Association, Washington, D.C., November 1982.

72. Olusola Ojo, "The Role of the Arab World in the Decolonization Process of Black Africa", Inter- national Problems, Vol. 20, Nos. 2-4, 1981, 73-84. On the Horn see Stephen O. Bamiduro, "The Arab Dimension of External Involvement in Ethno- Regional Conflicts in Africa". Paper presented at the 25th Annual Meeting of the African Studies Association, Washington, D.C., November 1982.

73. African Economic Development, No 17, 29 April 1983, 3.

74. Umunna Orjiako, "Black Africa and Israel (sic): Is it Time for Rapprochement"? Nigerian Forum, Vol. 2, Nos. 4 and 5, 1982, 538-539; and "Soli- darite Nuancee avec le Monde Arabe dans le Con- flict de Proche-Orient", Le Monde Diplomatique, 15 February 1982.

75. This position has been reiterated at every OAU summit in the past decade. See Weekly Review, 17 July 1981, 29-43. In a recent joint communique Niger and Saudi Arabia issued a statement con- demning Israel's 'settler colonialism' (New African, No. 177, June 1982, 19).

76. The OAU has tried to deal with this issue in the past. For a review see Yassin El-Ayouty, "OAU Mediation in the Arab-Israeli Conflict", Geneve Africa, Vol. 14, No. 1, 1975, 5-29. Also see Emeka Aniagolu, "Israel and the PLO: A Look at Recent Developments", Nigerian Forum, Vol. 2, Nos. 6-8, 1982, 746-751.

77. For example Jeune Afrique, No. 1138, 27 October 1982, 8-9.

78. See especially Nzongola-Ntalaja, "Africa and the Question of Palestine", The Search, Vol. 5, No. 1, 1982, 1-18. Best overview of this subject may be found in Sulayman S. Nyang, "African Opinions and Attitudes to the Palestine Question", The Search, Vol. 1, Nos. 3 and 4, 1980, 218-241. Also see S.K.B. Asante, "Africa in World Poli- tics: The Case of the Organisation of African

Unity and the Middle Eastern Conflict",
International Problems, Vol. 22, Nos. 2-4, 1981,
111-128.

79. Vincent B.K. Khapoya, "Africa and Israel in the
     Period of the Severance of Diplomatic Relations",
     Paper presented at the 23rd Annual Meeting of the
     African Studies Association, Philadelphia,
     October 1980.

80. OAU Foreign Minister's Council communique, as
     reported in the _Jerusalem Post_, 28 November 1982.

81. This was especially the case regarding responses
     to the Beirut massacres. See _Jeune Afrique_, No.
     1134, 29 September 1982.

82. A good overview may be found in Timothy M. Shaw,
     "Oil, Israel and the OAU: an introduction to the
     political economy of energy in Southern Africa",
     Africa Today, Vol. 23, No. 1, 1976, 15-26. Also
     reiterated in Jake Miller, "African-Israel Rela-
     tions: Impact on Continental Unity", _Middle East
     Journal_, Vol. 29, No. 4, 1975, 393-405.

83   Elisabeth Mathiot, "La Politique Israelienne en
     Afrique du Sud, en Afrique, et en Amerique
     Latine", _France Pays Arabes_, No. 102, August
     1982, 15-21. For a good overview see Rosalynde
     Ainslee, "Israel and South Africa: An Unlikely
     Alliance"? UN Department of Political and Se-
     curity Council Affairs, Centre Against Apartheid,
     Document 20/1981, July 1981.

84. For a critique of this policy see Naomi Chazan,
     "The Fallacies of Pragmatism: Israeli Foreign
     Policy Towards South Africa", _African Affairs_,
     Vol. 82, No. 327, April 1983.

85. The breakdown on African votes on the 1975 reso-
     lution, see Nadelman, "Israel and Black Africa",
     217. For a good analysis consult Samuel Decalo,
     "Africa and the UN Anti-Zionism Resolution, Roots
     and Causes", _Cultures et Development_, Vol. 8, No.
     1, 1976, 89-117.

86   For a recent example see John Henrik Clarke, "The
     Land Question in Palestine and East and Southern
     Africa: A Comparative and Historical Study of
     Two Colonial Tragedies", Paper presented at the

2nd UN Seminar on the Question of Palestine, Vienna, August 1980. For a refutation of this type of comparison see Flora Lewis, "South Africa: The Comparison with Israel is Unfortunate", International Herald Tribune, 1 February 1983.

87. "Israel Backs Up Separatist Movement in Africa", Nigeria: Bulletin on Foreign Affairs, Vol. 7, No. 1, 1977, 37-38.

88. Africa Now, No. 19, November 1982, 58.

89. Olusola Ojo, "South African-Arab Relations", Ufahamu, Vol. 6, No. 3, 1982, 121-133; Kunirum Osia, "Israel-South African Connection: Cause or Consequence of Black African Middle East Policy", The Search, Vol. 2, No. 4, 1981, 543-566; and Kunirum Osia, Israel, South Africa and Black Africa: A Study of the Primacy of the Politics of Expediency (Washington: University Press America, 1981), esp. 89-92.

90. Africa, No. 131, July 1982, 23. Also see Godwin Matatu, "The Star of David and Mobutu's Torch", Africa, No. 131, July 1982, 44-46.

91. A. Akinsanya, "On Lagos Decision to Break Diplomatic Relations with Israel", International Problems, Vol. 17, No. 1, 1978, 76-77. Hinted at in 'Sola Ojo, "The Arab-Israeli Conflict and Afro-Arab Relations", in Timothy M. Shaw and 'Sola Ojo (eds.) Africa and the International Political System (Washington: University Press of America, 1982), 139-167.

92. The interest orientation is also highlighted by Thomas Land, "Relations with Israel", New Outlook, Vol. 23, No. 2, 1980, 10-11.

93. For example, Kenyans are concerned with their relationships with the Saudis and with the U.S., the Ivory Coast is also concerned with its links with France, Senegalese considerations have a strong Islamic component, and the Nigerian interests include a heavy emphasis on OPEC problems of nuclear proliferation, and the South African problem.

94. All these issues are discussed in detail in "Commentary: Round-Table Discussion on the Estab-

lishment of Diplomatic Relations with Israel by Nigeria", <u>Nigerian Forum</u>, Vol. 2, Nos. 7-9, 1982, 645-730.

95. Orjiako, "Black Africa and Israel", esp. 535-536. Also see "Cote d'Ivoire: Normalisation avec Israel"? <u>Afrique-Asie</u>, No. 292, March 1983.

96. Aribisala, "Thought-Piece on the Question of Nigerian Israeli Rapprochement". Habib Boulares, "L.S. Senghor, Interview", <u>Jeune Afrique</u>, No. 272, July 1982, 22-25.

97. E.C. Ebo, "Extract from a Motion Moved in the National Assembly on the Renewal of Diplomatic Relations with Israel by Nigeria and Other African States", <u>Nigerian Forum</u>, Vol. 2, Nos. 7-9, 1982, 740-745, and the response by A. Bolaji Akinyemi, "Open Letter to Members of the National Assembly on Nigeria-Israel Relations", <u>ibid.</u>, 731-739.

98. Really highlighted by Aribisala, "Thought-Piece on the question of Nigerian Israeli Rapprochement", 525-526.

99. Skinner, "African States and Israel", highlights these differences, 3.

100. Some of the prevailing lack of sensitivity is stressed in Naomi Chazan, "Interview on Israeli-African Relations", <u>Haaretz</u>, 20 January 1983.

101. "Sharon's African Stage", <u>Jerusalem Post</u>, 21 January 1983.

102. These points are illustrated in Yehoshua Rash, "Les Annees Israeliennes en Afrique: Un Bilan", <u>Mois en Afrique</u>, Nos. 182-183, 1981; Dan V. Segre, "Cultural Colonization in Africa and Israel", <u>Jerusalem Quarterly</u>, No.14, Winter 1980, 18-27. There is a growing awareness that Israel lies between north and south and must find its appropriate niche in this configuration.

Chapter Nine

India's African Policy

Babafemi A. Badejo

Despite an enormous population and a low per capita
income, India has been able to achieve a number of
scientific and technological feats. These range from
the building of motor vehicles and aircrafts to the
launching of space crafts and communication satellites
and, perhaps most importantly, the detonation of a
"peaceful" atomic device. While many Africans are aware
of the Indian nuclear detonation, few are aware of what
strides India has made in the area of industrial manufacturing capacity. Impressed by these achievements,
it is not unusual for Indians to claim that India is
the world's tenth industrial power. While this claim
may be questioned, there is no gain-saying the importance of India's achievement especially when one consi-
ders that, unlike Brazil's effort, made possible due to
the operations of United States-based MNCs, India's has
been largely self-reliant albeit with minimal international cooperation and assistance. These realities
single India out amongst the amorphous bunch referred
to as the "Third World." So, while India cannot be put
on the same pedestal as the United States or the Soviet
Union, it is a power to be reckoned within the international arena. Hence this exploration of the patterns
of interaction between the subcontinents of India and
Africa.

From the onset, it needs be noted that problems
present themselves in any discussion of India's relations with Africa. For example, how does one discuss
India's relations with a continent comprised of over
fifty "sovereign" states? As a summation of varying
bilateral relations? Or does one look only at statements directed at the conglomeration "Africa?" Or if
one finds mainly references to Kenya, Zambia, Libya and
Egypt does one conclude that India has no "African
Policy," per se?

For our own purposes, we are concerned largely with
a discussion of India's policy towards Africa south of
the Sahara. In addition, bilateral relations between
India and specific African states will only aid in
occasionally illustrating issues that we see as applic-
able to most of Africa. In this regard, we devote
attention to India's ideological as well as economic

237

diplomacy in Africa. The discussion of India's ideological diplomacy ranges from her impact on African
nationalist struggles to non-alignment and the anti-
apartheid struggle. Our treatment of Indian economic
diplomacy involves an exploration of the varying
patterns of economic interactions with Africa, with a
view to ascertaining whether these interactions can be
seen as a model of South-South cooperation. This
dichotomous treatment of Indian policy in Africa can
also be seen in terms of periods of time. Thus,
India's ideological diplomacy falls largely in the
period before the Sino-Indian border conflict of 1962,
while her economic diplomacy can be seen largely as
falling within the period succeeding the 1962 conflict.
In examining these issue areas and periods, we believe
that India's policy toward Africa has been dictated
both by her domestic political economy, including
governing personalities, and by her economic capabilities. Important also have been India's reactions to
perceived incursions into Africa, both by the superpowers and China.

India's connection with Africa predates the colon-
isation of India and Africa.[1] But for our own purposes, we commence our analysis with the indirect effect of Gandhi and the post-independent Indian government on the anti-colonial struggle in Africa. As well,
we consider the impact of India on the foreign policy
stance of African states in the post-independence
period.

Mahatma Gandhi, as a young Barrister-at-law, went
to South Africa as an employee of a Muslim Indian community whose members were descendants of indentured
Indian agricultural labourers imported by South Africa
since 1860.[2] While in South Africa, Gandhi organized
Indians against the injustice of the racial laws of the
Union, as they affected Indians alone.[3] The method of
non-violent civil disobedience which Gandhi introduced
in South Africa was used again when he returned to
India to join the Indian Congress Party during the
anti-colonial struggle there.

Gandhi's method and the Indian Congress Party's
struggle for freedom impressed many African nationalists. Admiration was expressed across the continent by
such African nationalists as Obafemi Awolowo, Mbonu
Ojike, Adegoke Adelabu, Albert Lutuli, Kenneth Kaunda,
Julius Nyerere and Kwame Nkrumah who wrote:

After months of studying Gandhi's
policy and watching the effect it
had, I began to see that when backed by a strong political organisation, it could be the solution to
the colonial problem.[4]

It was in this light that Nkrumah launched "positive
action" in Ghana in early 1950, and Mbonu Ojike began
the famous "boycott the boycottable" drive in Nigeria.

The Ghandhian legacy of non-violence in the struggle for freedom became an important strain of post-
independence India's relations with African still
struggling for independence. Thus, when the Mau Mau
revolt was launched in Kenya, India's ruling Congress
Party denounced the revolt, calling it "undesirable and
harmful" and injurious to the struggle for freedom.[5]
Without an understanding of the influence of the
Gandhian method on post-independence India it will be
difficult to understand why an apparently anti-colonial
government supported the British colonial administration during the revolt.

The Algerian independence struggle also shared
Gandhian orientation. While Nehru from the onset
expressed support for the freedom of Algeria, he kept
insisting on the need for Algerian aspiration to be
realised without bloodshed.[6] On the question of recognition for the Provisional Government of Algeria
(GPRA), the Indian Government hedged. As Nehru argued:

> The question of an immediate recog-
> nition of the provisional Govern-
> ment of Algeria has rather diffi-
> cult aspects. It involves the
> recognition of a government which
> might be called a government exist-
> ing outside the territory which it
> is supposed to govern. The real
> test in our minds has always been
> how we can help in this matter and
> not be merely making a gesture
> without being able to help. There-
> fore, at present, we are not giving
> formal recognition to the Govern-
> ment.[7]

The refusal to accord recognition to the CPRA was in
accord with the position of the imperalists (including
France) who argued that they were not sure which group

with which to negotiate the terms of colonial freedom.
In any event, an Indian recognition of the GPRA would
have been more than a mere gesture since it would have
further legitimized the GPRA's claim that it represented the Algerian people.

Just as Gandhi's ideological legacy had an impact
on Indian government's responses to African problems,
Nehru's perception of the role of post-colonial states
in the international arena has significantly shaped the
post-independence foreign policy stance of most African
states. Of prime importance in this regard has been
Nehru's impact on the creation of a non-aligned
movement.

An important aspect of Indian foreign policy as
maintained by Nehru in most of his speeches was the
need for world peace. As Kimche noted, such a message
was not unconnected with what Nehru considered Indian
national interests. He was worried about the possible
effects of a war on the Indian attempt to build an
economic base.[8] Based on the premise that alliances
were essential for a World War, Nehru sought to isolate
the states emerging from colonialism from the East-West
Cold War. This, from Nehru's standpoint, would not
only disengage these states from possible war, but
would prevent such a war. In addition, non-alignment
as a foreign policy was to ensure the assertion of the
newly-won sovereignty of these nations in the international arena.

It is beyond the scope of this chapter to include a
detailed study of non-alignment as it concerns African
nations.[9] Suffice it to note, however, that most, if
not all, African states claim to be non-aligned as far
as the two superpowers are concerned. And apart from
such stated commitment to non-alignment, the summits of
the non-aligned nations, as an Indian diplomat pointed
out to us, constitutes an avenue for Indian interaction
with African heads of states,[10] and hence an aid to an
appreciation of African problems, significant amongst
them the anti-apartheid struggle in South Africa.

The anti-apartheid struggle signifies an important
aspect of Indian interaction with the African continent. It is on record that India was the first nation
to bring, in 1964, the unacceptable South Africa regime
before the United Nations. But just as Gandhi was concerned with the treatment of Indians, the Government of
India was concerned only with discrimination against
Asians of Indian origin in South Africa.

It did not take long, however, for the Government
of India to realise that the problem of racial equality
and its attendant conflicts cannot be seen in the
limited perspective of Asians of Indian origin alone.
Thus, in an address to the Indian Parliament in 1952,
President Rajendra Prasad noted that "the question is
no longer merely one of Indians of Sough Africa; it has
already assumed a greater and wider significance.   It
is a question of racial domination and racial intole-
rance.   It is a question of the future of Africans more
than that of Indians in South Africa."[11]

As the African independence struggles became heat-
ed, and some of the nations became independent, Nehru,
as the Chief Indian spokesman made various speeches
supporting the African struggle for freedom, especially
in Namibia, South Africa and Portugal's African colonies.   In as much as these speeches can be seen as an
important diplomatic support which the nationalist
movements needed, it is significant to note that the
speeches were not accompanied by concrete acts, and so
in effect constituted no more than moral lectures to
the international community.   When it came to the
question of material support for the liberation
struggles, India was found wanting.   In fact, when
asked to join Africans in the fight against Portuguese
colonialism, Nehru was reported as saying that the
liberation of Mozambique and Angola were African
problems just as Goa's liberation was an exclusively
Indian problem.[12]   This Indian attitude toward Africa
was to change only after the Sino-Indian conflict of
1962.

Prior to 1962, India had assumed that she had a
strong ally in Africa.   So when India was engaged by
Chinese forces over their border conflict, India
expected that most of Africa would openly support her
and count the Chinese as the aggressors.   Such was not
the case.   While African responses to the war varied,
it became clear that India was not to receive the support she expected.

The Nigerian Government, known at this time for its
anti-communism, condemned what its Prime Minister, Sir
Abubakar Tafawa Balewa, saw as Chinese intransigence,
and called on all friends of India to speak out in
defence of that which was right and the endurance of
world peace.   The Nigerian press was generally vehement
in denouncing China.   Ethiopia, Zaire, and Libya, also
denounced China.   Ghana and Guinea, however, worked
openly against what India considered her interests dur-

241

ing the crisis. Kwame Nkrumah's reaction was to write the British Prime Minister, Harold Macmillan, expressing his dissatisfaction with the possibility of British support being given to India in her fight against China. Guinea for her own part supported China's claims. In East Africa, the response was ambivalent. Professor Varma read such non-committal ambivalence into the reactions of Kenya, Tanzania, Uganda, Zimbabwe and Zambia. Though the francophone African countries except the Ivory Coast and the Niger Republic recognised Taiwan, they all refrained from a forthright condemnation of the Peoples Republic of China but belatedly expressed sympathy for India.[13]

What reasons can one deduce for Africa's response to the Sino-Indian border dispute? Alaba Ogunsanwo wrote:

> Chinese propaganda did much to discourage support for India. The Africa states had little adequate information on the issue other than what came in through Western propaganda. Of what they had the Chinese interpretation was the most persuasive. For instance, when the Tanganyika Government called on the Chinese and Indian envoys to present information, the Chinese submitted well-documented evidence. Maps, photostatic copies of treaties, illustrations showing the territory, disputed, as well as the lines of actual control by both sides prior to September 1962. The Indians could produce nothing to compare with it. This led Tanganyika to refrain from supporting either side. It was the same in Kenya. In East Africa, presence of unpopular Indian communities in those countries meant a rank-and-file welcome for the humiliation of India irrespective of who was in the right.[14]

In the aftermath of the war, the Indian Government decided to counter Chinese diplomatic efforts in Africa. China not only had strong propaganda machinery, but as well supported the armed struggles of African liberation movements. In addition, as Varma noted,

China had signed a Sino-Ghana Friendship Treaty promising a £7 million interest free-loan to Ghana as well as economic and technical cooperation. So India's attempt at stifling Chinese diplomatic efforts required: a) increased material support for the liberation struggle in Southern African and b) increased economic cooperation. The latter was also to involve Asians settled in Africa. The involvement of these "African Asians" was logical given the local resentment to them in East Africa. So, if these "Ambassadors of India" could now be seen as assisting in rather than exploiting the economic development of the countries of their settlement, then some African goodwill might find its place in India.

An attempt to counter Chinese propaganda portraying India as having joined the imperialist camp required that India step up its support for the African liberation struggles. India has since channelled funds through the OAU Liberation Committee, to assist liberation movements across Africa. Such contributions reportedly passed the Rs. 5 million mark by 1977. In the same year, India was reported to have budgeted Rs. 31 million for assistance to African liberation movements.[15] India is a regular donor to a certain number of the multilateral aid programs established by the United Nations for the liberation of Southern Africa. In addition, during one of his frequent visits to Tanzania, an Indian Minister of External Affairs under the Janata Party Government, Vajpayee, was quoted as saying that India would "definitely consider" requests for arms by the liberation movements in Southern Africa.[16]

Aside from direct material assistance, the Government of India has accorded SWAPO official recognition as the sole representative of the Namibian people. Thus SWAPO and the ANC have been able to set up offices in New Delhi. The Indian support for SWAPO, for instance, was reiterated by the Indian Minister of External Affairs during a Lok Sabha debate on appropriations to his ministry. In response to a charge that the Government of India was not doing as much for Namibia as it did for Angola, P.V. Narashimo Rao stated:

> Sir, we have also given material
> assistance to Namibia; channelled
> through their sole representative
> SWAPO. Now, I would not like to go
> into figures as to so many dollars

and things like that; but I would
like to say that we have given substantial financial support for the
UN Fund for Namibia; UN Institute
for Namibia; Special Non-Aligned
Fund for Namibia; Gifts of medi-
cines and blankets; and Grants-in-
aid to the SWAPO mission in New
Delhi. On all these counts what we
have done for Namibia is, I submit,
substantial and if more is needed
we are prepared to do more.
Recently, the representative of
SWAPO came and met me. When I went
to Lusaka, there again their representative met me and I told them
clearly that there is no question
of our not doing what is needed for
Namibia. Let their representative
come and meet us here in Delhi for
their office, for the conduct of
their struggle and whatever is
needed India will do. I would
like to repeat that promise that
whatever is needed India will do.[17]

Apart from tangible assistance, India sustained its
propaganda attacks on South Africa at every opportunity. For example, during the 1978/79 Anti-Apartheid
year, India set up a National Committee for the Obser-
vance of Anti-Apartheid Year under the chairmanship of
Mr. Asoka Mehta, a veteran of the Indian Council for
Africa. Throughout the year, this committee organised
seminars, rallies, exhibitions, film shows and meetings, all geared towards bringing the realities of
apartheid to the Indian people.[18] Nelson Mandela was
conferred the 1979 Award for International Understanding.

Just as India began warming up to the liberation
movements in Southern Africa in the post-1962 era, it
also started expanding economic relations with the rest
of Africa. Though the improvement in Indian economic
interaction started as an attempt to counter Chinese
economic inroads into Africa, it has since gathered its
own momentum.

Anirundha Gupta[19] who has keenly followed India's
relations with Africa, suggests that India embarked on
a selective economic interaction with Africa after
1962. According to him, India decided to reward coun-

tries that stood by her during the Sino-Indian war. He notes that India pledged increased technical assistance to Ethiopia and Nigeria. In addition, Gupta notes increased Indian concentration on Kenya, which according to him was openly anti-Chinese, and had a free economy as well as a sizeable Indian community willing to assist India's economic objectives in Kenya.

While it may be true that India was initially involved with these three countries after the Sino-Indian border clash, it seems to me that the emphasis on reward for those who supported India was wrongly placed by Gupta. If reward were the main reason, why then did India not involve itself in the Congo (Zaire), which was just emerging out of its own turbulence? The converse needs to be asked with regards to Kenya. Though Gupta offers additional reasons for the Kenyan case, there is no evidence that Kenya was openly anti-Chinese. In fact, what Gupta overlooks with respect to Kenya is that, not long after the clash, China announced a £3 million grant to Kenya with the promise of another £15 million in an interest-free loan.[20] At the Afro-Asian Conference in June 1964, China also expressed her willingness to give more interest-free loans and other forms of economic aid to Afro-Asian countries.[21] In effect, India found herself involved in aid-giving to Africa as a result of her obsession with China's African policy. However, this is not to downplay the importance of other objectives indicated by Gupta, such as the desire to improve the image of Indian settlers in Africa as a way of contributing to the development of their countries of residence.

The Indian obsession with China continued through 1968 and alternately relaxed and tensed until the Sino-Indian exchange of Ambassadors in April 1976.[22] Even after this time, however, there was no need for India to relax her economic interaction with Africa. This is partly because, China aside, India needed the African market for the export of her capital goods and semi-processed manufactures. What then has been the pattern of interaction? While one may find some evidence of Indian multilateral economic interaction with Africa, among them her grant of Rs. 5 million made to the United Nations Trust Fund for African Development and her involvement with African Development Fund and the African Development Bank, most of her economic activities have been at the bilateral level. Such bilateral relations have been multifaceted, ranging from Indian efforts to improve trade relations (i.e. the export of Indian capital equipment to Africa through tied grants and loans,), to her making joint ventures and offering technical cooperation in the way of personnel exchanges, to her executing turn-key and consultancy projects.

Trade between the two continents has been negligible. For instance, as Tables 9.1 and 9.2 show, Africa accounts for a tiny fraction of India's economic interaction with the world. This fraction, however, assumes significance when it is realised that Indian exports to Africa are made in the form of capital goods which as Gupta noted "are otherwise difficult to export."[23]

Table 9.1

Indian Exports

	Percentage Distribution						
	1973	1974	1975	1976	1977	1978	1979
Industrial Countries	55.4	51.3	45.8	51.4	52.7	53.9	54.8
Oil Exporting Countries	5.6	12.3	17.2	14.7	14.4	13.6	13.6
Africa	2.6	3.7	4.0	3.4	3.8	4.1	3.9
Asia	12.4	8.6	9.0	9.0	8.8	8.4	8.9
Others	24.0	24.1	24.0	21.5	20.3	20.0	18.8

Source: Adpated from IMF Direction of Trade Yearbook, 1980. Nigeria, Libya and Algeria are included in the oil exporting countries.

Table 9.2

Indian Imports

	Percentage Distribution						
	1973	1974	1975	1976	1977	1978	1979
Industrial Countries	63.8	49.2	61.0	60.6	53.4	54.4	51.4
Oil Export-ing Countries	12.8	25.7	20.4	22.8	21.0	17.8	23.4
Africa	5.5	3.5	1.9	3.7	4.5	4.7	4.7
Asia	3.2	1.9	2.2	2.8	5.9	8.4	7.0
Others	14.7	10.7	14.5	10.1	15.2	14.7	13.5

Source: Adpated from IMF Direction of Trade Yearbook, 1980. Nigeria, Libya and Algeria are included in the oil exporting countries.

Insuring this minimal trade interaction, India has had to provide credit facilities and, at times, grants tied to the purchase of Indian goods and expertise. This is due mainly to the poor economies of many African countries, and the need for India to compete with the West, which grants similar aid.[24] In effect, while India has always announced these credit facilities "as a gesture of goodwill," the double-edged nature of the grants must be borne in mind. While it is true Africa is receiving credit in a world where credit availability is getting tighter, India, which in the early years of her independence opposed tied aid, also benefits from the creation of an African market for her capital products.

Apart from offering credit facilities and other forms of aid to African countries, the Government of India has itself made direct foreign investments in Africa through some of her public corporations. As J.C. Srivastava points out in a contribution to a supplement on "India and Africa" in New Africa magazine,

247

these joint ventures cover a wide number of technical projects that include "paper and pulp, machine tools, razor blades, light engineering, tractor assembly, steel re-rolling, textiles--wool, synthetics and cotton, ready-made garments, jute products and sugar." These projects, confined mainly to Kenya, Nigeria and Mauritius (as evident in Table 9.3), are at various stages of implementation.

Indian equity in these ventures, some of which are private and some public, had until recently been tied to the share of Indian capital.[25] These too, had represented less than majority interest in the ventures. However, it is important to note that the joint ventures constitute a viable avenue for the export of Indian capital, and provide a source of foreign exchange from returns on investment. In effect, apart from the fact that the Indian Government and private Indian corporations have tended to hold less than majority interests, Indian involvement in joint ventures in Africa is no different from other foreign direct investment on the continent.

The joint venture arrangement is qualitatively different from technical assistance or cooperation which India could and does render for specified fees. Under technical assistance and consultancy arrangements, India has executed a number of turn-key and consultancy projects in Africa. These have included the construction of a railway line in Zambia, the setting up of textiles and sugar mills in Tanzania, the provision of consultancy services for the Nigerian Steel Industry, and the famous three year management of Nigerian Railways by Rail India Technical and Economic Services Ltd (RITES). These arrangements do not grant power of control over the ventures and thereby allow the African states (as was the case in the Nigeria Railways-RITES project), to decide the future of contrasts.

The struggle for, and achievement of, Indian independence has indirectly affected the nationalist struggles and eventual independence of Africa. Even in the post-independence period, India under Nehru's leadership made a lasting impact on the foreign policy stance of many African states.

India has also been a fervent supporter of the only issue which unites all of Black Africa: the liberation of Southern Africa. While such Indian support initially only took the form of condemnations made of aparth-

Table 9.3

<u>Indian Joint Ventures in Africa</u>

	In Operation			Under Implementation		
	No. of JVs.	Indian Equity (Rs. '000)	Percent of Total	No. of JVs.	Approved Indian Equity (Rs.'000)	Per-cent of total
1. Kenya	10	121,636	26.2	2	6,018	0.8
2. Nigeria	6	26,181	5.6	12	132,705	18.5
3. Mauri-tius	5	4,509	0.9	1	1,340	0.2
4. Uganda	1	2,807	0.6	-	-	-
5. Liberia	-	-	-	1	6,800	0.9
6. Seychelles	-	-	-	1	13,450	1.9
7. Tanzania	-	-	-	1	267	0.1
8. Bots-wana	1	500	0.1	-	-	-
9. Zambia	-	-	-	1	3,000	0.4
10. Senegal	-	-	-	1	169,000	23.4
11. Sudan	-	-	-	1	36,000	5.0
12. Others	-	-	-	3	-	-
Africa Total	23	155,633	33.4	24	369,180	51.4

Source: <u>New Africa</u>, No. 185, February 1983, p. 67.

eid at the UN and at other international fora, it has
for about twenty years now provided much material and
diplomatic assistance to the liberation efforts of
Africans. This material support, however, first arose
out of India's attempt to counter Chinese propaganda
which was depicting India as consolidating with the
imperialists.

In an effort to also counter what she saw as a
Chinese attempt to isolate her in Africa India, in the
aftermath of the 1962 conflict with China, began
expanding her economic interactions with Africa. She
has since granted tied aid to a number of African
countries, been involved in joint ventures with some
African states, and been responsible for turn-key and
consultancy projects in a number of African countries.

India's African policy from our analysis can be
seen as largely an attempt to counter the influence of
other powers in Africa. First was India's moral and
diplomatic support for the anti-colonial struggles of
African states. And in the post-independence period,
India's role in the establishment of the non-aligned
movement can be seen as an attempt to prevent either of
the two super-powers from carving out blocs of support
in Africa. However, the issue of whether India wanted
to lead this bloc is not explored in this study. Suffice it to note that India was also obsessed by what it
saw as a Chinese attempt to isolate her in Africa.
This Sino-Indian rivalry continued and melted into a
period in which India found itself competing with western industrial powers for the African market.

While the attempt at improved economic relations
with Africa so far may be commendable as an example of
"South-South" cooperation, the measures adopted have so
far been similar to those that the "South" has condemned the "North" for. Examples are tied aids which can
prevent the recipient from looking for the most efficient means of executing its desires, and equity shares
in so-called joint ventures, which allows some political power for India just as it would for an American
MNC. If Indo-African relations are to find a genuine
footing and not exist in a state of gradual
substitution of one master for the other, there will be
a need for creativity on both sides.

Notes

1. See Robert G. Gregory, India and East Africa: a history of race relations within the British Empire 1890-1939, (Oxford: Clarendon Press, 1971), 9.

2. Paul F. Power, "Gandhi in South Africa", Journal of Modern African Studies, Vol. 7, No. 2, (1969), 442.

3. See ibid. Power pointed out that Gandhi, though sympathetic to the lot of Africans, refused to see the struggle of Indians and Africans as one.

4. Kwame Nkrumah, Ghana: the autobiography of Kwame Nkrumah, (New York: Nelson, 1957), xiv.

5. Anirudha Gupta, "India and Africa South of the Sahara", in Bimal Prasad (ed.), India's Foreign Policy: studies in continuity and change, (New Delhi: Vikas, 1979), 267.

6. See Jawaharlal Nehru, India's Foreign Policy: selected speeches, September 1946-April 1961, (Delhi: Government of India Publications Division, 1961), 506-509. It seems, however, that Africans and Indians have since recognized that Gandhi's non-violence cannot be religiously upheld. Suspensions of his method have occurred in India's storming of Goa and her subsequent support for the armed struggle in Southern Africa. India's storming of Goa might also have encouraged movements that eventually liberated Portugal's African colonies.

7. Ibid., 509.

8. David Kimche, The Afro-Asian Movement: ideology and foreign policy of the Third World, (Jerusalem: Israel Universities Press, 1973), 314-325.

9. For a detailed discussion on Africa and Non-Alignment, see Bala Mohammed, Africa and Non-Alignment: a study in the foreign relations of new nations, (Kano: Triumph Publishing, 1982).

10. Author's interview with an Indian Diplomat at the Indian High Commission in Lagos. See also Gupta's account of Indira Gandhi's interactions with African Heads of States at the Lusaka and Algerian Non-Aligned Summits in Gupta, op cit.

11. As quoted in ibid., 264-265.

12. Lok Sabha Debates, Part II, Vol. I, No. 3, 16 May 1952.

13. See S.N. Varma, "India and Africa", International Studies, Vol. 5, Nos. 12, July-October 1963, 188-197.

14. Alaba Ogunsanwo, China's Policy in Africa (London: Cambridge University Press, 1974), 110.

15. See Shanti Sadiu Ali, "India's Support to African Liberation Movements", in R.R. Ramchandani (ed), India and Africa, (New Delhi: Radiant Publishers, 1980), 64.

16. Ibid.

17. See Government of India, MEA - 99/XP (Press)5/82, 7.

18. See Vanita Ray, "India--Africa Relations". Africa Quarterly, Vol. 18, Nos. 2 & 3, January 1979, 75.

19. See Gupta, op.cit., and Anirudha Gupta, "A Note on Indian Attitudes to Africa", African Affairs, Vol. 68, No. 275, April 1970.

20. K.B. Rai, "India's Stake in Africa", Africa Quarterly, Vol. 4, No. 3, October - December 1964, 156.

21. Ibid.

22. For more details, see Gargi Dutt, "India and China", in Prasad (ed), op.cit., 223-233.

23. Gupta, "India and Africa", 271.

24. Such credit has been extended to as diverse African countries as Kenya, Mozambique, Uganda, Seychelles, Mauritius, Ghana, Tanzania, and Zimbabwe. For the amounts and the various countries involved, see <u>Africa Research Bulletin</u>.

25. In 1978, the Indian government as part of a liberalising trend relaxed the rules to allow cash remittances to purchase equities overseas. However, I do not have data on the nature of Indian equities in joint ventures in Africa since 1978.

Chapter Ten

Some Possible Futures of Great Power Intervention in Africa

Amadu Sesay

> Many African governments are too
> politically, militarilly and econo-
> mically weak to defend themselves
> and their borders...many African
> governments lack legitimacy...they
> are guilty of political corruption,
> administrative incompetence, and
> economic mismanagement. Arising
> from this is the steady alienation
> of the ruling African elites from
> the generality of their peoples.
> In these circumstances, what you
> have is a power vacuum. Just as
> nature abhors a vacuum, so does the
> International System. As long as
> African leaders create a power
> vacuum, it follows logically that
> such a vacuum has to be filled...
> such is the nature of the state
> system. If it is either the West
> or the East that first moves, the
> other side will tempted to move to
> ensure proper balance of forces.[1]

Intervention is an important issue in contemporary
international relations. Since the end of the Second
World War, states have increasingly interfered in one
another's internal affairs so as to protect and promote
their national interests. A number of salient factors
are responsible for this phenomenon. First is the unprecedented increase in the number of state actors in
the international system. Second is the existence of
two super powers--the USA and the USSR--which both hold
vested international interests and unprecedented economic and military capabilities. As such, whether they
like it or not, some states are bound to be affected by
superpower activities in the world system. Closely
linked with the above factors is the emergence of two
rival global ideologies--liberal democracy championed
by the USA; and socialism/communism, whose major pro-
pagator is the Soviet Union. A third factor is the
unprecedented advancement in weapons of war, with the

emergence of nuclear weapons having made the prospect
of war between the major powers of the world unthinkable. Consequently, these powers have been compelled
to look for other ways to promote their interests in
various parts of the world. In addition, of course,
states do not always share the same interests, a fact
which has on many occasions led to conflict and collaboration among states in the international system, each
trying to use whatever means it deems fit and appropriate at any time to promote its own interests
vis-a-vis those of others.

Africa has been particularly vulnerable to great
power[2] intervention. Not only is it the least developed of all the continents, but it is also the weakest in
terms of political influence, and economic and military
capability. Thus, great powers have found Africa an
easier region than most to penetrate. The major objective of this chapter is to extrapolate on the future of
great power intervention in Africa based on past and
present incidents of such intervention.

i)   Definition of Terminology

The term intervention is popular among students of
international relations. It is not a term, however,
that is easily amenable to clear-cut definition. It
is, in fact, according to Richard Little, "associated
with a lot of contradictions." Little also contends
that once these contradictions have been "taken into
account, it is apparent that the word itself denotes
very little. Like many important terms used frequently, we find on closer inspection that it possesses no
acceptable meaning....Thus, a definition of "intervention wide enough to take in all the meanings attached
to the word will be masked by imprecision."[3] Not surprisingly, Little did not offer any straight-forward
definition of what constitutes intervention, offering
instead, three of its types: i) intervention at the
international systemic level; ii) intervention at the
domestic level; and iii) intervention at the individual (person to person) level. (We shall be concerned
here only with the first type). Little argues that
intervention occurs when state A gives economic or
military assistance to state B, or when state C inter-
venes militarily in state D. Using this case definition it becomes possible to build a typology of intervention covering various aspects of inter-state relationships in the global system.

Unlike Little, other scholars have defined intervention using its synonym, interference. According to R.J. Vincent, intervention is any "activity undertaken by a state...which interferes coercively in the domestic affairs of another."[4] However, not every instance of intervention or interference by one state in the domestic affairs of another is of a coercive nature. Thus, the massive injection of economic and financial aid by one country into another, either to prop a tottering leader or transport a new regime to power, may not be called coercive, yet it constitutes an act of intervention/interference. Again, the investment of huge sums of money in the economy of state A by state B or its nationals involves no coercion at all. Indeed, the only form of intervention obeying Vincent's definition is military intervention. This can be direct or indirect--i.e. when the soldiers of country A engage in combat in country B to assist that state, repel an invasion, or suppress a rebellion by its citizens. The French and Belgian paratroop drop in Kolwezi in 1978, made to help Mobutu crush an attempt made by Katangan exiles to take control of the Shaba Province, involved direct military intervention. Indirect military intervention occurred, by way of example, in the 1961 CIA-sponsored Bay of Pigs invasion of Cuba.

For the purpose of this chapter I shall define intervention to mean the interference or involvement of one state in the domestic affairs of another. Such involvement may be direct or indirect and may also be either coercive or non-coercive. It may be political, economic, humanitarian or military in nature. In other words, my definition of intervention includes the whole spectrum of inter-state activity. Thus such activities as "progaganda, espionage, discriminatory economic policies, assistance of legitimate governments, aid to subversive movements and support or denial of it to governments or opposition parties in domestic crises especially where such foreign support might have proved decisive,"[5] are regarded as intervention by this writer. With such a broad definition of what constitutes intervention, I can say that great power intervention in Africa refers to the interference--in various forms--by such powers in the domestic affairs of African states individually and collectively.

ii) Great Power Intervention in Africa: a historical perspective

While the focus of this chapter is on the future of great power intervention in Africa, a proper analysis nevertheless entails an examination of interventionist activities in the continent in both the past and present.

Great power interference in the domestic affairs of Africa is not new. We can trace it back several hundred years to such historical landmarks as the slave trade and the scramble for, and eventual partitioning of Africa which gave way to the colonial period. However, for the purpose of this chapter and analytical convenience I shall limit myself to the post-interdependence era--the period roughly from 1960 up to the present time (1983). One reason for the present restriction is that although Africans have reacted to various forms of foreign intervention in the past, they did so in their individual capacities and not as representatives of sovereign independent states--as independent actors in the international system.

Great power intervention in Africa in the post-independence era can be traced to two broad but inter-related factors: i) the domestic circumstances of African states; and ii) the international environment. The latter refers to the domestic circumstances of the intervenors; for example, the state of their economies, their ideologies and their various constitutional provisions.

iii) The Domestic Circumstances of African States

Many reasons have been suggested for Africa's vulnerability to great power interference. According to William Zartman, "foreign intervention occurs because African governments individually or collectively, for their own interests, are ready to engage external support , when these local interests happen to suit a particular foreign interest."[6] According to this argument, intervention is first made possible through collaboration between African and foreign leaders, sometimes for purely personal interests. Thus, if an African leader perceives his regime or personal safety to be at risk, he may engage the support of an external power to guarantee his safety and that of his regime. Whatever the reasons may be, foreign intervention is made much easier when Africans are willing to align their interest with those of the foreign power.

In his own analysis of the causes of great power intervention in Africa, Olajide Aluko has signaled among other things: the political, military and economic weaknesses of independent African states. Another consideration is the frequency African leaders systematically exploit their citizens for their own benefit. In addition, some regimes we administratively incompetent and are guilty of economic mismanagement.[7]

A factor contributing to the occurrance of great power intervention in Africa is the rapid turnover of leadership in various African countries.[8] This phenomenon leads not only to political instability but also creates power vacuums which invite foreign intervention. Another factor responsible for intervention is the existence of intra-African disputes. Many such disputes are the results of arbitrary colonial boundaries left by the great powers in the wake of independence in the 1960s. Despite an agreement by the successor regimes at independence not to revise their[9] borders in order to promote African unity and security, some states have nonetheless tried to modify their national boundaries. The most notable examples are the several attempts made by Somalia under different regimes to alter its boundaries with Kenya and Ethiopia. The attempt by Somalia's Siad Barre to change the Somalia-Ethiopia boundary in his country's favour in 1978 led to full-scale war between the two countries. In the process, both states received massive supplies of arms and ammunition from the Soviet Union.[10]

Yet another factor making for great power intervention in the continent is the presence of minority racist and colonial regimes. In the past, this presence has led to bitter wars of liberation, most notably in Southern Africa. In Angola, Mozambique and Zimbabwe, African nationalists fought against racist and colonial regimes with help from the socialist states: the Soviet Union and its allies as well as China. On the other hand, the colonial governments received support from their western allies and friends. At the moment, the wars in Namibia and to a lesser extent South Africa have attracted similar great power involvement in the continent. Finally, the unkind climatic conditions found in some parts of Africa-coupled with the continent's technological backwardness, have led to droughts, famine and starvation for millions of Africans. In the past, as is true today, such natural disasters have attracted massive financial, material and logistical intervention from the great powers.

iv) External Environment

It was said earlier that the nature of the international system has been responsible, to a large extent, for the occurance of foreign intervention in Africa. What I will consider, very briefly, is the domestic circumstances of some of the great powers--the intervenors--as they relate to their involvement in the continent. First, is the identification of the great powers with either of the dominant ideologies in the world system. Thus, great powers sometimes intervene in Africa either because they believe that their African ideological allies are in trouble or because they believe that a particular African regime does not conform with their own interests. In such circumstances, great powers may intervene to reverse the situation in their favour. Second, constitutional provisions of some great powers are such that it is not always easy for them to control the activities of either their nationals or MNCs based in their territories. Thus for a long time, Britain, Canada, and the US and other western great powers could not stop the recruitment of their citizens as mercenaries to fight against African freedom fighters in Zimbabwe and Angola. And one major reason why the western great powers have continued to assist racist South Africa is the presence of their MNCs in that country. Finally, on many occasions in the past, great powers have been 'forced' to intervene in Africa to protect their nationals or the interests of their MNCs. This was the situation in the Congo (now Zaire) in the early 1960s, and during the two Shaba crises of 1977 and 1978.

v) Typology of Great Power Intervention in Africa

From the above discussion I can identify several types of intervention. First, we have what we can call political/military intervention, usually occurring at the behest of either an African government in power or its opponents. Great powers intervene in such cases either to install/prop a friendly African government or leader in power, or to overthrow an 'unfriendly' government or leader at the request of local dissidents. This is one of the most popular forms of intervention in Africa. The great powers have supported and/or induced changes of government mainly by coups d'etat, either to unseat leaders perceived as hostile, or to install in power those perceived as pliant. In 1965, the CIA and the US government supported the over- throw of Nkrumah because of his socialist and pro- Eastern leanings. Similarly, the socialist regime of Milton Obote in Uganda was toppled by an externally engineered coup d'etat. But perhaps the most clear-cut cases of such interventions involve France and some of its former African colonies. A notable case was that of the Central African Republic under Emperor Bokassa. In 1979, under the operation code name "Barracuda," the French secret service--Service de Documentation Exterieure et de Contre Espionnage (SEDECE)--engineered the coup that toppled Bokassa, who had become an embarassment to President Giscard D'Estang.[11]   Bokassa was then replaced by the pliant David Dacko. In addi- tion, France for many years has stationed troops in Chad, Gabon, Senegal, Ivory Coast and Madagascar, to protect friendly regimes in those states. Finally, in 1975,   Savimbi and Holden Roberto invited some of the Western great powers--the UK, France and the US--to intervene on their behalf in Angola. Savimbi and Roberto enlisted this aid to combat the Popular Move- ment for the Liberation of Angola (MPLA), led by Augustinho Neto.

My second category of great power intervention may be called humanitarian intervention. Such involvement is normally a consequence of natural disasters such as drought, famine, and a conflict-induced refugee crisis. Humanitarian intervention became a prominent feature of great power policies towards Africa in the 1970s fol- lowing the Sahelian drought.[12]   Since the overthrow of Uganda's Idi Amin in 1979 by Ugandan exiles in Tanzania backed by regular Tanzanian forces, very serious cases of famine and starvation have risen along the Uganda- Sudan border. Starving refugees have spilled into neighbouring states, particularly into Sudan, and have aggravated the living conditions of local populations. The involvement of the great powers in relief program- mes has included the provision of food, and logistical support to distribute supplies. For instance in 1980, the EEC flew 38 tons of food daily to Soroti in Eastern Uganda.[13]   In June of the same year, Sudan organised an international conference to raise food and/or funds for its growing refugee population. Again, most of the donors were great powers, mainly Western: $4.2 million was received from EEC, 60 million Lira and 4,000 tonnes of wheat from Italy; £850,000 from Britain; while the US donated $100m in 1980 and the same amount in 1981.

261

Yet another type of intervention is the involving the nationals of great powers in their capacities as private citizens. This type is mainly indirect including, for example, the activities of mercenaries in the continent. Mercenaries may come to Africe for several reasons: adventure, high salary, or the feeling that they are fighting for a cause which serves their nation's interests. Examples of mercenary involvement in the domestic affairs of African countries abound: Congo (Zaire), Biafra, Angola, Benin and most recently, in Seychelles (1981). So far, all instances of mercenary intervention have involved the citizens of the Western great powers.[15]

The fourth type, economic intervention, goes back several hundred years and predated the slave trade and the colonial era. However, it was during the colonial period that it became institutionalised. Colonial economies were tied to those of the metropoles; and even after independence was achieved by African territories, vertical economic relations with the former colonial powers were continued. The citizens and companies of the colonial powers were also encouraged to invest in the colonies, with the result that, at independence, the economies of the African states remained in foreign hands: those of Britain, France, the United States, Germany and others; again, almost exclusively, Western powers.

Contemporary African economies have remained largely monocultural: they export raw products to the great powers in return for manufactured goods. With the ever-increasing prices being demanded for such products, African states have found themselves in almost perpetual financial hot water, often unable to pay for their imports. This has in many cases led to other forms of intervention, including the various rescue operations mounted by the International Monetary Fund and the World Bank. A recent important case involves Nigeria, which is to receive $2 billion from the IMF to pay off its debts.[16] It needs to be pointed out here that the Soviet bloc states and China are not yet members of these international financial institutions, which are dominated exclusively by western powers: the US, Japan, UK, France, Canada, Germany etc.

A fifth type of intervention can be either direct and indirect depending on the circumstances. It normally involves the activities of the secret services of the great powers from both the East and West, the KGB and the CIA. We have already illustrated the use to

262

which France has put its own secret service in the past
in its former African territories, and the CIA's role[17]
in Angola during the civil war there is well-known.
Suffice it to say that intervention using secret
agents/services is undertaken in most cases to protect
great power interests in Africa. Such protection may
involve ensuring that friendly African leaders remain
in power or that unfavoured regimes are ousted.

My sixth type of great power intervention results
from the presence of racist minority and colonial
regimes in Africa. As noted earlier, such interventions have taken place in Angola, Mozambique and
Zimbabwe. They are currently taking place in Namibia
and South Africa, with both superpowers involved.

Finally, great powers have intervened in Africa by
proxy using troops either from extra-African friends or
these of African allies. Two major instances of this
were: a) the Russian-sponsored Cuban intervention in
Angola (1975-1976), where Russia supplied logistics,
arms and ammunition as well as advisers, while Cuba
provided the troops that fought side by side with the
MPLA; and b) the use by France and the United States
of Moroccan troops and Egyptian pilots in Zaire, during
the first Shaba crisis of 1977, to shore-up the tottering Mobutu regime.[18]

vi) African Response to External Intervention:
past and present

African response to external intervention may be
classified as occurring: a) at the individual state
level and b) at the continental level through the
umbrella of the Organisation of African Unity (OAU).
For the purpose of analytical convenience, I shall
examine African responses to only three types of intervention: political/military, economic and humanitarian.
Africa's responses to interference in its affairs
have not been unanimous. This applies both to individual reactions and those made "collectively" by the
OAU. In both cases, reactions are influenced by several factors, among them, the identity of the interven-
or; the identity of the victim or target; the outcome
of intervention; and, finally, the motive for intervention. African responses are often reflected by the
ideological map of the continent as well as that of the
world system at large. A few examples will suffice.
In June 1978, in the wake of the second Shaba conflict,

President Senghor of Senegal said he was "disappointed in the West which had behaved illegally by letting the Soviet backed Cubans establish a foothold in Angola," "The Cubans," he said, 'would soon' be followed by East Germans." President Senghor warned that if it was true that the US did not intervene in Angola because it did not want its children to die in Africa, "in that case, in a few years' time, American boys will die in Germany and France and it will be too late." Senghor concluded the interview with a warning to the West that "the forces of communism are intent on waging an ideological struggle in Africa."[19]

In another interview, a prominent African had a contrary opinion. Mr. Leslie Harriman, then Nigerian permanent representative to the UN, said that the "Cubans have never attacked any sovereign state or crossed forcibly internationally recognised boundaries. On the contrary, what they have done is to assist oppressed people to gain their self-determination from colonial master."[20]

Again, in spite of his strong support for the free-dom fighters, President Kaunda of Zambia was willing to prevent a Soviet backed victory by the MPLA in Luanda. In the same vein, it was President Nyerere's ideological sympathy coupled with his strong support for libe-ration struggles in Africa that explained his strong support for the MPLA government. Finally, the emergen-cy session of the OAU called in February 1976 to settle the Angolan civil war broke up in disarray along ideo-logical lines. No agreement could be reached as to which of the liberation movements should be recognised. This was irrespective of the fact that two other move-ments, the FNLA and UNITA, were fighting side by side with South Africa, the continent's foremost enemy.

The OAU's Charter makes clear the Organisation's concern about external intervention in the continent. No doubt, one of the reasons for this concern had been the experience of African leaders in the Congo (Zaire). Article 11 clearly states that one of the purposes of the Organisation is to enable its members to "defend their sovereignty, their territorial integrity and independence." As well, African states have from time to time collectively taken positions on external inter-vention. At their second annual summit meeting in Accra in October 1965, they pledged among other things a) "not to tolerate the use of their territories for any subversive activity directed from outside Africa against any member state of the Organisation of African

264

Unity," b) "to oppose collectively and firmly by
every means at the disposal of Africa, every form of
subversion conceived, organised or financed by foreign
powers against Africa, the OAU or against members individually; c) to resort to bilateral or multilateral
consultation for the purpose of settling all differences between two or more member states of the Organisation of African Unity," and, finally, d) "not to give
any cause for dissension within or among member states
by fomenting or aggravating racial or religious,
linguistic, ethnic or other differences and to combat
all forms of activity of this kind." [21]

The Accra Declaration was in fact an admission by
African leaders that some of the root causes of intervention in their affairs by foreign powers were domestic. Given that the continent is a patch-work of
territory held loosely together by diverse racial,
ethnic, religious and linguistic groups, its edifice is
fragile and requires that pre-emptive measures be taken
for its protection. Thus, the Declaration was an
attempt to put a seal on all future developments within
the continent which might tempt the great powers to
intervene in its affairs. Significantly, however, the
Accra Declaration did not prevent externally sponsored
intervention in Africa. This was hardly surprising,
since other causes of intervention lay beyond the control of African states. Thus in 1967, mercenaries were
actively involved in Africa, fighting on both the
Federal and Biafran sides in the Nigerian civil war.
Perhaps the most daring case of external intervention
was the abortive Portugese-led invasion of Guinea,
Conakry, in November 1970. Not surprisingly, the mood
among African leaders was belligerent when they met in
Addis Ababa for their eighth annual summit. With specific reference to the activities of mercenaries, the
Heads of States reaffirmed a) "the determination of
African peoples and states to take all necessary
measures to eradicate from the African continent the
scourge that the mercenary system represents," b)
they reiterated the "irrevocable condemnation of the
use of mercenaries by certain countries and forces to
further jeopardise the independence, sovereignty and
territorial integrity of member states of the OAU;" and
c) "expressed total solidarity with states which have
been victims of the activities of mercenaries." [22]

What was becoming apparent by this time was that
Africa's collective interest in, and condemnation of,
foreign military intervention on the continent, was a
function of external intervention itself. Thus, during

the lull in the military activities of the great powers
in Africa in the period 1971-1974, Africa remained silent on the issue. However, 1975 saw the beginning of
the Angolan civil war and foreign mercenary intervention in that country. This was followed in 1977 by
another great power sponsored mercenary attempt to
overthrow the regime of the radical Benin President,
Musa Kerekou. In the same year, we had the first
Shaba crisis, to be followed almost twelve months later
by a second crisis in 1978. Indeed, by May that year,
direct and indirect great power military presence was
evident in the following countries: Angola, Ethiopia,
Guinea Bissau, Uganda, Chad, Mauritania, Gabon, Central
African Empire and, of course, Zaire.[23] The situation
was so serious that some people were talking about a
second Berlin Conference to redivide Africa.[24] More
important, perhaps, was the European proposal, led by
France, to set up a Pan-African peace force which could
be used to resolve intra- and inter-African disputes in
the future. Had that idea materialised, external
intervention in the affairs of the continent would have
become institutionalized.

When the OAU met in Khartoum in July 1978, attention was once again focused on the issue of great power
intervention in Africa. The OAU position on intervention at this time was rather contradictory. To be
sure, a resolution was passed condemning externally
sponsored intervention on the continent, but also recognising the right of every African state to seek
external assistance if it perceives that its interests
are threatened either by domestic or external forces.

The failure of the OAU to offer a blanket condemnation of external subversion in Africa was understandable
in 1978. Many of its members--especially the Francophone countries--had on several occasions been rescued
by France from being overthrown. As well, many African
leaders were not unaware that their standing armies
were at times unreliable and highly vulnerable to
external pressure. Furthermore, African Heads of State
were cognisant of the inability of the OAU to raise and
maintain a standing army to be used in emergencies. In
matters of internal and border conflicts, each state
was expected to be its own keeper. Finally, just
before the summit convened, over twenty African
states--mainly Francophone--had assembled in Paris to
hold a meeting with Giscard D'Estang on the Pan-African
defence force. All supported the idea of a Pan-African
Force for the continent. Although the OAU rejected the
call for a Pan-African peace force at the Khartoum

summit on the grounds that the continent's defence
needs should be catered for endogenously, it was obvious nonetheless that the issue had polarised the continent into two ideological factions.

By and large, the progressives, led by Julius
Nyerere of Tanzania, bitterly attacked the idea.
Nyerere warned other African leaders that "there should
be no mistake about the motives behind the whole idea
of a Pan-African force. Whatever the official
aganda...the Paris and Brussels meetings are discussing
the freedom of Africa. They are discussing the continued domination of Africa, and the continued use of
Africa, by Western powers. They are intended to be,
taken together, a second Berlin Conference." However
"until the OAU has made such a decision, there can be
no Pan-African security force which will uphold the
freedom of Africa..."[25]

In contrast to President Nyerere's outright rejection of the Western idea of a Pan-African Force, President Houphouet Boigny, whose country was represented at
the Paris talks, said the African countries that attended the meeting had "no complexes about it, since the
European members of NATO call on the US in case of
attack, and the Eastern European nations call on
Russia."[26] The Ivorian President's statement seemed to
have endorsed the division of Africa into ideological
blocs by the great powers. And as far as the moderate
leaders were concerned, they belonged to the Western
block and they liked it that way.

vii) Africa's Responses to Great Power Economic Intervention

Although African nationalists protested before
independence what they considered to be economic
exploitation by the colonial powers, most post-
independence African states have retained economic ties
left behind by departing European masters. In many
African states, the successor elites merely continued
the capitalist, free market economies which they inherited at the flush of independence, and often sought to
encourage foreign public and private investments in
their economies. In fact, for many years after political freedom had been gained by Africa, the only realistic approach to economic development was believed to be
continued reliance on external sources for investment,
loans, grants and aid.

The results of this policy have been important and resilient. First, African states discovered that although they had acquired the political kingdom, they remained economically dependent on their former masters. Besides, African economies were dominated by foreign multinational corporations (MNCs). A second result was that the continent's economy remained largely underdeveloped. Only a few African states, most notably Guinea and Tanzania, made any serious attempts to break away from dependence on their former colonial masters. However, as the Guinean example demonstrates, two decades after independence, even such a brave attempt was unsuccessful at laying the foundation for a more self-reliant country.

A number of crucial factors help to explain the slow response of African states to foreign economic domination and exploitation. First is what we may call the colonial inheritance factor. This refers to the provisions of independence constitutions given to the African states by the colonial masters. These guaranteed the activities of MNCs as well as the free enterprise economic system. In many of the independence constitutions, the successor regimes were made to renounce nationalisation as a policy. A second factor was the rather urgent desire of the new states to industrialise, which resulted in their trying to attract foreign investment to their territories as a means of promoting economic advancement. Indeed, for many years, massive injections of resources into the developing states by the developed North was seen to be the surest way to achieve economic growth in the poorer countries. Closely related to this was the over dependence by African states on MNCs for foreign exchange and economic activity. Thus, Mobutu discovered, to his chagrin, that his country was too dependent on Union Miniere to effect any meaningful control of its activities through nationalisation.[27]

Another factor is the collusion between ruling elites and MNCs in some African countries. As managers and board members of these enterprises, it was inexpedient for African governments to pass legislation which would adversely affect their profit margins. Finally, many African states were constrained by lack of finance to pay for the nationalised companies. In Sierra Leone, for instance, nationalisation of the Development Corporation, the subsidiary of Bethlehem Steel which was mining iron ore in the country, had to be cancelled in 1971 due to lack of funds. Nationalisations of foreign economic assets did not start in many African countries until many years after independence, and even then were not comprehensive.[28] In many cases, they were limited to the acquisition of majority shares by the African countries in the foreign enterprises; shares ranging from 51 to 60 percent. In 1971, for instance, the government of Sierra Leone acquired 51 percent share holdings in the assets of the diamond mining company, Sierra Leone Selection Trust (SLST), a subsidiary of De Beers Consolidated of South Africa. Nonetheless, it was obvious to most African countries in the 1970s that they should exercise much more control over their national economies and natural resources.

Many reasons were responsible for this change of strategy. First, by the mid-1970s it was obvious that western models of growth, which the majority of African leaders subscribed to for their countries' economic take-off, were failures in Africa. Second, the worsening world economic situation, which had been precipitated by the unprecedented rises in the price of crude oil following the Arab-Israeli war of 1973, left African countries amongst the hardest hit. Between 1974 and 1975, the UN was forced to make emergency arrangements[29] to ease the economic burden on the continent. Third, in 1974, the UN General Assembly passed Resolution 3281 (XXIX) which, among other things, announced that "each state shall freely exercise full permanent sovereignty, including possession, use and disposal, over all its wealth, natural resources and economic activities." The document also sanctioned the right of states to "nationalise, expropriate or transfer ownership of foreign property."

The more prosperous African states responded to the economic crisis by taking control of foreign enterprises. For instance, in 1977, Nigeria passed the Nigerian Enterprises Promotion Decree, reserving for Nigerians enterprises in 40 sectors ranging from garment-making to small-scale retail. The same Decree made it mandatory for bigger foreign companies to sell 60 percent of their shares to Nigerians. Foreign enterprises described by the Decree as complex in character were instructed to sell 40 percent of their shares to Nigerians. In all 59 enterprises were affected by the 60 percent order while only 39 were affected by the 40 percent rule.[30] For the majority of African states, however, it was "business as usual."

The attempts made by African states to control the activities of foreign economic interests on their ter-

ritories, either through nationalisation or indigenisation policies (as was the case in Nigeria), were not
very successful. In many African countries, nationals
acted as 'fronts' for foreign enterprises, negating the
spirit of the nationalisation or indigenisation. As
well, "host governments could not exercise effective
control over the joint ventures...because majority
equity control is not matched by increased indigenous
representation at the board or top-management
levels."[31] The net result was that the minority
partners finally wielded a more powerful veto than the
senior partners--the African governments. In that
respect, the economic hand of the clock remained in
more or less the same position as it was earlier in
many African countries.

     In addition to their individual responses, African
states tried collective action. Under the aegis of the
OAU and the United Nations Economic Commission for
Africa (ECA), a number of significant meetings were
held, particularly between 1979 and 1980, to devise a
programme that would lead to Africa's endogenous economic development. In March 1979, the OAU/ECA organised
a Futures Symposium in Monrovia to identify strategies
for Africa's self-reliant economic development. In its
report, titled <u>What Kind of Africa by the Year 2000?</u>,
the symposium recommended among other things the creation of "an African Common Market based on progresssive
co-ordination and integration...."[32] The Report also
recommended the creation of a unified African monetary
system by the Year 2000. Finally, the symposium called
upon African states to work towards self-sufficiency in
food production. Henceforth, it continued, "the degree
of a country's dependence for its food should be...con-
sidered as one of the most significant indicators of
its level of development."[33]

     When African leaders met in Monrovia in July 1979,
for the 16th annual OAU summit, among the issues discussed at length was the continent's economic development. The Assembly adopted the <u>Monrovia Declaration of
Commitment of the Heads of States and Governments of
the OAU on the Guide Lines and Measures for National
and Collective Self-Reliance in Economic and Social
Development for the Establishment of a New International Economic Order</u>. In adopting that Declaration,
the African leaders commited themselves "individually
and collectively on behalf of our governments and
peoples, to promote the economic and social development
and integration of our economies with a view to achieving an increasing measure of self-sufficiency and self-

sustainment." [34] It was also agreed in Monrovia that a special OAU economic summit should be held in Nigeria to devise a blue-print for the continent's economic development by the 2000. The special session took place from April 28-29, 1980 (it was not held in 1979 due to a transfer from military to civil rule in Nigeria, in September of 1979). The main outcome of the deliberations was the Lagos Plan of Action for the Economic Development of Africa 1980-2000 [35] (henceforth the Lagos Plan of Action). The said Plan identified four broad areas in Africa's drive towards economic self-sufficiency: a) self-sufficiency in food, b) self-sufficiency in energy, c) the promotion of inter-African trade as well as trade between Africa and the rest of the world on terms much more favourable to the continent, and d) the creation of an African Common Market by the year 2000. A detailed discussion and analysis of the Lagos Plan of Action is beyond the scope of this chapter. [36] However, if the provisions of the Plan were to be implemented in their entirety or in part, they would certainly have an impact on great power economic intervention in Africa in the future. If, for example, Africa is able to feed itself, there would be no need for it to continue to rely on the great powers for food imports. Moreover, an economically integrated African continent would be powerful enough not only to protect its weaker members but also to ward off various forms of great power economic intervention in the future.

viii) **Response to Great Power Humanitarian**
       Intervention

     The attempts made by African states to achieve self-sufficiency in food have been a total disaster. To date, no African state south of the Sahara can be said to be self-sufficient in food. Even Nigeria, potentially the richest and most powerful African state, has not succeeded in feeding its people independently, despite two successive food programmes designed to halt the annual drain of billions of dollars from the country to pay for food. (The first campaign was called Operation Feed the Nation (OFN), and was initiated by the military regime of General Olusegun Obasanjo. The current program.the Green Revolution, was introduced by the civilian regime of President Shehu Shagari). [37] Many other African countries have had to rely almost exclusively on the great powers either for grains to feed their populations or for the loans and grants which they use to settle their food bills overseas. There seems to be no end to this bleak scenario of reliance on the great powers by the African countries.[38]

A related problem is that of refugees. Africa has the world's largest refugee populations. The unfortunate people have had to rely on charity from abroad for their food and other needs. African states are too poor to either provide the money with which to buy food, clothing or tents, or they are unable to produce enough food to spare to meet the needs of the refugees. African attempts at solving this have been limited mostly to the hosting of conferences, at which appeals are made to the great powers to donate food or money to assist refugees. I have cited the international conference called by Sudan in 1980 to raise food and funds for its refugees. It is salient to point out here that before that conference, an OAU sponsored fund-raising meeting for African refugees was held in Geneva in April that year. At that time, it was revealed that the OAU would need $560 million to meet the immediate needs of the continent's homeless population. Interestingly, however, the only African contribution made at the time was one from Nigeria of $3 million. The majority of the other donors were outside the continent; the EEC $68 million, the US $285 million, Britain $13 million and France $2 million.[39]

I have in the foregoing pages tried to trace the history of great power intervention in Africa in the post-independence era. I have also identified several modes of intervention by the great powers, and the responses of Africans, with particular reference to the following; a) politically motivated military intervention; b) economic intervention; and c) humanitarian intervention.

I reached the conclusion that African states' response to all three types of intervention has been disappointing. In this final section of the chapter, I shall attempt to present possible futures of great power intervention on the African continent with regard to the three types identified above. The major objective in the following section is to identify factors both external and internal to Africa which are likely to explain the future of great power intervention on the continent.

ix) Possible Futures of Great Power Intervention in Africa

> "Our work has impressed us with the
> inherent difficulties of forecast-
> ing although we realise that ob-
> jects of forecasting vary greatly
> in their conjecturability. But the
> resulting skepticism regarding par-
> ticular or/and, more or less, all
> forecasting methods does not lead
> us to the conclusion that the
> attempt to forecast is worthless.
> As long as forecasting results are
> presented and used with adequate
> caution, planners can learn some-
> thing, even if nothing really
> solid, in their attempts to shape
> future development...."[40]

Making predictions about the future is generally a
hazardous exercise. It is even riskier when the prognosis concerns abstractions such as states and the
international system generally. However, making predictions about the futures of great power intervention
in Africa is much more hazardous for a number of
reasons. First, the nature of the environment within
which both the great powers and African states operate
is characterised by political instability, occasioned
either by communal violence or by the rapid turnover of
political leadership. Second, the sheer number of
states on the continent--fifty-one including the
Saharan Arab Democratic Republic (SADR)--makes any
comprehensive extrapolation difficult. These states
differ markedly in terms of their physical size, their
populations, their endowment with natural resources;
their economic, technological and military capabilities, and their ideologies and modes of development.
Third, because of their relative newness in the
international system, there seems to be a substantial
role for personalities in the policies of African
states. Any predictions about the future of Africa's
relations with the external world are thus dependent on
which personalities gain power. Finally, the futures
of great power intervention in Africa also entail two
other futures: that of the international system and
that of the great powers. Again, the problems inherent
in making predictions about the two environments are
daunting, to say the least. No one will say with any
degree of certainty what the world would be like in

twenty years time. The same applies to the great
powers.

Nevertheless, I believe we can still hazard some
scenarios on the futures of great power involvement in
Africa. Such prognoses would not be undertaken after-
all in an analytic vacuum. They will be largely based
on what I consider to be the objective as well as the
subjective circumstances of both the African states and
the great powers. We can conjecture scenarios for
great power intervention in Africa on the basis of
extrapolations from past and present patterns of
behaviour towards the continent. We can, in addition,
make assumptions about what Africa and the rest of the
world will be like by the year 2000.

As I have stated, a discussion of two environments
is crucial to any attempt to predict the future of
great power intervention in Africa: the domestic and
external environments of the African continent. The
futures of these environments would of course determine
the nature and scope of great power involvement in
Africa in the future. A brief examination of various
scenarios in both environments follows.

x) **Scenarios Relating to the Possible Futures of Great
    Power Intervention in Africa**

THE EXTERNAL ENVIRONMENT

Various scenarios can be suggested with regard to
the international system in future. First, we can
anticipate a continuation of the present loose bipolar
international system, with essentially its two dominant
powers, the US and the USSR. Such a scenario implies a
continuation of the present mode of great power
involvement in other parts of the world including Africa. It is assumed also that detente would continue. A
second scenario involves the emergence of a multipolar
system, with several new centres of power: China,
Europe, Japan and the Third World.[41] Indeed, it is
reasonable also to divide the Third World further into
three sub-groups of power and influence: Africa, Asia
and the Middle East and Latin America. The third and
final scenario concerns the international political
economy, which could be experiencing either a recession
or a boom. Either possibility would involve an
increasing search by the great powers for markets and
partners abroad. At the same time, other powerful economic centres would emerge in the Third World and in

Africa. The generation of economic giants in Africa--
which we may call New Industrialising Countries
(NICs)--will have profound consequences not only for
intra-African relationships but also for relations between the continent and the great powers. I will
explore this theme later. Suffice it here to say that
if any of the above scenarios should materialise, the
future of great power intervention in Africa is bound
to be affected accordingly.

THE DOMESTIC ENVIRONMENT

Both Zartman and Lemaitre agree that African states
will in the future be divided into three broad categories.[42] The first category is composed of the SICs or
NICs states. They are very few in number. The most
likely candidates for this category are: Algeria,
Nigeria, Zaire, Egypt, South Africa (shorn of its apartheid policies) and possibly Morocco and Zambia. These
are states with "a good chance of continued development
which would set them apart from the others with a sizeable GNP and a considerable economic weight that could
provide the means and aspirations for leadership roles
in Africa."[43] I should also add that this group would
include radical, social, transformationist, as well as
capitalist/conservative states. The second group of
states are the fairly prosperous ones. However, because of the variety of factors including their physical sizes and populations, they would not be candidates
for the leadership roles predicted to belong to those
in the first category. States in this category would
include Ivory Coast, Senegal and possibly Liberia. A
third category comprises the majority of African
states: those so poor that it may prove difficult for
many of them to survive as independent entities in the
future, especially in a period of world-wide economic
recession. These states will experience a "relatively
high rate of malnutrition, if not starvation, due to
stagnation in subsistence agricultural production, and
rising population rates, soil exhaustion, reduction in
world-wide food surpluses...increased balance of payments difficulties because of rising relative energy
and fertiliser costs; and a weak international market
for their low priority exports."[44] Because of their
economic backwardness, the poorer African states would
be in no condition to take advantage of a world-wide
economic boom even if one were to occur. They would
remain net importers of finished goods from either the
great powers or from local NICs.

The successful implementation of the OAU Lagos Plan
of Action, either in its entirety or in a substantially
modified form by the year 2000, could modify this
gloomy scenario. At the sub-regional level, I also
assume that integration schemes like ECOWAS in West
Africa, SADCC in Southern Africa and the projected
Central African Economic Community would have succeeded
in reducing the economic dependence of their members on
the great powers. Thus inside such continental and/or
sub-regional economic groupings, the lot of the poorer
members would be greatly enhanced as they fell under
the protection of those more powerful and prosperous.

A further scenario in the domestic environment
involves the future of the OAU. The ability of the
African states to ward off external economic and military penetration either individually or collectively
would depend on whether the OAU holds out together as a
strong and viable Pan-African body in future.[45]
Alternatively, the OAU could split into racial and/or
ideological factions. (Already, some black African
states are beginning to feel that the Arabs are intent
on breaking the OAU over an essentially Arab issue-the
Moroccan claim over Western Sahara and the latter's
admission into the OAU in 1982).

More specifically, an OAU dominated by progressive
African states would also be an inward-looking institution whose major objective would be to protect its
members, especially the very weak ones, from external
interference in their domestic affairs. We assume also
that the progressive states would make necessary amend-
ments to the Charter to reflect the contemporary needs
of the continent. On the other hand, an OAU dominated
by conservatives would tend to align with the great
powers both directly and indirectly. Under these circumstances, the interests of the weaker members would
be subordinated to those of the stronger, conservative
members. As well, Africa under a conservative ideological bloc of states could not effectively curtail
violence within and between African states.

My penultimate scenario deals with the future of
Southern Africa. Specifically, I am concerned with the
nature of change in Namibia and South Africa proper.
The installation of a black majority government in
South Africa through a negotiated settlement in that
territory would have a far-reaching impact on the future of great power intervention in the continent. It
is reasonable to expect that such a black government
would be acceptable to the Western great powers. Such

276

a government would also ensure a place for the whites
in the country and in positions of power[46] and influence
in the political and economic systems.   However, a
change of government brought about by a prolonged
guerrilla struggle in South Africa has two implications. First, great power intervention would be
inevitable in the transitional period. Second, the
post-revolutionary regime would be radical and marxist.
This would mean fewer ties with the West, closer ties
with the East but, at the same time, the country's
policy would be guided by Pan-African ideals, so it
would be much more inward-looking and independent. It
would team with other progressive regimes on the continent to ensure less great power interference in
African affairs.

     My final scenario concerns Africa's ability to feed
itself in the future. As was argued earlier, one form
that has become increasingly popular is humanitarian
intervention, provoked mainly by droughts and the
resultant starvation/famine in the affected areas.
Increases in this type of intervention allow us to project two scenarios, the first for seeing a continuation
of Africa's inability to feed its peoples and/or cater
to its refugees, the other seeing the continent
increasingly achieving self-sufficiency in food production by the year 2000. Of the two projections, the
first is the most likely. According to the World Bank,
incomes in Africa during the period 1985-1990 will be
much lower than they were in 1980 and Africa is also
expected to be the only continent where the birth rate
will continue to rise. The bank therefore concluded
that the general level of nutrition now[47] enjoyed by
Africa will be falling in the 1990s.   As well,
according to the ECA's Adebayo Adedeji, Africa in the
1980s and 1990 will experience sagging and sluggish
economic growth. Specifically, the continent is
expected to suffer "four devastating and debilitating
problems: chronic food deficits, pernicious droughts,
deteriorating[48] terms of trade and balance of payments
problems."   In 1982, Africa imported 23.9 million
tonnes of food, including 4.3 million tonnes donated by
the Food and Agriculture Organisation (FAO). The
Organisation's director predicted that donor countries
would have to step up their food assistance programmes
to Africa by as much as 7 million tonnes in 1983.
Circumstances are so bad that already a number of
African countries have begun experiencing critical
shortages and famine. The Central African Republic
recently appealed to the international[49] community for
assistance to help feed its people.   For those not

yet affected by droughts, the story is not much different. Sierra Leone has, for instance, depended on the
US for regular food supplies since 1977. From that
year to 1983, the US sent $13.6 million worth of food
to Freetown. And in 1983 alone, the value of food dispatched to Sierra Leone under the food aid programme
was $3.6 million.[50]

From the above discussion, I am left with the
impression that the African continent will for the
foreseeable future not be able to fend for itself. As
we will see shortly, this conclusion will have serious
implications for great power intervention in the continent in future.

xi) Some Possible Futures of Great Power Intervention in Africa

Given the foregoing scenarios for both the external
and domestic environment of African states, what are
the possible futures of great power intervention on the
continent? In attempting to answer this question, I
will confine myself   to three areas: a) political/
military intervention; b) economic intervention; and
c) humanitarian intervention. I will examine each in
turn in order to make prognostications about the
future.

POLITICAL/MILITARY INTERVENTION

Several futures are conceivable with regard to
great power political/military intervention in Africa.
First, if the international system is multipolar in the
future, the activities of the great powers outside
their own spheres of influence would be seriously curtailed. This includes any attempt by them to interfere
in the domestic affairs of African states. Consequently, they would have to team with regional hegemonial
powers to effect whatever changes they may desire. In
short, then, their intervention would be indirect,
effected through Africa surrogates and Trojan Horses.
This conclusion leads to the second possible future,
which concerns the emergence on the continent of two
sets of hegemonial powers; the conservative SICs and
the radical transformationist SICs. With particular
reference to the former, they would, as indicated
earlier, prefer to team up with conservative, capitalist forces outside the continent. However, as regional
powers, their interest would be primarily confined to
Africa. The less endowed, largely agrarian, African

278

states would be their main targets. They would want to see that friendly regimes are installed in those states for regional stability and prosperity. Consequently, they would be tempted to intervene in those states whenever they perceived a threat to their interests. Ideally, the conservative NICs would prefer to intervene single-handedly. However, under special circumstances, they would request aid from the great powers whose interests are expected to coincide. Such intervention would be limited largely to the provision of logistical support and strategic information, which would enable the African power to make a decisive intervention in the neighbouring state concerned.

Obviously, the futures of great power intervention in an African continent dominated by radical transformationist regimes would be quite different from those of conservative states. First, radical SICs would share direct links with external powers as much as possible. Theirs would be inward-looking economic and even political policies. They would tolerate less external interference in Africa's affairs because they would strive to strengthen African institutions such as the OAU as part of their goal of enhancing the political and economic stability of the continent. I thus envisage a strengthening of the OAU's conflict resolution machinery, which would prevent situations which have invited great power intervention in the past. Another possible line of action would be the establishment of a Pan-African Defence Force which could be sent to troubled areas on the continent. Under the transformationist NICs, great power intervention in Africa would be, if not entirely eliminated, better contained.

The third future belongs to South Africa. As already noted, there are at least two possibilities here. The first is a peaceful solution to the conflict which, if achieved, would eliminate the need for the Western great powers to intervene in the racial conflicts in that part of Africa. This would seem to support my first future scenario that great power intervention would be largely indirect.

Conversely, a military solution to apartheid would bring in its wake massive great power intervention in the continent. A possible scenario in this case would include open support for the nationalists by the Soviet block states and perhaps China, and support of all types would be offered by the West to the whites, who would probably be in alliance with conservative black, Indian and coloured politicians in the Republic. The novel feature of this case is the open military involvement of the Western great powers, whereas this has so far been discrete and limited largely to the supply of arms and ammunition. In the future, their involvement would take a more direct form; not only would their citizens be encouraged to fight with the whites, but their own soldiers would be involved as well. This would depend, though, on the Soviet Union and its allies' willingness to initiate and go as massively as they did in Angola. If they were to do this, involvement by Western great powers (who would not wish to risk a third Great War over the issue of South Africa) would be restrained.

Experience has shown, however, that the great powers do not accept defeat without a struggle. Thus in Angola, Mozambique and to some extent in Zimbabwe, where radical/transformationist regimes have been installed, the Western great powers have aided dissident movements in attempts to bring down and/or destabilise those regimes. In Angola, the UNITA movement is receiving assistance from the US and its allies, and in Mozambique, the Mozambique National Resistance Movement (MNR) is receiving support from the West and South Africa. A similar pattern is expected in South Africa if a radical transformationist regime is installed there eventually. The West would team up with the whites from that country in support of conservative dissident movements to destabilise the regime. The success of the great powers in achieving such an objective would, however, depend on at least two factors: a) the popularity of the new regime, and b) the support other states in the region were prepared to give it. If they were willing to give it support, it would be difficult for the dissidents to operate since they would be denied bases in neighbouring states. In short, the resistance would be short-lived.

Whatever happens in South Africa, one thing is certain: the scope and nature of great power military and political intervention on the continent would be quite different, in the future, from what it has been and is at present. Certainly, the blatant type of military intervention that we have witnessed in the past would disappear, to be replaced by intervention through proxies, the conservative NICs. Even then, intervention would be made on terms dictated by the NICs, who would control it tightly. The only exception would occur during an open racial war between blacks and whites in South Africa, when the Western great powers might be tempted simply to fortify the white resistance with their own troops.

ECONOMIC INTERVENTION

I envisage a diminishing role for direct great power economic inervention in Africa in the future, particularly as a result of the emergence of semi-industrialising African states (SICs) of both radical and conservative/capitalist allegience. The great powers would be much more circumscribed in a world economic recession. The SICs would divide the continent into spheres of influence, each of which would have preponderant influence in its own sphere. Within this area, direct great power intervention would be impossible without the consent and collaboration of the SIC concerned. Great power involvement in the economic activities of the African continent under these conditions would be mainly indirect. This applies even to the activities of their MNCs. Indirect participation by the great powers would more likely occur in the areas controlled by the conservative SICs. These states would be compelled by world economic trends to seek assistance from, or team up with, Western capitalist states. However, they would be in a much better and stronger position to control their foreign partners.

Private capital would continue to come to the continent but more slowly and irregularly, on terms acceptable to, and perhaps dictated by, the African countries. The reverse seems to be the case at present. This possibility for great power economic intervention is closely linked with the next one, which envisages a continent working rapidly towards economic integration and self-reliance, in accordance with the Lagos Plan of Action. If the Plan materialises--I am not in any way oblivious to the enormity of the obstacles to its success--the continent would by the year 2000 be covered by an African Common Market (ACM) similar to that in western Europe. Side by side with the ACM, the continent's energy and food needs would also be met endogenously, with the net result being increased economic status and bargaining power for Africa. Consequently, all funds coming into the continent would chanelled to a common fund/pool. Prosperous countries would also be in a position to protect weaker members of the continent from some of the blatant economic exploitation and interference they now experience at the hands of the great powers.

281

Even if the <u>Lagos Plan of Action</u> is not implemented in its entirety--and some scholars have argued that the ACM is not feasible, that Africa should work towards the creation of a Free Trade Area--[31] I still envisage a situation of greatly enhanced sub-regional economic integration. I have in mind such schemes as ECOWAS, SADCC and the projected Central African regional grouping. The effect of these sub-regional groupings on great power economic intervention in future would be the same as that of the continental association, at least for the particular regions concerned. Thus, in West Africa, we shall witness less great power economic interference, and the confinement of their role to their activities within global financial institutions such as the International Monetary Fund, or the World Bank. However, these institutions would be deprived of their veto powers as they are currently being exercised. They would not be able to make a <u>dictat</u> to the sub-regions because they would operate as economic units. As for foreign aid, this would perhaps continue to come in but not to individual countries. If at all, it would be given in the form of consortium arrangements for loans and grants because the sums involved would be too huge for individual countries to bargain for or absorb. I also envisage a continuation of great power technological involvement in the sub-regions, but in greatly attenuated forms, with the sub-regions in a much better position to choose their technology, bargain for it and even modify it to suit specific local needs.
In short, Africans would have much more control over their own economies and natural resources in future.

HUMANITARIAN INTERVENTION

Of the three types of intervention I selected for detailed examination, great power humanitarian intervention would seem to be the most persistent in future. Independent of the materialisation of some of the scenarios under political military and economic interventions, I foresee no immediate end to direct great power humanitarian intervention in the continent. Barring the success of the <u>Lagos Plan</u>, the food situation in the continent would remain bleak. The reasons for this are many and important. First, the African food crisis is not only a result of droughts. Wars, both within the between African states, corruption by government officials, falling world food reserves and outmoded technology all combine to form lethal weapons against the citizens of Africa. For the short-term as well as the medium and long-term periods, Africa would continue to

282

rely on the good will of the great powers in its war against pernicious droughts, hunger and famine. This seems to be the conclusion of World Population Bureau. According to this Bureau, although world food production is increasing at a rate of 1.5 percent per annum, Africa's rate of increase is much less than the world average, a mere ½ percent of 1.5 percent. Food production in the continent is also falling at an ever-increasing rate: from 7 percent in the 1960s to 15 percent in the 1970s. More important though, is the revelation that in Africa generally, people's Basic Human Needs (BHN) are only very nearly met if at all. The Report of the Bureau continued that East Africa is the worst hit area with people only receiving 83 percent of their minimum daily needs. The figure for West Africa is 96 percent.[52]

Given these circumstances, my conclusion is that great power humanitarian intervention in Africa will continue in the longer term period, with such intervention continuing to maintain its familiar pattern of donations of food and financial assistance to the stricken country/countries; provision of logistics of distribute the food and materials; and offering of loans/grants to African states otherwise unable to meet their rising food bills. As well, the activities of great power based voluntary organisations such as the Red Cross, OXFAM, the World Council of Churches and a host of others would continue in their usual pattern of involvement in the continent.

The scope and nature of great power humanitarian intervention in the future will be largely dependent upon the nature of the world economic system. If, for instance, African states were to experience a drought/famine during a world economic recession, their dependence on the rest of the world for food would be almost total. The above scenario would persist until African states joined together to grapple seriously with the endemic food crisis on the continent. Experience has shown that isolated attempts by single countries fail. The state concerned merely ends up wasting valuable money on schemes that result in increased dependence on the great powers not only for money, but also for the very food it has set out to increase.

283

Notes

1. Olajide Aluko, in New Nigerian (Kaduna), 17 July 1978.

2. For my purpose, the great powers are: the US, USSR, China, Britain, France, Canada, Japan, West Germany and Italy.

3. Richard Little, Intervention (London: Martin Robertson, 1975), 2.

4. R.J. Vincent, Non-Intervention and International al (New Jersey: Princeton University Press, 1974), 13.

5. Manfred Halpern, "The Morality and Politics of Intervention", in R. Falk (ed.) The Vietam War and International Law (New Jersey: Princeton University Press, 1968), 42.

6. I. William Zartman, "Social and Political Trends in Africa in the 1980s". in Colin Legum, I. William Zartman et al. Africa in the 1980s (New York: McGraw-Hill, 1979), 55.

7. See quotation for note 1 above.

8. By 1980, for instance, African states had experienced over fifty coups and attempted coups since the dawn of independence in the continent in 1960. See Daily Sketch (Ibadan), 13 April 1980.

9. See Articles II and III of the OAU's Charter for more details on this issue.

10. Although the Soviet Union initially armed Somalia soon after the socialist revolution in that country led by Siad Barre in 1969, Moscow changed sides in 1977 following the victory of the pro-Moscow faction within the then ruling Dergue in Ethiopia. For more details of Ethiopia's relations with the Soviet Union and Somalia, see Olusola Ojo, "Ethiopia's Foreign Policy since the 1974 Revolution" in Horn of Africa, Vol. 3, No. 4, 1980/81, 3-12.

11. Africa Now (London) July 1981, 53.

12. The countries affected by the drought include:
    Mauritania, Senegal, Mali, Upper Volta, Niger,
    and Chad. Others affected are Somalia and
    Ethiopia. For details on the drought and the
    relief activities of the great powres, see
    William A. Rance, "Lessons to be Learned from the
    Sahel Drought", in H. Kitchen (ed.) <u>Africa: from
    mystery to maze</u> (Lexington Massachusetts: D.C.
    Heath, 1976), Chapter 4.

13. <u>Africa</u> (London), No. 108, August 1980, 14.

14. <u>Ibid.</u>, 15-16.

15. The writer is not aware of any mercenary activi-
    ties by citizens of East European states in
    Africa.

16. See <u>The Guardian</u> (London), 6 May 1983.

17. See John Stockwell, <u>In Search of Enemies: the
    CIA story</u> (New York: Norton, 1978).

18. See <u>Africa Research Bulletin</u> (Henceforth <u>ARB</u>)
    Political Series, 1-30 April 1977, 4401 and 1-31
    May 1978, 4855-56.

19. <u>Daily Times</u> (Lagos) 6 June 1978.

20. <u>Ibid.</u>

21. <u>ARB</u> 1-30 October 1965, 379.

22. <u>Africa Contemporary Record</u> (London: Rex
    Collings), Vol. 3, 1970/71, C 4.

23. <u>The Guardian</u>, 22 May 1978.

24. <u>Ibid.</u>

25. <u>Daily Times</u>, 19 June 1978 and <u>Nigerian Tribune</u>
    (Ibadan) 24 June 1978.

26. <u>ARB</u>, 1-31 May 1978, 4860.

27. For Mobutu's experience with MNCs, see G. Lanning
    and M. Mueller, <u>Africa Undermined</u> (Harmondsworth:
    Penguin, 1979) Chapter 10.

28. See Adeoye Akinsanya, "Host government's response
    to foreign economic control: the experiences of

selected African countries", paper presented at an International Seminar on the Futures of Africa, Dalhousie University, Canada, May 1-4, 1981. See also his book, The Expropriation of Multinational Property in the Third world (New York: Praeger, 1980).

29. See Andrew M. Karmack, "Sub-Saharan Africa in the 1980s: an economic profile", in Kitchen (ed.) Africa from Mystery to Maze, 169.

30. See Adeoye Akinsanya, "Host government's response to foreign economic control", Table 3, No. 7.

31. Ibid., 15.

32. For details on the Symposium's proceedings, see What Kind of Africa by the Year 2000? Final report of the Monrovia Symposium on the Future development prospects of Africa towards the year 2000 (OAU/International Institute for Labour Studies, Geneva, 1979). The reference in question here is on p. 18.

33. Ibid., 24.

34. Preamble to the Lagos Plan of Action (Geneva: OAU/International Institute for Labour Studies, 1979), 5.

35. Ibid., for more details.

36. For a critique of the Lagos Plan of Action, see Amadu Sesay, "The OAU and Continental Order", in Timothy Shaw and 'Sola Ojo (eds.) Africa and the International Political System (Washington D.C.: UPA, 1982), Chapter 7.

37. One of the IMF's rescue plans for Nigeria involves $2 billion which is to be used to pay for imports including food items. See The Guardian, 6 May 1983.

38. For various predictions for the continent, see, the Annual Reports of the World Bank (Washington, D.C.). See the annual speeches of Adebayo Adedeji of ECA, especially in West Africa (London), 12 January 1981, 57-58 and 1 November 1980. See also the speech by Edouard Saouma, Director General of FAO in West Africa, 26 May 1980, 919; 1977 FAO Report titled The State of Food

and Agriculture (Rome) and Timothy M. Shaw, "On Projections, Prescriptions and Plans: a review of the Literature on Africa's Future", in The Quarterly Journal of Administration (Ife) Vol. 14, No. 4, July 1980, 463-84.

39. For details of the conference, see West Africa, 20 April 1980, 49-50.

40. Oscar Morgenstern, Klaus Knorr and Klaus P. Heiss, Long Term Projections of Power (Cambridge Mass.: Balinger, 1973), xv.

41. For more details on this type of system, see Steven J. Rosen and Walter S. Jones, The Logic of International Relations (Cambridge Mass.: Winthrop, 1977. Second Edition), 224-234.

42. See Philippe Lemaitre's chapter "Who Will Rule Africa by the Year 2000?", in Kitchen (ed.) Africa: from mystery to maze and I. William Zartman's "Social and Political Trends in Africa in the 1980s", in Legum, Zartman et al. Africa in the 1980s, 34.

43. I. William Zartman, "Social and Political Trends in Africa" in Legum, Zartman et al. Africa in the 1980s, 84.

44. Lemaitre, "Who will Rule Africa by the Year 2000?" 268.

45. I assume here that the OAU will eventually overcome its present problems resulting from its inability to host the 19th annual summit in Tripoli, Libya in 1982.

46. See, Timothy M. Shaw, "South Africa's Role in Southern Africa in the Year 2000", in Olajide Aluko and Timothy M. Shaw (eds.) Southern Africa in the 1980s (London: George Allen and Unwin, 1985).

47. See World Bank Report 1980, 86.

48. Adedeji Adebayo, in What Kind of Africa by the Year 2000?, 59.

49. New Nigerian, 7 May 1983.

50. West Africa, 23 May 1983, 1268.

51. See Ralph I. Onwuka, "An African Common Market or an African Free Trade Area Which Way Africa?" in Ralph I. Onwuka and Amadu Sesay (eds.) The Future of Regionalism in Africa (London: Macmillan) forthcoming.

52. See Daily Sketch, 18 May 1983 for more details on Africa's latest food problems.

Chapter Eleven

The Future of the Great Powers in Africa: towards a political economy of intervention

Timothy M. Shaw

"Great Power rivalry in Africa is
among the legacies left by European
statesmen who, a century ago in
Berlin, carved up the continent and
whole nations within it into tidy
colonial compartments, several with
frontiers still in dispute.
Russians and Americans attended
that inglorious conference but
stayed out of the scramble for
territories that followed. It is
one of history's ironies that
Moscow and Washington emerged, with
proxies to help them, as leading
contestants in the contemporary
struggle for position, presence and
power in Africa."

- Arthur Gavshon, Crisis in Africa[1]

"The foreign policies of the African Marxist regimes...are increasingly inconsistent with their proclaimed allegiance to nonalignment,
as well as with the interests of
the West.... Ideological consideration...are now dominating the
foreign policy of a number of African states. Such considerations
should also become part of
Washington's answer to the challenges they raise. And the myth of
an innocent Africa, preoccupied only
with economic development, should
finally be discarded."

- Michael Radu, "Ideology, parties
and foreign policy in sub-Saharan
Africa."[2]

"Ever since formal independence was
achieved in the 1960s, the African
economy has undergone an evolution,
the main lines of which have
remained fundamentally determined
by the economies of the centres of
world capitalism...a variety of
factors are resulting in real contradictions between the various
African countries. These include
the tendency towards a relative
diminution of the overall importance
of inter-African trade and trade
with Africa; the need for imperialism to maintain its domination over
Africa as a reservoir of raw materials; the extensive use of classi-
cal 'divide and rule' tactics;
interimperialist contradictions...;
and inequalities in economic potential between African countries...In
the medium term there is every
reason to believe that these general tendencies will continue to
dominate the evolution of Africa,
as they had done for the last 20
years."

- Elenga M'buyinga, PanAfricanism
or Neo-Colonism.

Paradoxically, as well as symbolically, ever since
independence, "intervention" has been a major issue in
Africa, for reasons of ideology as well as of policy.
The first twenty years of formal independence have
provided myriad instances of intervention; so we may
expect more cases in the future. This chapter is concerned with the incidence and impact of intervention in
the mid-term future--until the year 2000--a period
which includes 1984, the centenary of the Berlin Conference was well as the title of George Orwell's
futuristic and cautionary novel. However, Africa is
not likely to be recolonised in a formal manner;
neither is it about to become an advanced post-
industrial microchip planetary society. Nevertheless,
its future prospects are hardly auspicious, as Colin
Legum notes in his own preview:

...Africa is at a most difficult
and explosive stage of development.
During the 1980s quarrels within

290

one country or between hostile
neighbouring countries are likely
to erupt into violent conflicts....
Such conflicts will affect not only
the localities or countries directly involved, but in many cases also
will provoke foreign intervention.
This is not to say that Africa will
be the passive victim of international power politics. On the
contrary, African factions will
actively seek foreign military and
economic assistance to bolster
fragile positions, as they have
frequently done already....In
short, the outlook for Africa in
the 1980s is for continued internationalisation of predictable
local conflicts.[4]

i) **Towards a Political Economy of Intervention:**
    strategic and structural

This chapter has identified five main themes as a
way of examining the future of intervention on the
continent. These are by no means exhaustive, neither
are they, I trust, entirely orthodox. Rather, they
constitute a tentative attempt to go beyond orthodox,
state-centric "high politics" as adjuncts of "intervention" to examine its roots in the structures of Africa's incorporation in the world system: the unconventional, non-state centric "low politics" of much intervention. First, then, I treat intervention as a structural as well strategic relationship. Second, I suggest that it arises from continental contradictions as
well as from extra-African interests and intentions.
Third, I indicate that its incidence and character
depend on particular stagers in the global cycle.
Fourth, I point to the regional as well as continental
implications of intervention. And finally, fifth, I
reflect on the importance of modes of analysis in
approaching the future of Africa: different perspectives throw up dramatically distinctive scenarios. In
short, the chapter constitutes an attempt to go beyond
the conventional lament about the superpowers in Africa
towards an understanding of the diversity of interests
and connections involved: coalitions favouring or dis-
favouring certain patterns of intervention in Africa up
to the end of the century.

Given Africa's inherited and intrinsic integration
in the world system, the catalyst for particular interventions can be continental or external, economic or
political, and short- or long-term. Whilst in general
substructure determines superstructure, in several
instances, the reverse may be true. Not that we can or
should altogether ignore substructural situations--modes
and relations of production--merely that we should
accurately identify the locus of intervention. Given
the growing economic marginality of the continent as a
whole it is rather hard to insist that substructure is
the basis of all interventions. Yet to ignore it as a
factor, particularly during the present conjuncture, is
to overlook crucial relationships, ones which may
become more salient before the end this century.

The first theme of this chapter is, then, that
military intervention is more likely than structural
intervention in the future of a) the revival of the
cold war, b) the demise of most African economies,
and c) the intensification of contradictions and conflicts on the continent within as well as between
states. Legum amongst others has pointed to the growing interrelationship between local and global
tensions, and so to the "logic" of superpower interaction:

> Africa's post-colonial conditions
> of political instability will, if
> anything, be greater in the 1980s
> than in the two previous decades...
> The African continent will not
> remain isolated from the conflicts
> in the rest of the world community
> notwithstanding the pan-Africanist
> aspiration towards non-alignment.
> Only the achievement of genuine
> detente between the West and the
> Soviet bloc will lessen the
> interests of the major powers in
> the continent....
> Even if the major Western powers
> should wish to disengage from an
> interventionist role in Africa, it
> is hard to see how their global
> interests will allow this to happen
> so long as the Soviets, at least,
> remain unwilling to match such a
> Western disengagement.
> In brief, issues related to Africa
> are likely to engage a great deal

of international attention in the 1980s.[5]

The second theme suggested here is that intervention in the future will be strategic rather than
structural because of continuing changes within the
continent's political economies: the contradictions of
underdevelopment and decline will increase its vulnerability unless alternative strategies of self-reliance
are adopted (see Section v) below). And unlike earlier
decades, such economic difficulties may not call forth
a positive response from increasingly isolationist
interests in the North, notwithstanding internationalist efforts like the Brandt Commission. As I. William
Zartman cautions:

> In Africa, with the likely return
> of ideological politics, the rise
> of distributional issues, and the
> generation of new counter-elites in
> the 1980s, the coming decade will
> find the continent as vulnerable to
> subversion and opposition movements
> in exile as it was in the early
> 1960s....[6]

And because of the revival of cold war concerns
along with the demise of detente such strategic
"openings" may indeed be acted upon during the 1980s
whereas they were sometimes overlooked in earlier more
benign times.

No matter what the period, intervention in Africa
has rarely been a local or parochial affair; it has
reflected continuing extra-continental differences and
disputes too. The global balance and African configuration have usually been interrelated. This interrela-
tion is likely to be a feature in the future as it was
in the past, with profound implications for international as well as African affairs. The present period
of renewed East-West and West-West tensions holds
particular fears for Africa's tenuous sovereignty and
autonomy, as noted in the final section.

Patterns of intervention are inseparable not only
from inter-imperial rivalries but also from related
contradictions at the periphery: the intensification
of class formation and antagonism particularly in
periods of economic contraction. To be sure such
tensions may be both repressed and diverted: one-party
state structures and military regimes have repressive

capabilities while ideologies associated with integration, ethnicity, racism, religion and developmentalism
have diversionary potential. But contradictions become
harder to contain as a) the honeymoon post-
independence political period recedes and b) the
expansionary post-independence economic period passes.
In short, the African crisis poses major possibilities
of both challenge and response, insatability and intervention. As M'buyinga asserts in his critique of the
elusiveness of either change or cohesion on the continent since independence:

> ...what has happened in Africa
> during the past 20 years, as far as
> pan-Africanism and African unity
> are concerned, is fundamentally the
> consequence of the development of
> classes and class struggles in our
> continent.[7]

Such a radical appreciation takes us some way away from
exclusively strategic concerns and towards a redefinition of the security on the continent, discussed in
sections iv) and v) below. Here, however, we merely
note the prospect of increasingly antagonistic social
relations at the periphery as the African crisis continues and intensifies.

A third theme of chapter treats. Africa's status in
the cycle of economic expansion and contractions as the
global situation within which intervention may or may
not occur.

If intervention can be conceived in both structural
and strategic terms in general then it can surely be
related at both levels to different periods in the
world system. Such a correlation with changes in
global cycles--from economic expansion to contraction
and from strategic detente to confrontation--has
important implications for projecting the future as
well as explaining the past. In general throughout the
post-war period there seems to have been an inverse
relationship between structural and strategic interventions: in good economic times the former dominates
over the latter--i.e. economic "benignness"--whereas in
bad economic times the latter dominates over the
former--i.e. military "malignness." These tendencies
would seem to be related to a) conditions at the
global level and b) contradictions at the continental
level.

In periods of economic expansion inter-imperial rivalries are benign so although structural involvement is high strategic intervention is low. Conversely, in times of economic contraction, such as the present period, inter-imperial rivalries are active so strategic intervention is high yet structural intervention is low. Hence one crucial factor in predicting the future of intervention would seem to be a stage in economic cycle, especially when downturns produce internal conflict--i.e. potential for external military involvement--whereas upturns may mitigate and moderate domestic antagonisms. We can "test" such a "theory" by distinguishing between the expansion of the 1960 and the contraction of the 1970s; i.e. between the first and second decades of independence. Such a chronology or categorisation may enable us to project alternative scenarios for the remaining two decades to the end of the century: if contraction continues then strategic, rather than structural, intervention will increase in the mid-term future.

The world systems perspective advanced by Immanuel Wallerstein lends support to such a scenario, with additional emphasis on the uneven impact of different stages on different groups of countries. In the current, third, phase of the continent's incorporation the impact of contraction will be less severe at the "semi-periphery than at the periphery. South Africa and Nigeria will continue to emerge as industrial producers for domestic and regional markets. But the overall contraction will bring to a head those sometimes latent tensions within and between states as class and country struggles intensify: "In the coming 50 years this incorporation will take one of two forms: dependent development or revolutionary transformation as a part of a network of forces within the world economy as a whole, which will further the transformation to a socialist world system."[8] Given the continuing integration of the semi-periphery--the Newly Industrialising/Influential Countries (NICs)--into the capitalist nexus and the dialectical inclination of the periphery--the Least Developed Countries (LDCs)--towards self-reliance, such divergence lays the basis for continental conflicts at the levels of both ideology and economy. It also suggests that the apparent revival of the radical-conservative division in Africa has deeper roots than just individuals and policies: possible structural bases with profound implications for future interventive incidents and outcomes.

The transition from an expansionary to a contracting stage in the global economy has posed major challenges for analysis as well as for praxis. In particular, submerged contradictions in both centre and periphery became more manifest and antagonistic after the 1960s: inter-imperial rivalries at the centre and assorted class contradictions (both within and around the indigenous bourgeoisie) at the periphery. Notions of "interdependence" began towards the end of the 1970s to yield to ideas of competition (among the advanced industrialised states) and dependence (between centre and periphery). Country, corporate and class relationships were no longer seen to be mixed-sum, but zero-sum, in character. Muted antagonisms became overt, with profound implications for contemporary and anticipated interventions. M'bunyinga provides a nice overview of this post-independence period, particularly in its classic "neocolonial" form:

> In their efforts to dominate the so-called underdeveloped countries, the various imperialist bourgeoisies both collaborate and compete amongst themselves. The resulting interimperialist contradictions are permanently manifest in the periphery, notably in Africa. Science and technology have permitted an unprecedented development of the forces of production which has consigned a variety of industries to the museum....It is, therefore, not surprising that the imperialist bourgeoisie, in its quest for maximum profits, should ship such outdated 'classical' industries out to the dominated regions, notably to Africa. Of course, this in no way modifies the relations of domination and exploitation which have existed for so long between this bourgeoisie and the peoples of Africa.

The fourth theme presented here is that conflicts over borders, development directions and external associations tend to concentrate at the regional level. Not that either national or continental levels are unimportant, but the regional level does tend to be the one at which local country and class interests intersect with external county and corporate interests. This

level has always been salient in post-independence
Africa but its importance has grown as "middle powers"
have emerged in each region both to lead the group and
to be subjected to various extra-continental pressures.
For inter-imperial rivalries in the North increasingly
concentrate on competition for exchange with and
influence over the middle powers of the South:
Algeria, Nigeria, Zaire and South Africa in the four
major regions, with Ivory Coast, Kenya and Zimbabwe in
an aspirant category.[10] Based on the contemporary
history of regional conflict and cooperation on the
continent, albeit at the level of superstructure,
Zartman asserts that "the development of (sub)
regionalism is likely to form one of the predominant
patterns of inter-African relations in the 1980s".[11] And, as
we shall see, Southern Africa is isolated by most scholars as
being primus inter pares: the bellweather region for the 1980s.

Aside from these empirical questions about the
incidence and impact of intervention to date, a final
fifth theme is that of mode of explanation as well as
of projection. The prevailing paradigms of systems
analysis and developmentalism are under attack in the
international relations and the African studies
fields.[12] Zartman represents both of these conventional positions, albeit in a relatively enlightened
"internationalist" form.

Preferred mode of analysis is inseparable, of
course, from both projection and prescription.
Zartman's espousal of of "decolonisation" as the motif
for the continent by contrast to "dependency" suggests
that Africa's ability to control intervention is
increasing: "decolonisation has its own logic, wherein
each step creates pressures for the next and reduces
the possiblity of counteraction by retreating post-
colonial forces."[13] Dependence, for Zartman, fails to
capture current tendencies whereas decolonisation
reflects contemporary arrangements: "Capitalising on
its increased independence, Africa is able to exact a
higher and higher price for a lessened European presence. Thus it can be seen that the dependency
approach at best describes a static moment, while the
decolonisation theory accounts for changing relations...."[14] So instead of being critical of Eur-
Africanism, Zartman can be positive as a liberal
internationalist: "From an evolutionary point of
view, therefore, the Lome Conventions are a welcome
development. Neither...neocolonial association
nor...institutionalisation of dependency...."[15]

By contrast, a more radical perspective sees
dependence as the major factor in underdevelopment and
so permissive of intervention, especially in its
structural guise. In response to such a mode of analysis, the praxis proposed by the Economic Commission for
Africa (ECA) and the more "progressive" states is self-
reliance: disengagement from rather than further,
albeit rationalised, incorporation within, the world
system. Not that self-reliance by itself guarantees
either development or socialism; but it is a precondition for both. Such a transition may have an exponential impact on dependence as African   relations
come to replace extra-African ones, recognising that
intra-continental intervention is only marginally
preferable to that from outside (see Section iii)
below. But the possibilities of such "horizontal"
exchange are peculiarly affected by the outcome of the
struggle in the Southern African region. As Langdon
and Mytelka indicate:

> Such South-South trade in the
> African context could be especially
> useful on a continental basis. But
> the prospect of such development
> depends heavily on successful over-
> throw of the white-run regimes in
> Southern Africa. The possibility
> of that taking place is likely to
> be a central focus of much inter-
> national concern in Africa, on many
> levels, throughout the 1980s.
> Self-reliant black regimes in
> Namibia, Zimbabwe and South Africa
> would make an immense contribution
> to alternative development strategy
> for all Africa,   but considerable
> conflict will occur before sub
> regimes finally emerge.[16]

We turn to the relationship between region and
continent in section v) below. Before reflecting on
Africa's neocolonial inheritance, however, we pause to
note two characteristic features of the continent's
situation and condition: its essentially "Western"
orientation and its continuing ability to surprise
because of its unpredictability.

The still ubiquitous character of Western association with Africa--the basis of structural "intervention"--has been well-captured by Zartman, who, despite
his emphasis on decolonisation, identifies its major
contraction:

Africa is a nonaligned part of the
Western world. Its background,
values, dependencies, exchanges,
and aspirations are primarily with
the West, as it works out its own
nature and concerns.[17]

So Western intervention is inclined to be less visible
and more continuing than that from the East; that is,
if anything in Africa displays real continuity.

Despite all the analyses of and debates over
Africa, the one feature which still stands out about
the continent is uncertainty. And given the interrelatedness of Africa and the rest of the international
order in whatever period, this uncertainty or unpredictability is of global concern. As Gavshon cautions:

The contemporary African experience, therefore, suggests that
the only certain thing in a changing continent is uncertainty; and,
paradoxically, that the progress
depends on the degree to which its
people face up jointly to adver-
sity. For the superpowers, bracing
for a new phase of confrontation in
the 1980s, that could be a reminder
and a warning.[18]

Throwing caution about such uncertainty to the wind,
however, this paper attempts to extract continuities
from Africa's history of intervention and so project
such trends into the mid-term future: from structural
benignness to strategic malignancy.

ii) Inheritance of intervention: neocolonialism

The basis of any reliable projection is historical
data. Although any comprehensive set of scenarios for
the future of intervention would go back of precolonial
and colonial antecedents, here I start with its salient
"neocolonial" variant. The neocolonial period, of
circa 1960 to 1975, has its roots, of course, in earlier
epochs. But intervention during the precolonial centuries was legitimised by recourse to Europe's "civil-
ising mission" and during the colonial decades by
recourse to Eurocentric "international" law. In the
sixties, intervention was internationalised once more,
although it was largely structural because of the
unnecessity for strategic involvements, Congo notwith-

standing. "Independence" meant that intervention at least became an issue--neocolonialism is not quite colonialism and that more African and other actors could become involved in "plunder" on the continent.

Two almost continuous trends are thus discernable over patterns of both strategic and structural intervention in Africa since the early 1960s. First, the number of involvement actors--state and non-state--has grown consistently. And second, the range of coalitions which include African participation has also grown ineluctably. First, non-colonial countries and corporations, notably American[19] and Japanese, have become involved, along with non-capitalist and non-major states (eg. Russia and Cuba, respectively). And second, African militaries and regimes--particularly the military, bureaucratic and national fractions--have become partners in complex coalitions over, say, intervention in Angola, Chad, the Horn, Sahara and Shaba, let alone Southern Africa. In all instances except the last, such grouping have increasingly broken into two antagonistic coalitions, broadly separated into "moderate" and "radical" factions; only over the quintessential "PanAfrican" issue of Southern Africa has the conservative coalition been so much of a minority.[20]

The role of countries, corporations and classes other than those of the super- or great-powers should not be assumed to be either subordinate or "proxy." Indeed, national armies and classes of both middle and African powers are quite capable of deciding to intervene first, anticipating support from major allies. But such assistance is not always forthcoming, as South Africa discovered, belatedly, in Angola, and as Tanzania realised in Uganda. Nevertheless, the intricacies of the world system do provide considerable leverage for more minor actors to secure the involvement of more major interests especially when the snowball effect turns a winning coalition into a landslide.

Given the political importance of the continent's 50-odd states, as well as their relative economic unimportance--diplomatic centrality combined with economic marginality--"Africa policy" is a fixed item on the agenda of non-African actors, although its place is very changeable.

The options confronting non-African decision makers can be divided into three main choices, ranging from "interventionist" through "internationalist" to "isola-

tionist." In practice, very few interests--country,
corporate or class--have consistently advocated either
of the extremes, preferring instead some mix of
emphases, befitting Africa's rather peripheral and
transitional status. And within this mix the salience
of issue areas may vary over time. If towards the
"radical" isolationist end of the spectrum we identify
Basic Human Needs (BHN) and "Afro-centric" positions,
then at the "conservative" interventionist end we can
place geostrategic or globalist and credibility pos-
tures. Somewhere in the middle--"moderate" or inter-
nationalist--part of the spectrum lie "tempered ideal-
ist" and "helping Africa to transform itself" attitudes,[21] quintessential "liberal" positions. In
general, the superpowers with their strategic imperatives tend to be closer to the interventionist pole
than major or minor powers; and corporations with their
economic criteria tend to be so rather than governments, especially those bits of government concerned
with assistance and development: the "internationalist" or "Basic Human Needs" advocates. Finally,
assorted non-governmental organisations tend to be more
"progressive" and to advocate isolationalist or Afro-
centric values. The variety of positions, particularly
the range found within the advanced industrialised
capitalist states, leads to mixed messages or multiple
advocacy: in the US governmental system for instance,
let alone within the broader American political economy, a whole host of "Africa policies" can be identified.

The salience of Africa in extra-continental perceptions and politices is not, of course, a fixture; hence
it movement up and down the foreign policy agenda.
Rather, there are continual debates within major
countries and corporations over "Africa policy." One
of the most celebrated in recent times was, of course,
that in Carter's America, between "globalists" and
"Africanists"[22] over Angola. W. Scott Thompson, given
his own hawkish tendencies, comes down hard on the
latter "Andrew Young" faction

> ...The Carter administration was
> never comfortable looking at Africa
> geopolitically. The old dichotomy
> between ideals and substantive
> interests began to be seen as a
> conflict between siding with
> 'Africa' and assuming a 'globalist'
> position that, by implication and
> without any necessary connection,

301

was associated with a benign
approach to South Africa.[23]

Thompson does not hide his preference for Reagan's
realpolitik in treating African and related "cold war"
issues; indeed he advocates a continued "hard-nosed"
globalist approach for the 1980s, with minimal regard
for African sensibilities or subtleties:

> ...the United States for the first
> time has a strategy with respect to
> Africa...US policy toward Africa is
> more strategic in conception than
> is US policy toward any other
> region...the question for US
> strategist is not how does America
> fit into Africa's perspective, but
> rather how does Africa fit into
> ours.[24]

Such a conservative position emphasises the strategic
issue-areas whereas more liberal policies focus on
political or economic concerns.

If the conservative interventionist view of Africa
emphasises its strategic status and the radical isolationist critique its economic position, the liberal
internationalist perspective is essentially political
in concern. In considerable contrast to Thompson,
Zartman expresses this middle-ground well in the case
of the US.:

> In the context of the global
> balance and beyond it, America's
> interest in Africa is primarily
> political: it lies in a need to
> monitor the continent's chaotic
> development in order to help avoid
> destabilising crises which would
> subvert African progress and suck
> the US into unwanted but unavoid-
> able intervention...the US has no
> direct responsibilities in Africa
> and, on the other side of the coin,
> cannot count on African states as
> allies.[25]

Liberal-cum-internationalist premises, as Thompson
indicates, have been under seige during the Reagan
administration with its cold war mind-set. Yet they
still represent powerful forces within the American

establishment and would claim longer-term rationality
(for the "national interest") and affinity (for things
"African"). Jennifer Seymour Whitaker articulates this
alternative internationalist-cum-trilateralist position
well: "the need to minimise the military competition
in Africa and to pursue political and economic alternatives rooted in African realities springs...from calcu-
lation of real US options."[26] So the internationalists
advocate political rather than either strategic or economic forms of intervention appropriate to a continent
still essentially within the Western sphere. But as
the neocolonial period drew to a close with major
crises or challenges in, say, Angola and Ethiopia, so
the political-first position came under attack from
both interventionist and isolationist elements: internationalism is a tenuous policy in an illiberal world.

Despite successful Soviet commitment in Ethiopia
and Angola, Africa remains, as already suggested, an
essentially "Western" oriented continent: "EurAfrica"
is the major North-South connection, increasingly reinforced since the Second World War and the independence
era by American and Japanese involvements concentrated
in diplomatic and economic issue areas, respectively.
The division of labour within the Western world with
regard to Africa is, then, of considerable importance,
affecting and reflecting national policy preferences:
Franco-American cooperation in Sahara and Shaba; Anglo-
American cooperation over Zimbabwe; and "Contact Group"
interaction over Namibia. The form of Western collaboration over change in South Africa remains to be
seen. Meanwhile, aside from Franco-African summits,
official multilateral economic relations are coordinated in several fora--IBRD/IMF meetings, Lome II EEC-
ACP institutions, and the OECD development committee
and "Cooperation for Development in Africa", now joined
by ECA, SADCC and ECOWAS advocacy.

By contrast to the diversity of Western linkages,
the Soviet Union has fewer and weaker partners on which
to call--just COMECON, including Cuba, now that China
is estranged. Although, it has tried occasionally to
multilaterise its relationships--see the January 1969
Khartoum conference--and despite continuity in collective
and progressive lusophone institutions, the Soviets
essentially coordinate a host of bilateral connections.
Moreover, except perhaps in Addis Ababa and Luanda they
lack the ready informal access which Western diplomats
still enjoy throughout most of the continent. Having
supported ZAPU for so long, the Soviets were particularly resentful of being sidelined by the Front Line

States (FLS), British and Americans during the Lancaster House Conference on Zimbabwe. Indeed, one trump card which the Reagan administration seems determined to throw away by reintroducing "globalist" calculations into America's Africa policy is a distinction between the superpowers: it is in Russian interests alone to equate the two blocs on the continent, given the head-start of the West. One indication of the relative unawareness of the Soviet connection with the continent is the limited spectrum of its own debate about alternative Africa policies.

Given the character of its own political economy and the (limited) history of its ties with Africa[27] the links of the Soviet Union are essentially political and military, with the latter becoming the more important as political relations have proven to be so unreliable. Although select trade, aid and communications links have been gradually growing, the centerpieces remain politico-strategic. By contrast the other superpower's relations are more variable, with an important economic-corporate component. Those of European powers are, on balance, more economic than either strategic or political whilst that of Japan is almost exclusively economic in character. These inter-imperial distinctions may vary over time as competition continually changes the ranking of Africa on the global agenda--but overall Africa will remain rather marginal for almost all actors, except perhaps, selective European countries and corporations.

So if Africa poses perplexing problems for the US, as reflected in its continuing policy debate, it also does for the USSR: the imminent end of national liberation movements with the remaining struggles in Namibia and South Africa (see section v) along with the independent streak in even avowedly "Marxist-Leninist" regimes make any prospective Soviet impact quite problematic. Soviet intentions and achievements relate to the continuing debate around Gorshkov's papers and the blue water navy. The Soviet attempt to identify and encourage "non-capitalist" states has been inconclusive:[28] individual, ideological and institutional instabilities upset to careful policies. For a while, approximately the decade 1965 to 1975, the Soviet Union yielded pride of revolutionary place to China, and after Afghanistan it may yet do so again.

But from the mid-1970s, reinforced by Angola and not harmed by Zimbabwe, the Soviets have been able to

improve their visibility and record in Africa. In the
early 1970s several regimes proclaimed themselves to be
Marxist-Leninist. But, as Robert Legvold indicates:

> ...1974 marks a watershead....1974
> is the year of the Ethiopian
> 'revolution': the year Benin pro-
> claimed its goal socialism; it is
> the year of the Soviet-Somali
> Treaty of Friendship and Coopera-
> tion; and the year of the Second
> Congress of the Congolese Workers's
> party. Combined with continued
> progress in Guinea, Tanzania and
> Somalia, these events apparently
> persuaded Soviet observers that the
> African revolution had gathered its
> second wind.[29]

However, Soviet policy remains essentially pragmatic, having learnt reluctantly in Ghana, Nigeria,
Somalia, Uganda and elsewehre that African leaders are
both nationalist and mercurial. Its renewed stake,
brought about by the appearance of more genuine
Marxist-Leninist regimes in the mid-1970s to replace
those "revolutionary democracies" "lost" in the mid-
1960s, is rather cautious: "By and large, as the
Soviet leaders know, change in Africa unfolds at its
own pace and in its own fashion."[30]

The above argument essentially suggests that
Western intervention has become more strategic and less
structural in form since independence as African political economies have asserted themselves while Soviet
involvement has consistently been strategic and diplomatic. The argument also suggests that Western
debates (and actions?), reflective of the evolution in
the global economy, have become more extreme rather
than moderate, particularly since Angola and the demise
of Carter's more "Afro-centric" criteria; i.e. that
much of the decade of the 1970s was a peculiarly benign
period in terms of America's Africa policy. The trauma
of Vietnam changed the calculus of risk in Africa and
elsewhere at least for a while. The more malign character of the present and prospective periods reflects
the revival of strategic doctrines and responses related to economic contraction among the industrialised
states at the centre.

iii) Variation in intervention: post-noecolonialism

As the African continent becomes more divergent
and diverse so patterns of intervention change. Three
particular developments are already discernible in the
post-neocolonial period of 1975 onwards. First, structural intervention has been superceded as the dominant
form by strategic intervention. Second, both superpowers and assorted great and middle powers have begun
to be active strategically on the continent. And
third, African states, both NICs and LLDCs, have been
interventive on their own continent usually, but not
always, in their own particular region. Paradoxically,
then, economic dislocation and recession from the mid-
1970s on has had the effect of increasing strategic
rather than structural intervention: inter-imperial
rivalries and the NIC/LLDC divide have exacerbated
political rather than economic differences.

Although Africa may be at the periphery of the
world system, because of global interrelatedness
outcomes there can affect relationships elsewhere as
well as vice versa. Events in the Horn and in Southern
Africa, especially Angola, served in the late-1970s to
intensify the confrontation between the superpowers;
conversely, superpower competition in the early 1980s
has, in turn, exacerbated tensions in the Sahara and
Chad as well as along the borders of South Africa.
Gavshon suggests, however, that, given Africa's economic crisis the political instability, the superpowers
may still have a mutual interest in limiting bipolar
tensions on the continent, with important implications
for the rest of the world system:

> In the final two decades of the
> century, whoever occupies the White
> House or Kremlin, it seems certain
> that a new phase of interdependence
> faces the nations. Pressures are
> building up on East and West alike
> to contribute substantially towards
> evolving a new international econo-
> mic order that would make that
> concept of interdependence a real-
> ity. East and West have the choice
> between controlling, if not aban-
> doning, their rivalries in Africa
> and elsewhere or risking the break-
> down of national and international
> systems.[31]

Any such revival of detente may be difficult to
realise, however, given the intensity of issues in
Africa and the involvement of African as well as non-
African actors in antagonistic coalitions. Raymond
Copson reflects the prevailing wisdom that the post-
neocolonial period will be quite conflictual, particularly in Southern Africa but also around Libya's self-
proclaimed "sphere of influence:"

> In view of the weaponary and man-
> power available to several African
> countries, and the strong griev-
> ances that mark some African dis-
> putes...it is clear that armed
> international violence is possible,
> primarily at four major flash-
> points: the regions bordering
> South Africa and Namibia; the Horn
> of Africa; Libya's borders and the
> borders of the Libyan sphere of
> influence, now extending into Chad;
> and Morocco's borders, including
> the borders of Morocco's sphere in
> influence in the former Spanish
> Sahara. Three of these potential
> flashpoints have been constant
> sources of tension in Africa inter-
> national politics over the past two
> decades[32].Only the Libyan challenge
> is new.

However, not only is Libya's interventive posture
novel, the assembly of antagonistic coalitions over
Southern Africa, the Horn and the Sahara has also
reached a new stage of sophistication, reflective of
intensifying ideological divisions on the continent.

Legum also recognises that conflict in Africa will
intensify in the present decade, yet his reasons for
speculating thus lie with orthodox factors such as
ethnicity and nation. Nevertheless his own concluding
speculation is apropos: "Africa's postcolonial conditions of political instability will, if anything, be
greater in the 1980s than in the two previous
decades."[33]

Legum not only bases his assertion of increasing
conflict on rather orthodox sociological rather than
more radical class analysis; he also offers a rather
idiosyncratic chronology of foreign intervention to
date, suggesting that Western involvement ended and

restarted later than other observers; he also is more
one-sided in apportioning "blame" for such intervention, despite Reagan's assertive "leadership" of the
NATO powers:

> In the 1950s and 1960s the major
> Western powers and the Soviet block
> intervened actively....However, in
> the later part of the 1970s the
> Western powers began to show them-
> selves to be much less ready to
> become directly involved in local
> power struggles, while the Soviets
> became more adventurous....Unless
> there is a major reversal of this
> trend in Western policies in the
> 1980s initiatives for outside
> intervention with the Chinese and
> some of the Western nations poss-
> ibly reacting to their moves in
> particular circumstances.[34]

Legum also provides a broader set of issues inviting
such involvement, not just the orthodox range of
African "flashpoints" nor his own set of internal
"sociological" factors:

> Five issues are likely to keep Africa high on the
> agenda of international decision-making in the
> 1980s:
>
> 1. 'Ocean politics', a crucial aspect of the
>   global power struggle.
>
> 2. The racial confrontation in Southern Africa,
>   which will almost certainly reach its climax
>   before the end of the next decade.
>
> 3. Afro-Arab politics.
>
> 4. Sino-Soviet rivalry for influence in the Third
>   World.
>
> 5. The North-South dialogue...[35]

Most analysts assume the agenda items to consist of
regional wars as opposed to more structural issues,
although clearly intervention and interaction treat
both. One of the reasons for such an assumption can
be found in the growth of intra-African military
involvement outside national boundaries and without the

approval of either neighbours, regional organisations or continental "wise men": a dramatic redefinition of "pan-Africanism."

So a new phenomenon in post-neocolonial Africa--although in many respect a return to pre-colonial relations of regional conflicts and coalitions [36] --is the possibility of intra-continental "intervention." As Zartman indicates, "Intervention by one African state's army in another's problems made its appearance[37] in the late 1970s and has since increased." The involvement of Libya in Chad and Tanzania in Uganda, for example, are suggestive of a new type of "Pan-Africanism": unilateral intervention as opposed to collective "peace--keeping" under OAU auspices. The joint "EurAfrican" involvements in Katanga/Shaba represent half-way forms: neither unilateral nor collective, but usually "legitimised" through Franco-African arrangements.

The propensity for such intra-continental incursion is a function of a) superpower detente and disinterest; b) African instabilities on the one hand and capabilities on the other; and c) elusiveness of some effective collective organisation. A more controversial fourth element may be adduced: ambitious leaders seeking aggrandisement even at the expense of "brothers" territory and integrity --the transformation of Pan-Africanism into Pax Africana.

Legum also points to the growing African involvement in so-called "interventive" coalitions, although characteristically he may date its appearance differently from Copson, Zartman and other analysts:

> One of the mythologies of contemporary Africa is that the continent is the victim of exploiting foreign powers. But an objective analysis will show that this belief is a post-colonial hangover from the days when Africa was indeed the passive victim of the major powers. The situation today is that foreign intervention recurs because African governments, individually or collectively, for their own interests, are ready to engage external support....[38]

309

But whilst the weakness of PanAfrican structures and economies may be permissive of intrusion, the very instability and incoherence of many polities make its extension, in either spatial or chronological terms, problematic.

The future of such intra-continental intervention is limited, then, by the very same factors which made it possible in recent years. First, superpower detente is in decline and the disinterest of other countries and corporations is uneven: strategic African classes, cities and minerals still attract extra-continental attention. Second, despite continental instability and decline some states have achieved a degree of order and power, particularly those with petro-dollars. Third, the influence, even presence, of the OAU can no longer be assumed after the Tripoli fiascos and related ineffectiveness. And fourth, ambitious leader are unlikely to disappear whether the external situation is unpropitious or not. In short, both African and external proclivities towards intervention are likely to be strengthened through the 1980s despite (or even because of) economic difficulties. Indeed, the very divergencies on the continent between NICs and LLDCs may embolden the former towards involvement in the latter, albeit under the guise of regional or continental "integration."

So despite the considerable political and economic costs involved, we may expect a continuity of Libyan-type interventions, even if not Tanzanian-style ones, notwithstanding the involvement of the TPDF in the Seychelles and Mozambique as well as in Uganda. And we may anticipate further external "adventures" by Algeria, Morocco, and Nigeria and possibly by Zimbabwe, particularly once its southern border has been effectively secured. Such a scenario stands in contrast to the projection of Copson who argued in 1982 that, aside from conflicts in Northern and Southern Africa,

> Elsewhere on the continent, the
> prospects for armed international
> violence are quite limited over the
> remainder of the decade--limited by
> the modest capabilities of the
> African states and by the genuine
> reluctance of black Africa regimes,
> which do share a certain sense of
> solidarity with one another, to
> become involved in costly disputes
> that could threaten domestic

310

political stability and damage
prospects for economic development.[39]

One technique both to recognise linkages and to
restrain adventurism which has become quite popular of
late in Africa is the establishment of mutual defence
agreements, as well as of potential regional defence
associations such as that envisaged through ECOWAS.
The early Kenya-Ethiopia (1963) and Sene-Gambia (1964)
treaties have since been joined by Egyptian-Sudanese
(1977), Guinea-Liberian (1967) and Mozambique-Zimbabwe
(1981) accords; all efforts, albeit somewhat idealistic,
to restrain unilateral definitions of pax Africana.
The twin issues of Pan-African interventive inclinations and security arrangements raise one further
related question: are military governments on the
continent more prone to adventurism than civilian
regimes? We have already raised the issue of whether
the appearance of more radical "Marxist-Leninist"
systems increases the prospects of division and intervention. Here we treat an analagous issue: are great
power perspectives and propensities affected by the
incidence and activity of militaries in and around
African polities?

Not only should we be cautious in ascribing intervention in the past and future to the inclinations and
master-plans of major powers given the range of their
"Africa policy" debates, noted in the previous section.
We should also be sceptical about whether military
governments are more likely to be interventive than
civilian ones as often assumed in the literature.
While Henry Bienen is realistic about the increasing
capabilities for intra- as well as extra-continental
involvement, he is cautious about their likely incidence, as well as their impact on non-African powers:

> There are good reasons to predict
> that Africa faces more, not less,
> interstate conflict. Growing eco-
> nomic differentiation proceeds
> apace within Africa. States
> increasingly have the wherewithal
> to translate disagreements into
> economic and military actions....
> military factors in Africa can no
> longer be seen as just matters of
> domestic politics; they play a
> vital role in Africa's inter-

311

national relations and must affect
the calculations of other nations
that deal with Africa.[40]

Nevertheless, military regimes are no more or less
inclined to external adventures or missions than
civilian ones, according to Bienen, notwithstanding
their growing direct and indirect role in governments:

> ...we do not find that African
> military regimes align themselves
> in clear-cut ways in either inter-
> African affairs or global
> politics...African militaries do
> not appear as distinctive actors in
> the foreign policy process,
> although more attention should be
> given to military styles of
> decision making.[41]

While military involvement in African government
may be of marginal importance in explaining or predicting either intra- or extra-African interventions,
ideological orientation may be of increasing salience,
especially in the post-neocolonial period. This is so
when ideology is reflective of distinctive political
economies rather than of just individual leadership
preferences. Increasingly intense and antagonistic
contradictions   in both centre and periphery (not
forgetting the emergent African semi-periphery), as
well as increasingly divergent economic performances
and prospects, have exacerbated differences between
Africa's political economies. The target of intervention is decreasingly homogeneous as the neocolonial
period yields to a post-neocolonial order. Given new
tensions within as well as between African political
economies--the issue of the proletariat and peasantry
is treated in the next section--"security" may yet have
to be redefined on the continent.

iv) Intervention in a post-expansion, post-detente
world

Intervention as sustained and sudden involvement
in the territory, polity and/or economy of another
state has become more problematic over time: the
number of states, issues and actors makes it ever more
complex and problematic. Not that less certainty about
outcome reduces its incidence: intervention has always
been a high risk policy. But the range of interventive

interests and strategies is likely to expand as the
elusiveness and ambiguousness of power permit small as
well as big states, regional as well as global actors
to intervene on the continent. Indeed, it is one indication of the continent's relatively low level of military capability that Libya, Morocco, or Tanzania can
intervene at apparent will in regional disputes. Yet
the development of country and class coalitions poses
problems for both the regulations and sustainment of
such interventionist actions: a dramatic redefinition
of 'good neighbourliness."

    The revival of the cold war in the 1980s also
serves to increase the stakes in Africa: any extra-
continental involvement is again seen through globalist
perceptions to be zero-sum both inside and outside
Africa itself. Intervention from such a perspective,
as indicated in the above section on policy-making, is
never benign nor limited; it is always one move in a
comprehensive master plan. Just as European balances
in the 1880s were interrelated to colonial acquisitions
in Africa so in the 1980s some external actors-
superpowers and others-attach importance to hegemonic
associations with African leaders, movements and
minerals. Such high stakes are unfortunate for at
least two reasons, however.

    First, Africa's economic crisis is so severe that
any distortion from its constitutes a further setback
to the satisfaction   of the Basic Human Needs (BHN) of
most of its peoples. Both the OAU Lagos Plan of Action
and the World Bank's Agenda are responses to this
intensifying condition of inadequate and uneven
growth.⁴² The major debate between and about these two
perspectives and prescriptions is not over whether
Africa should develop but how. The latter, IBRD
Agenda, proposes further structural intervention--more
commodity exports for more manufactured imports along
with less public sector involvement and more foreign
assistance--whereas the indigenous Lagos Plan advocated
disengagement as a means to control the incidence and
impact of structural intervention: a retreat from an
unhelpful inheritance of incorporation.⁴³ Although
neither of these two sets of economic proposals directly addresses the issues of foreign intervention and
domestic militarisation, such phenomena can only
further divert and retard Africa's economic recovery;
the disarmament/development dialectic or debate has
hardly been recognised yet on the continent.

But second, given Africa's economic strengths, its
political stability is so fragile that external inter-
vention--strategic as well as structural--could become
very routine, almost habitual. As economic condition
and political conditionality are so closely interrelated, external involvement with one necessarily affects
the other; and both, separately and together, encourage
extracontinental attention. Given the morass that
foreigners may enter, extreme caution is adviseable;
yet as recent political and economic crises indicate
such caution is remarkably absent. So both superpowers
may prolong their considerable respective involvement
in Ethiopia and Zaire in the hope that some returns
will thereby be gained despite exponential military and
financial debts. In such special situations, strategic and
structural causes become almost indistinguishable: neocolonialism
verging on outright colonialism remains alive and well in certain
cases.

Although all instances of continental conflict and
external involvement, including the Horn and Shaba are
important for the future of Africa, two continuing
regional crises have achieved a particular salience,
which will continue for the foreseeable future: the
Middle East and Southern Africa. Both involve long-
term issues of land, race and rights--i.e. real human
development--the continuous attention of regional
organisations and global actors, and certain inter-
connections (e.g. South Africa and Israel, and the PLO
and the ANC). Moreover, both are considered as bellweather cases determining the direction of the continent as a whole. Zartman, for instance, has pointed
to regional trends as significant for continental
direction, an "eventful" transition in Southern Africa
having profound implications for radical change elsewhere:

> The African continent is an open
> field of opportunities and traps
> for foreign powers, and particu-
> larly for the US. It should be
> noted that there would be nothing
> but traps if the Southern African
> conflict turned to revolution and
> an OAU--Pretoria war. In that
> case, the US would probably not
> live up to African desires and
> would suffer badly in its African
> relations....The manner in which
> Zimbabwe attains independence is

314

crucial to the political direction
of Southern Africa, a negotiated
(political) transition providing a
more 'moderate' member of the
Southern region than a guerrilla
(military) takeover. On the other
hand, the revolution in South
Africa has already begun and will
render increasingly difficult the
search for <u>interlocuteurs valables</u>
should the government ever decide
on meaningful reforms.[44]

However, it is not clear, despite alarmist analysis
of the strategic mineral and Cape route questions, that
the Soviet Union and its allies would automatically
benefit from a transformed South Africa.[45] Just as
Zimbabwe under Mugabe is above all else a nationalist
regime so we might expect a liberated "Pretoria" to be
similarly inclined. The ANC is a very long-standing
and sophisticated party, as indicated by its history of
political debates and recent strategic actions; it is
no more likely to become a "puppet" of the USSR than
its present Nationalist Party predecessors are of the
UK or the US. The very sophistication of the South
Africa political economy--I treat proletarianisation
later in this section--makes simplistic scenarios
inappropriate.

By contrast to the relatively benign, political
emphasis of Zartman--the liberal position--Geoffrey
Kemp prefers a more activist, strategic role for the US
in South Africa and else-where centered around specific
and general interests. This stance serves to legiti-
mise post-Carter initiatives in and around Africa:

In the broader geopolitical context
of the Southern seas, appropriate
military policies for the US are
more clear cut. In order to
balance and deter the Soviet Union,
low-keyed US initiatives to maintain a military footing in the
South Atlantic and the Indian Ocean
should be continued.[46]

In addition to the factor of strategic balance and
gamespersonship, other commentators have revived cold
war ideological disputes, in part reflective of a growing debate in Africa itself between moderates and radicals.

Michael Radu articulates the restored paranoia of
"anti-communism" as applied to contemporary Africa,
grossly underestimating the tensions within the radical
coalition:

> Faithful to their perception of the
> international arena as the focus of
> class struggle, the African
> Marxists...see international rela-
> tions as close to a zero-sum
> gane...
>
> The use of 'proleterian inter-
> nationalism' to justify Soviet-bloc
> interventions in Africa was often
> mentioned, although its implica-
> tions for the future, as preparing
> the gound for a possible de facto
> extension of the so-called
> Brezchenev Doctrine to at least
> some African 'progressive' regimes
> were often underestimated. What
> has gone largely unnoticed...is the
> emergence of a network of ties
> among the members of the 'progress-
> ive' group...support for nourishing
> Marxist groups in their attempts to
> gain power, and as defence of the
> existing Marxist regimes.[47]

And Radu sees such socialist regimes as more securely
entrenched in power than their non-socialist counterparts: fixtures on the African scence. He asserts
that they are more "socialist" than "African"--and so
lie outside the confines of any "Afrocentric" orien-
tation--and thus, given their "alignment", (see his
opening citation) should be subjected to direct and
indirect isolation by the US:

> Internal militarisation, increas-
> ingly level of cooperation among
> African revolutionary regimes and
> between them and the communist
> states, and the presence of foreign
> military and security personnel on
> their territory are all factors of
> regional and continental instabi-
> lity.[48]

Zartman, from a liberal "Africanist" perspective,
is much less certain than Radu about either the cohe-

siveness of the radical coalition or its intentions; so
he is likewise less strident in calling for a renewed
"cold war" reaction from America:

> ...the ad hoc factions of the OAU
> have not turned into alliances that
> either dominate or divide the mak-
> ings of the OAU or replace it as an
> active international organisation.
> The moderate 'axis' of Morocco-
> Senegal-Ivory Coast-Gabon-Zaire,
> which the radicals recognise, or
> the radical 'bloc' of Madagascar-
> Angola-Mozambique-Congo-Benin-
> Algeria-Libya, which the moderates
> fear, turns out to be ragged, ad
> hoc, and subject to notable defec-
> tions or 'paired' neutralisations.
> Although it may not be cohesive,[49]
> Africa has not fallen apart.

Nevertheless, despite internal fragmentation the two
coalitions are seen, at least by each other and by
extra-continental associates, to be cohesive and
continuing groupings. Over current African
flashpoints-Chad, the Horn, and Sahara as well as the
Middle East and Southern Africa--they tend to adopt
antagonistic positions, positions which underlay the
demise of the aborted Tripoli OAU summits: the issue
was as much factionalism as Gaddafi, although the two
are closely interwoven.

The increasing self-consciousness and mutual support of the antagonistic coalitions in Africa raise
important issues for both policy (see previous section)
and projection (see next section). If the moderates
have identified with the EEC and "Franco-African"
arrangements then the "radicals" have common interests
with COMECON and "Tricontinental" institutions.
Although Africa as a whole remains pervaded by Western
influences, the appearance of more radical regimes
through guerrilla struggle has tilted the balance
somewhat away from an early Western dominance. As
Zartman notes,

> The end of the 1970s thus saw
> Africa divided along cold war
> dimensions as it had never been
> before.[50]

Yet he points to the special conditions of Angola and
Mozambique which did not prevail in Zimbabwe and need
not do so in the liberation of the rest of Southern
Africa. So, unlike Radu's fiercely anti-communist
stance or Legum's renewed fears of the USSR, Zartman is
considerably more relaxed about Soviet (and African)
possibilities and intentions: "the latter half of the
1970s represented a high-water mark for Soviet penetration into Africa, at least until the South African
target opens up in the 1990s."[51] However, aside from
general economic and political difficulties, there is
one structural change occuring which might ostensibly
open the continent to more radical--but not ncessarily
Soviet-supported or--manipulated--pressures.

One particular result of both economic contraction
and type of political economy has been the proletarianisation and alienation of labour in Africa, particularly Southern Africa. The "labour aristrocracy" of the
mines and factories has been superceded by an impove-
rished urban workforce and a growing pool unemployment.
In turn, alienated and unemployed proletarians are
likely to engage in various kinds of industrial and
political actions, as seen in strikes, food riots and
political protests, which the **Lagos Plan** is designed to
forestall. Such class actions have become more frequent and violent as IMF-style desubsidisation and
devaluation policies erode further the precarious
living standards of non-bourgeois classes.[52]

And if the plight of the proletariat is serious
then that of the peasantry is even more so as indicated
in the World Bank's **Agenda**: commodity prices continue
to tumble and rural infrastructure is falling into
decay. The only "rational" strategy--to ensure the
satisfaction of BHN--is for the peasantry to abandon
(if free to do so from governmental regulations and
pressures) cash crop production (except, perhaps, for
urban dwellers within the country) and return to sub-
sistance agriculture for the extended family.[53] Such a
revival of rural self-reliance poses fundamental
challenges to the bases of African political
economies--international exportation for foreign
exchange and national extraction for bourgeois
affluence. Without cash crop production, transporta-

318

tion, and exportation, both national economies and
national bourgeoisies become rather vulnerable; hence
the imperative, in terms of both "national interest"
and bourgeois predelictions, to revive commodity trade
as advocated by the World Bank.[54] Yet the workers and
peasants, for both short- and long-term reasons, are no
longer so impressed by either World Bank or national
plans. One result of the current crisis, according to
M'buyinga,

> ...is inevitably an ever-increasing
> awareness on the part of the
> African workers and poorer peasant-
> ry that irreducible contractions
> put their interests in opposition
> to those of both imperialism and
> the African neo-colonial bourgeoi-
> sie. The latter may be equally
> dominated by the foreign imperial-
> ist bourgeoisie, but they can
> always take troubles out on the
> African workers. Within the limits
> imposed by imperialisms, the neo-
> colonial African bourgeoisies
> strive to organise an African
> market, notably a labour
> market...[55]

So intensifying internal contradictions, given
Africa's extroverted and vulnerable economies, will
increasingly involve external policies and relations:
foreign affairs, including intervention, will no longer
be an exclusive preserve of the bourgeoisie, whether
civilian or military. But this is just one of several
possible predictions about the mid-term future of
intervention in Africa; others follow in the concluding
section.

**v) Intervention projected: contradictions, coalitions
and corporatism on a world scale**

Pliny the elder captured the essence of the continent back in the first century AD when he complained:
ex Africa semper aliquid novi.[56] Yet even the very
novelty of continental affairs should be amenable to
certain forms of projection and speculation. It is
quite certain, for example, that no African state other
than South Africa will become industrialised by the
year 2000. Further, some African peoples will still
not have their basic needs met by the end of the century.[57] And if the structural constraints on develop-

ment are so clear, then the politics of poverty can likely be envisioned: political instability will continue to be endemic and populist pressures will lead to both revolution and repression.[58] Clearly, however, we need to be more specific in our predictions and, for the purposes for this paper, speculate on implications of such continental conditions for the incidence of intervention.

The future of intervention in Africa will, unless novel, unforeseen elements and events intrude, be a function or continental trends and global developments. Neither of these problematiques, nor their interrelations, can be easily or confidently previewed. However, a select set of factors can be identified recognising that these may a) be interrelated and b) be rearranged over time. Given the approach adopted throughout the paper these are subdivided into strategic and structural types.

In terms of strategic issues, the global balance of power and the (related) continental configuration will be most salient, with regional balances--Southern Africa, the Horn, North Africa and West Africa--being both causes and results of continental and global situations; and in turn, such situations are affected by current perceptions of technological needs, investment protection, mineral imperatives and military capabilities.[59]

In terms of structural issues, the global economy and (related) continental characteristics are most salient, with two sets of tensions among "middle powers" being crucial, especially in a period of economic contraction--interimperial rivalries at the global level, and NICs versus LLDCs at the continental level.   In turn, these are connected with changes in a) economic issues and negotiations (e.g. NIEO, EEC-ACP, GATT, UNCTAD, etc.) and b) class and corporate strategies and struggles (e.g. the rise and role of the national bourgeoisis and types of joint ventures and company policies).[60] In both sets of issues, technological and financial developments are crucial conditioners of diplomatic, strategic and economic relations: perceptions as well as expectations of technological change (e.g. what roles for petroleum and copper in the post-industrial age?) and financial difficulties (e.g. how to renegotiate debts and salvage investments?) profoundly affect broader policies.

In all such considerations, two basic underlying issues can be abstracted, both being of fundamental importance for patterns of and prospects for intervention on the continent, whether the intervention is strategic or structural, and whether internal or external origin. These crucial "systemic" variables are both related to stage or cycle in global and continental orders: a) whether the two strategic balances are moving towards or away from equilibrium and b) whether the two structural systems are in periods of expansion or contraction.

In terms of both the global and African situations, the post-war period from about 1960 to 1975 was, as already indicated, one of strategic balance and economic expansion. Since then, in a post-detente, post-Bretton Woods era, the strategic situation has moved away from equilibrium and the economic condition has moved towards contraction. The latter period is characterised by more conflict both within and around Africa. The underlying question about the future of intervention is whether the remaining two decades of the twentieth century will be characterised more by pre-or post-1975 type relations. For the purpose of this analysis I have called the initial, post-independence period "benign" and the later, post-neocolonial period "malign."

Strategic

As already indicated, the propensity for intervention, both intra- and extra-continental, has increased in the current malign period of renewed superpower confrontations and intensified inter-imperial rivalries. With major domestic difficulties--unemployment and deindustrialisation in the US and unproductivity and religion in the USSR--both super-powers are unlikely to moderate their central ant gonism from global reaches. Moreover, inter-imperial rivalries including other countries and corporations will exacebate such tensions, leading to alternative antagonistic coalitions over African disputes. And such continental conflict will be plentiful, not just in established "flashpoints" like Southern Africa and the Horn but also along the West African coast and in the Sahel, exacerbated by divergent economic performances and prospects. The tendency for African and non-African interests to coincide will be reinforced, with special emphasis on the role of NICs like Algeria, Egypt, Nigeria and

Zimbabawe, all of which will develop further their own
"military-industrial complexes."[61] Conflict over strategic mineral and foreign capital will continue, but in
changeable forms as attention shifts from copper to,
say, uranium or from direct investment to collective
debts.

The African response to such a history and continuity of interventive acts has also been high on the
PanAfrican agenda both before and after independence.
In recent post-independence times, African leaders have
been continually exercised by the issue of security,
for both national and personal reasons. But precisely
because of their contradictory position in the world
system--particularly dependence upon external exchange
and support--they have never been able to reach an
effective consensus. Plans for an African High Command
and for peacekeeping forces have come and gone; effective action usually depends on influential statesmen and
an extra-continental involvement, with legitimisation
following rather than preceeding crisis diplomacy.
Thus far, despite a widespread awareness of the
problem, there has been no "security summit" along the
lines of the Lagos economic meeting. The effective
forums for such actions have been the FLS grouping on
the one hand and the Franco-African summits on the
other. The OAU has debated the Indian Ocean as a "zone
of peace," seeking to exclude the bases and activities
of the "Big Powers," and at Freetown in mid-1980 discussed the establishment of an "OAU Political Security
Council" designed to respond with "the necessary speed
and effectiveness to political cases and problems of
security on the African continent." Such a Council
would be oriented towards safeguarding "the territorial
integrity and political independence of member-
states"[62] but its prospects of establishment let alone
effectiveness remain problematic given broader fissures
within the OAU structure.

The problems of an indigenous response to security
threats, including interventive acts, is likely to be
compounded by shifts in the continental strategic map.
For, with the imminent independence of Namibia and the
eventual liberation of South Africa, guerrilla struggle
will no longer be associated with orthodox nationalist
movements. Instead, it will come to be directed at
unpopular indigenous regimes, at its already has been
in Uganda and Zaire. So "security" will gradually be
redefined away from orthodox issues of national
sovereignty and boundaries and towards questions of
class and repression: who defines and benefits from

the "national" interest?[63] A particularly central
issue will be, as indicated in the previous section,
the place of proletariat in African political economics
and foreign policies. Thus the strategic and the
structural will become ever less distinguishable:
economic prospects affect military balances in both
Africa and elsewhere.

Despite the overall trend towards malignancy some
countervailing elements of benignness will remain,
however; for example, as indicated above, traditional
"Pan-African" attempts at conflict resolution and
peace-keeping at both continental (OAU) and regional
(ECOWAS) levels. And each antagonistic coalition will
always seek collective African legitimacy for its
actions through such established institutions. Yet the
strategic situation will, ineluctably, become more
intense and controversial as the threats become intra-
rather than inter-national in origin, "by-products" for
both general economic difficulties and particular economic forces.

Structural

As already suggested above, economic intervention
will become more uneven as external interests both wane
and concentrate: wane in terms of overall interests in
Africa yet concentrate: on particular states,
resources and sectors as global demands shift. As a
strategic situations becomes more malign the economic
one tends to benignness at least from the perspective
of the African periphery. The post-neocolonial period
of global contraction and continental decline is
characterised by disinterest in the Fourth World punc-
tuated by particular concerns, such as with petroleum
production and import absorption. Inter-imperial
rivalries are not focused on who can be most generous
in economic crisis situations such as the Sahel or the
Horn, although there are elements of both inter-state
and inter-non-state competition over aid to drought
victims and to refugees.

Rather, inter-imperial rivalries are concentrated
on the NICs, the few remaining areas of growth in a
contracting continent. So both countries and corporations seek to attract the foreign exchange earnings
and capital investment potential of, say, Algeria and
Nigeria even if they are more cautious about, say,
Angola and Libya. And they also continue to support
regional centres such as the Ivory Coast and Kenya.

323

The remaining forty-odd states--the Fourth World of LLDCs--are treated to "benign neglect"--triage--as they lack the foreign exchange, strategic minerals or industrial sectors to attract external interest.

Moreover, even in the NICs, the prospects for sustained economic intervention are reduced by the rise of a national bourgeoisie, in its entrepreneurial, political and military forms: penetration is only secured through collaboration with such indigenous class fractions. Just as strategic intervention requires at least formal African state association so structural involvement requires African class cooperation. An "Afrocentric" policy merely means, then, identifying and attracting positive African countries classes with which to cooperate. Given the diversity of actors and interests on the continent some such positive elements may always be found through which to "legitimist" intervention of both kinds: selective "indirect rule" in a post-neocolonial world.

It is within such a context that Africa's own plans for continental security-an African High Command--and continental economy--the Lagos Plan of Action--take a particular relevance. The only way in which the continent can insulate itself from negative changes in the global economic environment given its disappointing rate of development is through disengagement. So the Lagos Plan progresses from analysis through policy to praxis:

> The effect of unfulfilled promises
> of global development strategies
> has been more sharply felt in
> Africa than in the other continents
> of the world. Indeed, rather than
> result in an improvement in the
> economic situation of the contin-
> ent, successive strategies have
> made it stagnate and become more
> susceptible than other regions to
> the economic and social crises
> suffered by the industrialised
> countries. Thus, Africa is unable
> to point to any significant growth
> rate, or satisfactory index of
> general well-being, in the past 20
> years. Faced with this situation,
> and determined to undertake
> measures for the basic restruc-
> turing of the economic base of our

continent, we resolved to adopt a
far-reaching regional approach
based primarily on collective
self-reliance.[64]

In particular the Lagos Plan seeks to respond to
and reduce external historical, economic and policy
pressures given-with pregnant strategic implications--
their negative impact to date:

> ...Africa, despite all efforts made
> by its leaders, remains the least
> developed continent...Africa was
> directly exploited during the
> colonial period and for the last
> two decades; this exploitation has
> been carried out through neo-
> colonialist external forces which
> seek to influence the economic
> policies and directions of African
> states.[65]

However, in response to such an inauspicious
inheritance self-reliance will not always be either
consensual or comprehensive given divergencies of
capabilities and policies (and prospects). Nonetheless
as a direction for the continent it holds out some
promise whereas otherwise unfolding trends point
towards unpromising patterns of further dependence, at
least for the collectivity. Yet the very factors which
increase Africa's vulnerability--underdevelopment,
extroversion, divergence--also reduce its prospects for
collective self-reliance: too many indigenous
interests would be affected, unless, that is, domestic
pressures force a change in the national calculus.

Such plans for structural (and so strategic)
self-reliance are, of course, formulated and advanced
by elements, albeit relatively progressive ones, within
the African bourgeois. There are, then considerable
limits on their "progressive" content once the issues
move beyond collective nationalism. Only the excluded
non-bourgeois classes--the workers and the peasants--
can really define a radical foreign policy, one which
eschews indigenous as well as external intervention and
exploitation. Regretably, whilst it is quite clear
that there are Revolutionary Pressures in Africa[66] they
will remain too weak and diverse and be subject to too
much coercion and repression, to be effective in the
mid-term, except in one or two particular cases like

325

Ethiopia. For the one certainty in this otherwise
uncertain world is that the rich and powerful, whether
African or otherwise will not abandon affluence and
influence readily. A luta continua!

Notes

1. Arthur Gavshon Crisis in Africa: battleground of East and West (Harmondsworth: Pelican, 1981) 15.

2. Michael Radu "Ideology, parties and foreign policy in sub-Saharan Africa" Orbis 25(4), Winter 1982, 991 and 992.

3. Elenga M'buyinga Pan Africanism or Neo-Colonialism: the bankruptcy of the OAU (London: Zed, 1982) 124, 125, and 126.

4. Colin Legum "Communal conflict and international intervention in Africa" in Colin Legum et al Africa in the 1980s: continent in crisis (New York: Mc Graw-Hill for Council on Foreign Relations 1980s Project, 1979) 23-24. Emphasis added.

5. Ibid. 65-66.

6. I. William Zartman "Coming political problems in Black Africa" in Jennifer Seymour Whitaker (ed) Africa and the United States: vital interests (New York: New York University Press for Council on Foreign Relations, 1978) 89.

7. M'buyinga Pan Africanism or Neo-Colonialism 4.

8. Immanuel Wallerstein "The three stages of African involvement in the world economy" in Peter C. Gutkind and Immanuel Wallerstein (eds) The Political Economy of Contemporary Africa (Beverly Hills: Sage, 1976) 8.

9. M'buyinga Pan Africanism or Neo-Colonialism 79-80.

10. See Timothy M. Shaw "Regional cooperation and conflict in Africa" International Journal 30(4), Autumn 1975, 671-688 and "Towards a political economy of regional integration and inequality in Africa" Nigerian Journal of International Studies 2(2), October 1978, 1-28.

11. Zartman, "Coming political problems in Black Africa" 95.

12. See Timothy M. Shaw "Beyond the conventional: towards a political economy of the perphery" Radcliffe Presidential Conference on Challenging Conventional Wisdom, Cambridge, April 1983.

13. I. William Zartman "The future of Europe and Africa: decolonisation or dependency?" in Timothy M. Shaw (ed) Alternative Futures for Africa (Boulder: Westview, 1982) 261.

14. Ibid. 275.

15. Ibid. 277. cf on "EurAfrica", Timothy M. Shaw "EEC-ACP interactions and images as redefinitions of EurAfrica: exemplary, exclusive and/or exploitative?" Journal of Common Market Studies 18(2), December 1979, 135-158.

16. Steven Langdon and Lynn K. Mytelka "Africa in the changing world economy" in Legum et al Africa in the 1980s 211.

17. I. William Zartman "Issues of African diplomacy in the 1980s" Orbis 25(4), Winter 1982, 1028.

18. Gavshon Crisis in Africa 43. cf. Gerard Chaliand The Struggle for Africa: conflict of the great powers (London: Macmillan, 1982).

19. On decolonisation as a reflection of American hegemony rather than African nationalism see Gilbert A. Sekgoma "Decolonisation: towards a global perspective, 1940-1978" in Timothy M. Shaw and Sola Ojo (eds) Africa and the International Political System (Washington: University Press of America, 1982) 41-67.

20. See Timothy M. Shaw "International organisations and the politics of Southern Africa: towards regional integration or liberation?" Journal of Southern African Studies 3(1), 1976, 1-19 and, with Agrippah T. Mugomba, "The political economy of regional detente: Zambia and Southern Africa" Journal of African Studies 4(4), Winter 1977/78, 392-413.

21. For a useful typology of such alternative, but not always exclusive, positions see Helen Kitchen (ed) "Options for US policy toward Africa" AEI Foreign Policy and Defence Review 1(1)

passim. See also her "Six misconceptions of Africa" Washington Quarterly 5(4), Autumn 1982, 167-174.

22. See David Ottaway "Africa: US policy eclipse" Foreign Affairs 58(3), 637-658. cf. L.H. Gann and Peter Duignan Africa South of the Sahara: the challenge to Western security (Stanford: Hoover Institution, 1981).

23. W. Scott Thompson "US policy toward Africa: at America's service?" Orbis 25(4), Winter 1982, 1015.

24. Ibid. 1022- 1023. Emphasis added.

25. Zartman, "Coming political problems in black Africa" 89-20.

26. Jennifer Seymour Whitker "United States policy toward Africa" in her collection on Africa and the United States 242. Cf. Festus U. Ohaegbulam "Africa and superpower rivalry: prospects for the future and possible remedies" Journal of African Studies 8(4), Winter 1981/82, 163-175.

27. On pre-revolutionary connections between Tsarist Russia and Africa, especially with the Ethiopian empire, see Edward T. Wilson Russia and Black Africa before World War II (New York: Holmes & Meier, 1974). cf. Deepak Nayyar (ed) Economic Relations between socialist countries and the Third World (London: Macmillan, 1982).

28. See, for instance, Mai Palmberg (ed) Problems of Socialist Orientation in Africa (Stockholm: Almqvist & Wiksell, 1978). cf. the more "official" line in Gleb Starushenko Africa Makes a Choice: the development of socialist-oriented states (Moscow: Novosti, 1975).

29. Robert Legvold "The Soviet Union's Strategic Stake in Africa" in Whitaker (ed) Africa and the United States 163.

30. Ibid. 165. cf. the "Cold War" orientation of Peter Janke "Marxist statecraft in Africa: what future?" Conflict Studies 95, May 1978 and David Rees "Soviet strategic penetration of Africa" Conflict Studies 77, November 1976.

329

32. Raymond W. Copson "African Flashpoints: prospects for armed international conflict" Orbis 25(4) Winter 1982, 903-904.

33. Legum "Communal conflict and international intervention in Africa" 65.

34. Ibid. 48.

35. Ibid. 49.

36. On these see Timothy M. Shaw "The actors in African international politics" in Timothy M. Shaw and Kenneth A. Heard (eds) Politics of Africa: dependence and development (London: Longman, 1979), 357-396.

37. Zartman "Issues of African diplomacy in the 1980s" 1030.

38. Legum "Communal conflict and international intervention in Africa" 55.

39. Copson "African Flashpoints" 905.

40. Henry S. Bienen "Military rule and military order in Africa" Orbis 25(4), Winter 1982, 964-65.

41. Ibid. 965. cf. Bruce E. Arlinghaus (ed) Arms for Africa: military assistance and foreign policy in the developing world (Lexington: Lexington, 1982).

42. See OAU Lagos Plan of Action for the Economic Development of Africa 1980-2000 (Geneva: International Institute for Labour Studies, 1981) and World Bank Accelerated Development in Sub-Saharan Africa: a agenda for action (Washington: IBRD, 1981).

43. For critiques and comparisions see Timonty M. Shaw "Debates about Africa's Future: the Brandt, World Bank and Lagos Plan blueprints" Third World Quarterly 5(2), April 1983, Caroline Allison and Reginald Green "Accelerated Development in Sub-Subharan Africa: what agendas for action?" IDS Bulletin, January 1983, and "Special double issue on the Berg Robert and the Lagos Plan of Action" Africa Development 7(1/2), 1982, 1-206.

44. Zartman "Coming political problems in Black Africa" 113. For more on the comparison between "eventful" and "uneventful" scenarios in Southern Africa see his "Social and political trends in Africa in the 1980s" in Legum et al Africa in the 1980s 109-119.

45. See Larry W. Bowman "The strategic importance of South Africa to the United States" African Affairs 81(323), April 1982, 159-191. cf. L.H. Gann and Peter Duignan South Africa: war, revolution or peace? (Stanford: Hoover Institution, 1978).

46. Geoffrey Kemp "US Strategic interests and military options in Sub-Saharan Africa" in Whitaker (ed) Africa and the United States 150.

47. Radu "Ideology, parties and foreign policy in sub-Saharan Africa" 987.

48. Ibid. 991. For a more balanced, albeit non-radical, interpretation see Crawford Young Ideology and Development in Africa (New Haven: Yale University Press, 1982).

49. Zartman "Issues of Africa diplomacy in the 1980s" 1042.

50. Ibid. 1039.

51. Ibid. 1041.

52. On the case of Zambia, for example, see Jane L. Parpart and Timothy M. Shaw "Cycles, contradictions and coalitions: class fractions in Zambia, 1964-1984" in Irving L. Markovitz (ed) Studies in Power and Class in Africa (forthcoming).

53. See Timothy M. Shaw "Beyond Underdevelopment: the anarchic state in Africa" African Studies Association Washington, DC, November 1982.

54. See Accelerated Development in Sub-Saharan Africa 45-80.

55. M'buyinga Pan Africanism or Neo-Colonialism 125.

56. Natural History Book 8.

331

57. See Barry B. Hughes and Patricia A. Strauch "The future of development in Nigeria and the Sahel: projections from the World Integrated Model (WIM)" and Florizella B. Liser "A Basic Needs Strategy and the Physical Quality of life Index" in Shaw (ed) Alternative Futures for Africa 179-236.

58. See Claude Ake A Political Economy of Africa (London: Longman, 1981) 176-189.

59. See Timothy M. Shaw and Don Munton "Africa's Futures: a comparision of forecasts" and Timothy M. Shaw and Paul Goulding "Alternative scenarios for Africa" in Shaw (ed) Alternative Futures for Africa 37-130.

60. For an overview of these see Timothy M. Shaw Towards an International Political Economy for the 1980s: from dependence to (inter) dependence (Halifax Centre for Foreign Policy Studies, 1980).

61. On the general question of such "complexes" in the Third World, including the cases of Egypt, Nigeria and South Africa(pp. 179-202 and 285-327) see Edward A. Kolodziej and Robert E. Harkavy (eds) Security Policies of Developing Countries (Lexington: Lexington, 1982).

62. "On the proposal for the establishment of an OAU Political Security Council (CM/Res. 789 [XXXV] "OAU Council of Ministers, Freetown , June 1980 in Colin Legum (ed) Africa Contemporary Record, Volume 13, 1980-81 (New York: Africana, 1981) CII.

63. On such issues of the "new security" in post-neocolonial Africa see Timothy M. Shaw "Unconventional conflicts in Africa: nuclear, class and guerrilla struggles, past, present and prospective" Jerusalem Journal of International Relations (forthcoming).

64. Lagos Plan of Action 5.

65. Ibid. 7.

66. See Claude Ake Revolutionary Pressures in Africa (London: Zed, 1978).